The Response
of Social Work
to the Depression

Jacob Fisher

Foreword by
Clarke A. Chambers

The Response
of Social Work
to the Depression

Schenkman Publishing Co.   Cambridge, Massachusetts

Library of Congress Cataloging in Publication Data

Fisher, Jacob, 1905– (Feb. 4)–
   The response of social work to the Depression.
   (University books)
   Bibliography: p.
   Includes index.
   1. Social service—United States—History—20th
century. 2. Public welfare—United States—History—
20th century. 3. Depression—1929—United States.
4. Social workers—United States—Political activity.
I. Title.
HV91.F56   361'.973   79-21359
ISBN 0-8161-8413-5
ISBN 0-87073-891-7 pbk.

Contents

Foreword

The social service professions have traditionally pursued two major strategies—the one to provide assistance to persons in need, the other to promote broad reforms designed to ameliorate harsh conditions or to reconstruct unjust social arrangements. At times of rapid social change or of economic crisis it has often seemed that the two components were mutually exclusive and even opposed. During the decades that straddled the turn of the nineteenth and the twentieth century, for example, some social work leaders insisted that needy individuals and families required services that would assist them to function better in a society whose institutions and values were taken as given, while others proclaimed that the social environment itself was at fault and that the best way to ameliorate personal difficulties was to remedy basic institutional flaws.

It was the latter group that pressed for legislation to protect women and child laborers, to provide financial assistance to dependent children through mothers' assistance programs, and to initiate comprehensive systems of public assistance and social insurance. The Committee on Standards of Living and Labor of the National Conference of Charities and Correction—led by such notable social actionists as Florence Kelley, Paul U. Kellogg, Owen Lovejoy, John Kingsbury, Henry Moskowitz, and others—proposed in 1912 a platform of "Social Standards for Industry" that called for a living wage, reasonable hours of labor, government regulation of industrial conditions, the prohibition of child labor, and systems of social insurance to cover the hazards of industrial accidents and occupational disease, sickness, old age, and unemployment. When Theodore Roosevelt and the Progressive party embraced its essential planks, many distinguished reformers and social service workers rallied to his cause. The Bull Moose party went down to defeat, but the welfare measures it endorsed remained on the social agenda of progressive social workers through the conservative years of the 1920s and many of them were subsequently realized during the era of the New Deal. The persistence during the 1930s of social action—both liberal and radical—as one responsibility of professional social work is a central theme of this book.

Again in the tumultuous years of the 1960s traditional priorities of the profession—to provide ever more efficient and humane services to persons and groups in need—were challenged by radicals who, spurred by the civil rights movement and by the "War on Poverty," demanded the empowering of dispossessed groups in American society: blacks, Chicanos, American Indians, the welfare and working poor, and recipients of Aid to Families of Dependent Children. Proponents of direct action used tactics of confrontation to publicize their goals before the National Conference on Social Welfare, just as leaders of the rank-and-file movement had stirred the annual convention of the National Conference of Social Work in 1934, and as advanced progressives had seized the initiative in 1912.

Yet the "priestly" and "prophetic" functions of social work had historically more often been intertwined and mutually supportive than antagonistic. What Mary Richmond, the founder of social diagnosis and modern scientific case work, labeled the "retail" and the "wholesale" phases of social service established a dialectic that informed both service and action. Practitioners learned by daily contact with persons in need the complex ways in which individual lives were conditioned by external forces and circumstances over which they had little control. Enabling individuals and families to secure larger measures of self-determination required not only the strengthening of internal resources but adjustments in neighborhood, community, and society as well. Public health bore on personal hygiene; household cleanliness and public sanitation were seen as inextricably intertwined. Insecurity of employment and exploitative conditions of labor constituted chief factors determining levels of family income and standards of employability. A caring society had to provide both floors below which citizens could not be allowed to fall and ameliorative services for those who lived along that margin of existence. For many social work leaders, service and action were perceived not as polar opposites but as points along a continuum marked by amelioration ("patching up" and "scavenger" work), cure, prevention, and constructive policies designed to advance programs of social health.

It is also the case, however, that in different eras the profession of social work tended to emphasize one factor and then another. Surely in the decade of "normalcy" following the First World War, social service focused heavily (if not exclusively) on the inward factors of personality adjustment, and psychiatric case work became the rage. If a handful of activists kept alive the impulse for reform, the twenties were generally inhospitable to concerns of labor, housing, social insurance, and protective legislation. The social science theories that informed the profession disciplined their devotees to objectivity and impartiality. Socialized by formal training and practical experience to maintain social distance and to strive for objective analysis, social workers, longing for recognition as truly professional persons, were generally little inclined to engage them-selves with issues of class, race, social power, and property. Social workers generally, in whatever era, did indeed so strongly reflect a prevailing middle-class ethos that only a few rare souls in any generation were able to transcend its limitations and bias. And those few drew inspiration and authority from Freud, not Marx. However advanced their progressivism might be (Florence Kelley, Jane Addams, and Robert Hunter for example thought of themselves as democratic socialists), rarely did they challenge frontally the basic arrangements of the prevailing economic system. That strategy remained to the rank-and-file movement in the 1930s.

Prosperity left America ill-prepared for the shock of economic depres-sion; as panic deepened into widespread unemployment and want, the nation was slow to recognize the extent of despair and slow to devise remedies. The heroic measures of the early New Deal did much to relieve human suffering through direct relief and public works projects but after years of hard times, unemployment and deprivation had been overcome only in modest degree. The Social Security Act of 1935 provided compen-sation for unemployment, insurance against old age, and federal funds to assist dependent children, but it offered future promise more than imme-diate performance; not until after the Second World War did it begin to provide that maintenance of purchasing power that had been its declared goal.

It was in such a context of modest and partial reforms that Grace L. Coyle, a pioneer leader of group work, lashed out against colleagues who continued "to pick up the pieces without ever attempting to stop the breakage. . . . The real situation which faces us as social workers," she declared in the May 1937 issue of the *Survey*, "includes a society potentially rich but actually poor, wasteful of its material and human resources, torn by class and racial conflicts, its cultural life on the whole meager, vulgar and disintegrated."

It is this subject—the complex roles of social work during the Great Depression—that Jacob Fisher explores in this book, which is part history and part memoir. And fortunate we are to have his account! The first generation of professional social workers, from the 1890s down into the 1930s, gave us many first-hand accounts that mingled historical narrative and personal reminiscences. Jane Addams, Mary Simkhovitch, Lillian Wald, and Edward Devine (among others), recorded events of their lifetimes from their own special coigns of vantage. Bertha Reynolds in *An Uncharted Journey* and Helen Hall in *Unfinished Business* enriched our understanding of social welfare in social work's second generation, and their stories and perceptions of the 1930s provided significant insights into domestic and foreign affairs in those troubled years. Scattered here and there in articles and essays one can find other testimony of the turmoils and tensions of the Depression era, witness of what it was like to be a professional social worker at a time when traditional main-line practices no longer sufficed. Jacob Fisher now portrays events of those years from the perspective of the radical left.

Readers of this book might do well to begin with Fisher's moving and disarming autobiographical account of his coming of age in the 1920s: *On Vanishing Ground* (Fairfax, Virginia: Piney Branch Press, 1979). Among many themes of family, schooling, and growing up, the book details the circumstances (part chance, part design) that led him to a Bachelor of Science degree from the Washington Square College of New York University in 1926 and a Master's degree from the Graduate School of Jewish Social Work. The latter chapters also provide a self-knowing account of his early perceptions of the field of social work and the attraction exercised for him by the left in the opening years of the Great Depression.

He took a position as case worker and supervisor for the New York Jewish Social Service Association, 1928–1934, shifting to a position as research analyst for the Council of Jewish Federations and Welfare Funds in the years 1934–1940. He worked as statistician and analyst for various bureaus of the Social Security Administration, from 1940 to 1954, when he was suspended as a "security risk" for his activities during the 1930s. The spirit of McCarthyism reached a crescendo in 1954; Fisher resigned and was not able to find work in his own field until '57, when he joined the staff of a consultant firm where he remained until his retirement in 1973.

During the thirties he was caught up in those events and movements that provide the themes for this book. Active in the rank-and-file movement, he edited early issues of its journal, *Social Work Today*, and subsequently was a member of its Board of Editors. President of the New York Social Service Employees Union, 1937–1939, he also served as Vice-President of the New York State Industrial Union Council of the CIO, 1938–1939, and as President of the New York City Joint Council of the United Office and Professional Workers of America, 1939–1940. Membership on the Executive Committee of the Social Workers Committee to Aid Spanish Democracy, 1936–1939, put him at the center of concern for the fate of social democracy that moved so many antifascist radicals in those years. These experiences and activities provide an angle of vision for this book.

The story he tells is founded on first-hand observation and participation; it is based as well on a rereading of the historical record with the perspective that the passage of nearly fifty years can bring. Fisher writes with a vividness and passion that deeply-felt experiences afford, but there is nothing of the apologetic in what he sets down; his account never slips into polemic nor does it become self-serving. He serves up sparkling vignettes of significant persons who so rarely find their way into traditional histories: Mary van Kleeck, Harry Lurie, Grace Marcus, William Hodson, Bertha Reynolds, and a host of others. Students of Depression history will be introduced as well, to fresh, new perceptions of such New Dealers as Aubrey Williams. Fisher provides rich detail on the structure and function of social work, and on the variety of associations and journals through which social work defined itself. His sensitivity to the ideological and practical difficulties attendant upon organizing professional persons into unions constitutes another theme.

Historiographers have come to appreciate the complex ways by which assumptions regarding culture and society contemporary to a given era serve, with the passage of time, to define critical scholarly interpretations of events in that earlier age. One is not surprised to learn, therefore, that the left-leaning positions held by the rank-and-file movement, critical of New Deal welfare policies, exhibited a degree and a kind of radical skepticism which revisionist historians picked up in the sixties. This observation is not meant to suggest that Jacob Fisher, writing in 1979, is a proponent of a "new left"; nor is it meant to imply that revisionists of the sixties borrowed their ideas directly from "old left" critiques of the thirties. Jacob Fisher is probably unfamiliar with the writings of Barton Bernstein on the New Deal, and there is no clear evidence that Bernstein has studied in any detail the rank-and-file movement in social work. But the recent past and the present are nevertheless entangled.

This book, then, enlarges and enlivens our understanding of that remarkable decade about which so many millions of words have been written. Some of it covers relatively familiar ground: the emergence of public assistance and social security as chief issues to which social workers, like citizens generally, had to respond; the return of social work, with new emphases and new perspectives, to a reconsideration of the tension between direct practice and direct action, and their intermingling. Other themes have been less frequently explored (and then rarely with the telling detail that Fisher commands): the strained relationship between established professionals in public welfare and civil servants who were not certified or accredited by graduate degrees, a phenomenon that took precedence, during the Depression, over concerns in earlier eras regarding the relationships between professionals and volunteers; the processes by which professional persons became radicalized by events and by intense ideological argumentation; the role of an informed, radical minority in shaping issues and in defining the terms of political debate; and the delicate and shifting balance of liberal, radical, and Communist factions within the "popular front" coalitions of the mid-thirties. As one whose memory of that time is acute, Fisher knows that the decade was not all of one piece, but rather that it was marked by rapid and often erratic shifts of mood and temper. The mingling of history and reminiscence will provoke recollections in other readers who, like the author, were passionately engaged in the contests of those years. For younger readers his account will provide still another angle of insight on events of an era whose impact they feel even if they do not fully comprehend it.

Finally, in an era of consolidation and retrenchment not unlike the twenties or the fifties, it is good to be reminded of a radical tradition of protest, action, and involvement that is also part of the heritage of the social service profession.

CLARKE A. CHAMBERS
Professor of History, and
Director, Social Welfare History Archives Center
University of Minnesota, Twin Cities

Introduction

The subject of this book is the transformation wrought in social work by the Great Depression of the thirties. No decade before or since has seen as many changes in the role of the profession, its size and structure, basic philosophy and outlook, and so strong an influence on government programs.

The thirties were unique in the nation's history in several respects, all having an impact on social work. Mass unemployment, its most notable feature, was unprecedented in the millions of lives touched by it, in the scale of deprivation and suffering endured, and, in its first years, in the sense of drift in national purpose induced by the seeming inability of business or government to affect it. Out of this harrowing experience emerged broad public acceptance, by 1933, of an immense expansion in the activities of the federal government in the economic and social life of the country.

Not least in importance among the many measures undertaken to restore the economy, to raise purchasing power, and to meet need was the assumption of federal responsibility for public relief to families and individuals in want. This was expressed initially in direct grants and later in emergency work programs; in permanent federal programs for sharing the cost of cash grants to defined groups of unemployables in the needy population; and in the establishment of a social security program, providing benefits not based on need but on loss of income through unemployment, retirement by reason of age, or death of the family earner. Under the Social Security Act a federal-state-local partnership in public assistance was instituted. By the end of the decade, there was a public welfare department in almost every county in the country, whereas only a few hundred had existed at its beginning. Program procedures, particularly the determination of eligibility and size of grant, as well as criteria in the selection of personnel, derived largely from social work standards inherited from an earlier period.

To meet the demand for personnel in the new public assistance programs, the number of social workers, including paraprofessionals, doubled and tripled in the course of the decade. The American Association of Social Workers, the principal professional organization, doubled in size. Training programs proliferated. Seventeen new schools of social work were opened; established schools increased their enrollment.

Of far-reaching consequence for the profession's doctrinal ambience was a significant shift in the relative importance of the public and private sectors of social work, as reflected in the number of families served, personnel employed, and expenditures. To cite one index, the proportion of assistance payments to needy families from voluntary sources dropped from one-fourth at the beginning of the decade to one percent or less by the end. Increasingly, social work opinion-makers were employed in public rather than private agencies, influenced by developments in the public rather than the private sector in social work.

A decade marked by ferment in political and economic ideas was bound to affect social work's views about the nature of the economy and its own role in effecting change. The thirties witnessed even more than did the Progressive Era (roughly 1900–14) a turn to the left in the thinking of liberals. The fundamental ethos of the prevailing economic order was questioned, and calls for a radical reconstruction of society were voiced. Since social work has traditionally identified itself with the liberal strain in American thought, it is not surprising that the leftward swing in liberalism was reflected in the views of a number of prominent social workers.

The shift to the left was most pronounced in the Rank-and-File Movement. The Rank-and-File Movement challenged established social work thinking at every point, but most emphatically in its belief in an alliance with the labor movement and the organization of trade unions to strengthen the economic security of the newly employed thousands in public agencies. This book, among other topics treated, traces the origins and changing views of the movement, its relations with the professional organizations in social work, and the influence of each upon the other, a subject either ignored or skimped in histories of social work covering those years. As a manifestation of the emergence of a dissenting left in the profession in the thirties, the movement had a significance greater than the number of social workers identified with it, never more than a minority. Its support of more comprehensive social welfare and social insurance programs than were acceptable to the administration or to the profession in the thirties, its emphasis on nondiscriminatory treatment of minorities among recipients and staff, and on the right of public assistance families to voice their grievances and have them adjusted, anticipated developments enacted or attaining program form in later decades. These aspects of the Rank-and-File movement give it a particular interest for the student of long-range trends in social work, and confer on it an importance not evident when perspective is limited to a single decade.

Some remarks may be in order concerning the sequence in which the subjects discussed in the book are presented.

As the thirties recede in memory, the decade acquires in the popular mind a unity of shape, texture, and flavor that blurs and conceals the changing contours of the economic and political landscape of those years; the variety of daily experience from place to place, year to year, and from one social class to another; the shifts in contemporary perception of the significant problems of the day; the diversity in issues that seemed to demand action, stirred expectations, aroused response.

The main features of this popular view of the thirties have become encapsulated in such labels as "Hard Times," "Decade of Despair," "the Red Decade;" and in the belief that Franklin Roosevelt and his New Deal saved the country in the end from the Depression, despair, and the Red threat.

There is a kernel of truth in some of the labels but, as the account which follows indicates, the reality bore little resemblance to the myths that have come to encrust the period.

In retrospect we may distinguish four periods in the thirties: the Hoover years, 1929–33; the first New Deal, 1933–35; the second New Deal, 1935–37; and the years 1937–40, a mixed period characterized by recession and recovery, a growing concern with international developments seen as a potential threat to America, the outbreak of World War II, and an accompanying increase in preparations for defense.

The overlap in dates is deliberate. History is not a walk from one sealed chamber to another. The events characteristic of a particular period have their beginnings in the preceding period; carry over in diminished strength into the next period. This was particularly true in the thirties, marked not only by quick shifts in economic and political climate, but also by striking variations in the rate of change among different aspects of national life.

Strictly speaking, the decade may be viewed as having run either from January 1, 1930, to December 31, 1939, or alternatively, from January 1, 1931, to December 31, 1940; both interpretations are acceptable in Webster. But as the foregoing paragraph suggests, the terms "the thirties," and "the Great Depression" and the word "decade" are used somewhat loosely here to embrace events from the fall of 1929 to the end of 1940 and occasionally beyond.

The features specific to each of the four periods reflect in their differences the changes that took place in the decade in the nation's economy; in its politics; in the relations of government to business, labor, agriculture, and other special interest groups; in the relations of the federal government to the states and localities; and in the ideas people had about these subjects. To examine these differences even in summary is to put at rest any notion of an underlying unity in the decade as a whole.

It makes sense to consider social work in a similar sequence. The response of social work to the Depression varied from one period to another, affected by the changing economic and political climate, and by shifts in administration policy and in programs to meet need. Such unity as may be found may be traced to the shaping effect of liberal thinking on social work views in each of the four periods treated. The thirties illustrate, as did the Progressive Era, the strong influence of liberalism on the profession's basic outlook and on its understanding of social work's role in society. With conservatism in politics occupying as low a place in public esteem as at any time in American history, the nature of the liberalism in the ascendancy in the thirties is of first importance in understanding its major role in the legislation passed, in public programs to relieve want, and in social work thinking, as well as in understanding the decade as a whole.

It was a liberalism which, in summary, stressed human as against property rights; equality of access to employment and educational opportunities, to the protection of the law, and to voting; legislation to promote better housing and health programs, and economic security when unemployment, illness, disability, old age, or death of the wage earner interrupted family income; governmental guarantees of labor's right to organize and to bargain collectively; development of the nation's resources to raise the standard of living; such intervention in the economy as was deemed necessary to promote the general welfare; a foreign policy emphasizing the peaceful resolution of international disputes, nonintervention in the affairs of other nations, self-rule in the colonial world, and opposition to Fascism and other manifestations of totalitarianism.

These are recognizably loose terms, subject to many interpretations, perhaps because it has been characteristic of liberalism to avoid orthodoxy, to change with the times, and to welcome a wide range of ideas, from the mildly progressive to the radical. It was indeed this openness to unconventional thinking and the appeal of radicalism to many liberals which was most characteristic of liberal thought in the thirties, particularly in the early years. It led to temporary alliances, happy and unhappy, with Communists around specific issues, to experiences, some of them productive of heartbreak and sober second thoughts later, and in the late forties and early fifties, to attacks on liberals as coconspirators with Communists against the nation's security. Some of the individuals involved as activists and participants in the thirties, and as victims in the fifties, were social workers.[1]

The principal sources used in the preparation of the present account are the contemporary publications listed in the bibliographical references which precede the notes in back of the book. I have drawn freely on my own recollections of the period as a participant in a number of the activities described. Acknowledgment is made to Dr. Leslie Alexander of the Bryn Mawr Graduate School of Social Work and Social Research for making available to me photocopies of documents from the Social Welfare History Archives Center at the University of Minnesota, which she assembled as part of her research for a doctoral dissertation on the history of the union movement in voluntary social work. I am indebted to George Wolfe, old friend, cherished colleague in the thirties, for his kindness in reviewing an earlier draft and calling my attention to deficiencies whose correction has contributed to fuller coverage and better balance in the treatment of the subjects covered in the book. It is more than a sense of uxorious duty that moves me to express appreciation also of the help of my wife, whose suggestions and own memories of the times lifted me over many a rough spot in this narrative.

I The Hoover Years, 1929–33

Chapter 1

A World Turned Upside Down

The Hoover years from the beginnings of the Depression in the fall of '29 to the inauguration of Roosevelt in March 1933 were probably among the worst in the nation's history in the extent of the decline in economic activity, the magnitude of unemployment, the scale of the destitution experienced, the sense of drift in national purpose, and, with some exceptions, the passive acceptance of a shrinking standard of living and a loss of faith in the country's future.

When the decade opened, America, the success story of modern times, the land of opportunity, the pot of gold at the end of the rainbow for European immigrants for a hundred years or more—first in the world in national income, in national wealth, and in industrial and agricultural production—the cocky America which bestrode the world like a colossus in the twenties—this nonpareil America appeared to have lost its way. Stock value plunged. Factories and mines curtailed hours, closed. Railroads cut back schedules, abandoned branch lines. Businesses went into bankruptcy. Banks failed. Millions lost their jobs, exhausted savings and credit, borrowed, went hungry.

It was a world turned upside down. Just as America had climbed to the top the fastest, it now plummeted to the bottom the fastest, perhaps because it had farther to fall to hit bottom. In places history seemed to be racing back to America's beginnings, like a movie reel run in reverse. By 1932 money was so scarce for some people, barter replaced it as a medium of exchange. People traded services for food and fuel. Carpenters repaired houses, shoe workers patched shoes, tailors mended clothing—for potatoes, eggs, apples, wood. Economists tended to view such reversions to a premoney economy as symbolic of the collapse of the modern commercial-industrial order of the last four centuries. But since economists were held in low regard for their dismal record in predicting the early end of bad times, few now listened to them. The more hopeful, more acceptable view of barter was that taken by such a well-known social worker as Joanna Colcord, director of the C.O.S. (Charity Organization Society) Department of the Russell Sage Foundation, who in 1933 praised what she called cooperative production exchanges as constituting "a more effective program than social work itself ever developed for conserving self-respect and general morale of people out of work."[1]

The collapse shook every nook and cranny of the economy. There's always a living on the farm, a tobacco planter told Edmund Wilson in the course of his travels through the country for the *New Republic* in 1931, but most farmers had another story to tell. Crop prices, chronically depressed all through the twenties, dropped below the cost of production. A bushel of corn, for which the grower got 80 cents in '29, fell to 32 cents by '32; a bushel of wheat, from $1.04 to 38 cents.[2] Rather than sell at such prices, farmers burned their wheat, cotton, and corn; doused their fruit with kerosene; dumped their milk. The paradox of food destroyed or allowed to rot while the hungry starved was not confined to the United States. In Brazil in '32 the government dumped at sea or burned 13 million bags of coffee to raise the price.[3] It was the height of economic absurdity.

Moral Lessons

Hope in Washington for a halt in the downward spiral remained steadfast, sustained by brief upturns at sporadic intervals. But a new note had crept into the principles espoused by the Republican party. The business of America is business, Coolidge had said, and the G.O.P. in the twenties saw and proclaimed itself as the party of American enterprise, American growth, and American prosperity. After 1929 a change occurred; the Republican party now viewed itself increasingly as the guardian of the country's basic moral values, particularly the work ethic and the frugality ethic, imperatives deemed essential to the salvation of America in hard times.

Campaigning for the Senate in New Jersey in the fall of 1930, Republican candidate Dwight Morrow, one-time Morgan partner, with a distinguished career in corporation law and government service, saw virtues in the Depression. Too much prosperity, he said, ruins the character of a people. The men and women who had built the country were reared in adversity, he reminded his audiences.[4] He knew his history. The Puritans had experienced hard times in their first years and had had to call on all their resources to meet with patience and steadfastness the trials they endured in settling the land. And how many of the later arrivals in colonial America had come here as indentured servants, whose heavy work and frugal maintenance during the three to seven years of their indenture were deemed morally uplifting because they taught them industry, forbearance, and thrift, virtues they lacked in the old country, where they had been for the most part the scum of the earth, the unemployed, vagrants, felons awaiting trial or commitment, and discharged prisoners. One could call up, too, the travails undergone by free immigrants in their initial years here, from the early days of the republic right down to the present.

The President, too, appealed to history. Speaking at Valley Forge on Memorial Day in 1931, Hoover discovered in the sufferings of Washington's soldiers camped there in the bitter winter of 1777–78 the triumph of character and idealism over the counsels of despair and the temptation of material comfort. The lesson of Valley Forge, said the President, was that in a time of trial and stress the path to a nation's greatness was independence, self-reliance, steadfastness. America was going through another Valley Forge. He called on his fellow-countrymen to prove worthy of Washington and his men by resisting the lure of Depression panaceas, particularly the rosy illusion that government can do better than the individual himself in thinking and planning his daily life.[5]

These uplifting words were addressed to the nation at large; to the business community the President felt compelled to say very little. In his eyes its leaders knew what they had to do and could be counted upon to do it. He shared their strong faith in the ability of the economy to overcome its difficulties on its own, given time and no intervention by government. Classical laissez-faire economics, some critics called it, fit for the nineteenth century but not appropriate to the crisis America was undergoing. The term carried no pejorative meaning for Hoover, to whom it had the appeal of having provided the solution to other depressions in the past, and he was sure it would do so again in the current setback.

Hoover, a self-made man with a poor-boy background as humble as Andy Jackson's or Abe Lincoln's, a millionaire before he was forty, found it reasonable to attribute his success and the prosperity of the America of the twenties to the free rein given the American entrepreneurial spirit, "rugged individualism" (one of his favorite expressions), the American system, the American way, which encouraged the best men to rise to the top. (The idea that all men are equal, he had written in 1922 in *American Individualism*, was "part of the claptrap of the French Revolution.") It was responsible for giving this country the highest standard of living in the world. He had seen it all happen in his lifetime; in the twenties there had been more cars on the road every year, more telephones in use, more radios, more refrigerators, more phonographs, more electric lights. American industry had poured out from a seemingly bottomless cornucopia a flow of consumer goods that made life better, happier for everyone. It would do so again, if let alone. This was why he vetoed Senator Norris's bill to erect a government plant at Muscle Shoals, Alabama, to make and sell power and fertilizer. He was opposed, he said in his veto message, "to the Government entering into any business the major purpose of which is competition with our citizens. . . . The real development of the resources and industries of the Tennessee Valley can only be accomplished by the people in that valley themselves."[6]

The economy was sick, in this view, because the country's superb, efficiently run industrial machine, its productive agriculture, its well-organized transportation and communications complex had yielded by the end of the twenties a volume of goods and services beyond the capacity of the country and its customers to absorb. The lack of capacity lay primarily abroad. The more he thought about it, the more he was inclined to find the major causes of the Depression in forces outside his beloved, well-nigh perfect country. The debts accumulated by countries in the World War, the revolution in Russia, the disturbances in China and India, the overproduction of raw materials in South America, Africa, Asia, were all brutal assaults on the laws of supply and demand, causing prices to fall worldwide and a drastic decline in the ability of foreign countries to buy American goods.

There was little the government could do about overproduction and depressed prices abroad. As far as this country was concerned, the illness of excessive inventories could be cured only by an old-fashioned self-purge in the form of reduced production and lowered prices. As inventories declined under the twin pressures of a limitation in the supply of new goods and the growth in sales generated by low prices, recovery would set in, as it had in similar circumstances in the past (1921, 1914, 1908, 1893, to list the most recent four recessions).

The government, the President asserted over and over again, had nothing to contibute to this automatic process, other than a modest increase in public works. "The sole function of government is to bring about a condition of affairs favorable to the beneficial development of private enterprise," he said in 1931.[7] In the same year he vetoed a bill to establish a nationwide employment service, sponsored by Senator Wagner of New York in 1931, on the ground it would interfere with the free market in jobs, an essential feature of the American enterprise system. We must not be misled by the claim that the source of all wisdom is the federal government, he had said at Valley Forge, in what must have struck some Democrats as a parody of the philosophy voiced over a century earlier by the founder of their party, the Jefferson who believed the less government the country had the better. The government would intervene at most now only to bail out with interest-bearing loans the banks, the insurance companies, and the railroads. A bill to permit such a departure from Adam Smith and David Ricardo was passed in January 1932, after over two years of steady descent into the pit of what seemed to some a bottomless depression. Most reluctantly, Hoover signed it.

Thus was created the Reconstruction Finance Corporation, with $2 billion in loan authority, the major effort of the Republican administration to decelerate and if possible to arrest the descent. Hoover's doubt of its necessity was reflected in his address to a national conference of bankers and industrialists he called that August. With unemployment at 12 million, he told his guests that the major crises of the Depression had been overcome and that only one more push by industry was needed to restore 1929's prosperity.

The largely Republican press of the country shared the President's faith in a self-healing economy, which Hoover glimpsed in every favorable news item, however scanty. The answer to the question, What is news?—a hardy perennial among reporters and editors—was influenced in the early thirties by considerations of national morale, and a tender concern for faith in America, for its greatness, and for the feelings of Mr. Hoover. A plant reopening, if only on half time, drew front-page headlines. Its closing again a few months later was buried in a two-line story on page 23.

Chastened by premature announcements from the White House of corners turned and economic chart lines changing direction, business leaders with some exceptions preferred to remain silent. ("The fundamental business of the country . . . is on a sound and prosperous basis," the President had said right after the catastrophic fall in stock prices in 1929.[8] On March 8, 1930, he told the country the crisis would be over in sixty days; followed on May 1 by an assurance to the U.S. Chamber of Commerce that the worst of the Depression was over; a cheerful message to be repeated in the spring of '31 and '32.) They had taken credit for boom times in the twenties; now they had nothing to say. The old faith in ever-rising sales and profit margins, in ever-rising stock prices, in a future of stock splits and new issues had vanished. There was nothing to replace that faith, to account for the irrationality of falling stock prices, falling sales, company deficits, absent dividends. They preferred to let Hoover do the talking; he had been elected to do just that. If what he had to say was not quite in substance and tone what they expected when he was elected in '28, that was Hoover's tough luck, no worse than their own.

So they preferred to keep their heads low, their voices muted. And they didn't like to see their names in the paper. They were sensitive. They had no taste for such nasty descriptions of the big businessman as Edmund Wilson presented *New Republic* readers with when reporting on the trial in 1933 of Charles E. Mitchell, former president of the National City Bank, indicted for financial shenanigans after having sold the American public $15 billion of stock in auto companies that went broke and of bonds in South American countries now insolvent or undergoing revolutions. "Enormous, with no necks," said Wilson, "they give the impression of hooked, helpless frogs, or of fat bass or logy groupers, hauled suddenly out of the water, and landed on the witness stand, gasping. They pant, they twitch in the chair, they make gestures finlike and feeble—one can imagine behind their jowls great gills that are vainly trying to respire the alien air.''[9]

When the farm on which John D. Rockefeller was born in 1839 near Richford, New York was put up for public auction in September 1932, for nonpayment of $47.29 in taxes, the family was not moved by sentiment or filial piety to buy it. There would have been publicity. There were no bids and the town took possession of the farm,[10] one of thousands all over the country that met the same fate that year.

Fatalism, Faith

"Fatalism" perhaps best describes the mood of the public at large as the Depression deepened. Half-lulled by the periodic cheerful news of a plant reopening, comforted by Hoover's likening of their distress to the trials endured by the nation's early settlers and the soldiers at Valley Forge, heroes all, numbed by their frustration in their search for work, people for the most part, contemporary accounts attest, accepted their lot as an act of God. The laid-off steel puddler, the short-week bookkeeper, the high school graduate futilely seeking his first job, felt defeat, shame, but seldom discontent, and outrage hardly ever. They were too overwhelmed by their personal experiences, by the depressing news in the daily paper, to seek an explanation. When they did, they sought it generally in the personal; in the throw of the dice of change, which gave you nothing and your neighbor the one vacancy in the plant for which a thousand job-seekers had applied; in being born under the wrong sign of the zodiac; in being Wednesday's child; in anything but the way things were ordered in the country. Some blamed their own foolish behavior for their lack of money; when they had had it they had spent it on such nonessentials as a car or a radio. Millions with deep religious convictions took their plight as a punishment for their sins. There was a revival of faith, particularly in Jesus, not "the Man Nobody Knows," as Bruce Barton had called him in his best-seller of that title in 1925, Jesus the supreme salesman, the greatest ad man of all time, but Jesus the comforter, the comforter of the poor, a poor and humble man himself.

The poor needed faith to stay alive because for many that was about all they had. By early 1933 unemployment reached 13 million, one in every four persons in the labor force.[11] Many people still with jobs were working two and three days a week only. Wage cuts of 10–20 percent seemed to become a standard feature of every renewed union contract. Wage levels had dropped to half or less of what they had been in '29. The rate for sawmill operators in Pennsylvania was down to 5 cents an hour; in

Connecticut some sweatshops were paying young women 60 cents to $1.10 for a fifty-five-hour week.[12] Hundreds of thousands of youngsters were on the road in search of jobs or a handout. Apple sellers became a familiar sight on Wall Street. ("Many persons left their jobs for the more profitable one of selling apples," Hoover was to say later in his *Memoirs*.[13]) The Salvation Army's bread lines and soup kitchens of 1930 were being replaced by emergency relief offices issuing vouchers which could be cashed at the corner grocery store.

By winter of '32–'33 millions of families were on assistance. Nothing on this scale had ever been seen before in the United States. Poverty was nothing new in the nation's history, but it was either hidden in the hollows of Appalachia and in the seldom visited and seldom described homes of tenant farmers and sharecroppers in the deep South, or, where visible and publicized, confined pretty much to the big-city slums. The slums were the older decayed neighborhoods into which penniless immigrants had poured by the millions; in the late nineteenth and early twentieth centuries the overcrowding, the bad sanitation, the high incidence of disease, the airless unlighted rooms and their use both for sleeping and for work taken home had been written up and portrayed in photographs by such journalists and photographers as Jacob Riis and Lewis W. Hine. An optimistic America saw the slums as temporary way stations out of which most immigrants and certainly their children would move as they mounted the first rungs of the ladder of opportunity offered all newcomers to the golden land. Immigration laws enacted in the twenties, reducing the flow of newcomers to a trickle, would in time eliminate the slums, their sponsors said. But as long as they existed, they remained for most Americans all through the twenties, as they had been earlier, synonymous with poverty, disease, and crime, particularly poverty, and provided appropriate justification for the annual Community Chest drive.

Poverty had also been associated in the public mind with homeless derelicts who in good times and bad were to be found on the Bowery in New York and in the skid rows of all large cities; grimy, ragged winos and other alcoholics, huddled in the doorways of empty stores, tippling out of bottles concealed in brown paper bags, who slept in these same doorways summer nights and on sidewalk subway gratings winter nights, kept warm by the tepid air rising from the station below, and who were kept alive by the coffee and soup lines run by the Salvation Army and municipal shelters for the homeless. The Bowery bum type was now so lost in the larger miseries of the Great Depression that he made the news only when found dead after drinking the wood alcohol squeezed out of a Sterno can. Gone too from the papers as too commonplace were the early stories of bread lines for the homeless, overcrowded public lodging houses, and the use of municipal barges for persons with no other place to sleep.

The New Poor

The families on relief in '32 and '33 were different. The slums still held many, but like a deep wound whose blood stains bandage and clothing, the need for assistance had seeped out into adjacent neighborhoods and beyond, into lower-middle-class areas, the nearer rundown suburbs abandoned long ago by the affluent, into small towns, mill towns, company towns, and into the countryside. The family earner whose lack of a job drove him to apply for public aid was a bricklayer, a store clerk, a truck driver, a telephone operator, a machinist, a typist, a cloak cutter, a copper miner, a coal miner, a loom fixer, a tool-and-die maker, an assembly-line operator in an auto plant, a printer—occupational groups hitherto almost never touched by want.

Perhaps the most visible evidence of the new poverty was the emergence in city dumps, on railroad embankments, and even in the drained, abandoned reservoir of New York's Central Park, of packingcase, tarpaper, and tinsheet huts known as Hoovervilles and serving as shelters for an occasional family, but mostly for homeless unemployed men, no longer confined to skid row because no longer the traditional derelicts. Unlike the families on relief in their own homes, concealed in their anonymity from public view, whose members could not be distinguished by dress or manner from others in the crowd on any street in the neighborhood, their residents seemed to flaunt their destitution, their squalor; the Hoovervilles were a little bit of Latin America's shanty-towns transplanted to North America, unabashedly wretched in appearance, cold and drafty in winter, unbearably hot in summer, their grounds strewn with empty tin cans, bottles, and the leavings of garbage (after all, their occupants foraged for food in the public dumps), overrun with rats, an eyesore, an insult to the American way of life as depicted by Norman Rockwell on the cover of the Saturday Evening Post, and deservedly torn down at periodic intervals by offended authorities.

New, too, was protest. Fatalism may have been the predominant mood of the country at large, but here and there another note emerged, one of outrage, expressed publicly. The protest was not confined to those unlikely rebels, the farmers who burned their wheat, dumped their milk, stoned state troopers protecting dairy truckers defying the milk strike; or tenant farmers, some with rifles, who raided the general stores in England, Arkansas, one day in January 1931 for flour and lard to feed their hungry families.[14]

In the larger cities there were hunger marches and demonstrations before city hall and the relief offices; demands were voiced for an end to evictions for nonpayment of rent, for jobs on work-relief projects, for more adequate and more regular assistance allowances. In the winter of

'32–'33 police were called out in New York to scatter neighbors and sympathizers blocking evictions; Chicago reported several instances in which the padlocks were knocked off the emptied flat and the furniture was put back as soon as the bailiff and his crew had left; in Chicago, too, club-wielding police expelled picketing relief recipients who had occupied a welfare office to demand restoration of cuts in their grants; fire hose was used to disperse five thousand jobless besieging Seattle's city hall; and in Illinois the governor called out the National Guard to meet the threat of a mass descent by the unemployed on the state capitol at Springfield.

And in the summer of 1932 some twenty thousand unemployed World War veterans, accompanied in some cases by wives and children, descended on Washington to ask for immediate payment of the "adjusted compensation certificates" due them in 1945, and called by them their overdue war bonus. They were treated gingerly by the District police, but Hoover refused to meet with their representatives, Congress adjourned without acting on their request, and in the end the White House ordered the army in to disperse the bonus marchers with teargas bombs, bayonets, and tanks, evict them from federal buildings they had occupied, and put to the torch the shacks and tents in which they were encamped near the Capitol and along the Anacostia River. The embittered members of the Bonus Expeditionary Force went home, a target now of administration charges that they were criminals and Communists.

To many newspaper readers the charge of Communist inspiration, if not leadership, in the Bonus Expeditionary Force and other manifestations of discontent seemed plausible in the light of the fact that the Communist party had held a demonstration in front of the White House as early as March 6, 1930, and had organized a mass meeting in New York's Union Square on the same day, attracting 35,000 participants. Both ended when the police waded into the crowd with billy clubs and blackjacks, and in Washington with teargas bombs as well; such violence appeared to the reading public as almost provoked by the recalcitrant behavior of the demonstrators in refusing to disperse when ordered.

When 3,000 unemployed auto workers converged on the Ford Rouge River plant in March 1932, they were repulsed with water from plant fire hoses and gunfire from the Dearborn police which left four dead and many wounded; the funeral services for the four who died featured a large red banner, a picture of Lenin, and the Russian funeral march of 1905. It was the Communists, too, who organized the periodic hunger marches to bread lines, relief offices and employment offices, marches quickly dispersed by the police who had learned how to cope brutally and effectively with such demonstrations. And although the Communist party succeeded in drawing only several hundred persons to Washington in response to a call for a national hunger march on the capital December 31, 1931, suggesting waning rather than waxing influence among the unemployed, the image of a Communist worm in the heart of every rotten apple in the sickly looking social barrel lingered and disposed most people to take an indifferent if not unfriendly attitude toward all protests by the unemployed and persons on relief.

This view was not incompatible with the relative infrequency of protest, indicative to some extent of the small size of the minority which felt impelled to express protest. Indeed, against the vast background of a nation in which millions were unemployed, millions in need, millions on relief; a society which tolerated a miserable and degrading relief system, and indifference on the part of the federal government—against this background, the protests which took place seemed quite insignificant in number and size.

Atypical as they may have been, the occasional manifestations of protest contributed nevertheless to the sense of desperation felt by mayors and governors as they scraped the bottom of the tax barrel to meet the ever-mounting burden of relief. An increasing number began to see in federal help the only way out of what was viewed now as a national and not a state or local problem.[15]

The Last Puritan

But an administration in Washington committed to private initiative in economic affairs and to local responsibility for meeting the needs of the unemployed turned a stone face to any suggestion of federal aid. The relief of want fell within the voluntary sector in the philosophy which inspired Hoover's vision of the relations of the individual and society. The man who had made his international reputation as head of the American Relief Administration in postwar Europe, which fed 300 million people with food bought with federal dollars, now saw nothing but evil in the use of federal funds to relieve hunger in America. For the national government to step in was to violate one of the basic premises on which American civilization rested; at the most such intrusion should be limited to local and state governments. In endorsing the January 1931 campaign of the Red Cross for $100 million to aid drought victims, he appealed to the "heart of the nation" to respond generously, affirming that there could be no higher duty than to feed the hungry.[16] "If the day should ever come," he said later that year, "that voluntary agencies of the country, together with local and state governments, are unable to find resources to prevent hunger and suffering, I will ask the aid of every resource of the federal government. . . . However, I have faith in the American people that such a day will never come."[17] Even so minimal a gesture as federal coordination of voluntary efforts distressed him, and it was only with the greatest reluctance that he had been induced in October 1930 to appoint an Emergency Committee for Employment, fearful that such national recognition of what blared from every newspaper headline would only make matters worse. The principal function of the committee was to exhort cities and counties to do their best to relieve want, a task so meaningless its chairman, Arthur Woods, soon resigned.

When the People's Lobby, headed by noted educator and philosopher, John Dewey, asked him in 1931 to call a special session of Congress to appropriate $3 billion for public works and $250 million to subsidize a proposed system of state unemployment insurance programs, his response was, "I know of nothing that would so disturb the healing processes now undoubtedly going on in the economic situation. We cannot legislate ourselves out of a world depression; we can and will work ourselves out."[18]

In the fall of '31 the Woods Committee was succeeded by the President's Organization on Unemployment Relief, headed by Walter S. Gifford, president of the American Telegraph and Telephone Company. The new committee, like the old, was designed to promote voluntary giving; its chairman issued a call for "faith, hope, and charity." It was, its critics affirmed, only an advertising gimmick. In launching the Welfare and Relief Mobilization of '32, still another appeal for voluntary contributions for unemployment relief, Hoover said the winter of '32-'33 would be the last of the Depression; few people believed him.

When drought killed cattle and crops in the Southwest, Hoover asked Congress to appropriate funds for loans to farmers for seed, cattle feed, fertilizer. Democrats seized the opportunity to say Hoover thought it humane to feed starving cattle, wicked to feed starving children. Hoover was trained as an engineer but he had learned enough zoology to distinguish between cows and people. Deeply hurt at the Democrats' accusation, Hoover said cows had no tradition of local responsibility and self-help; people did. Cows had no moral fiber that risked being destroyed; people did.

In the end, as giving by the public proved inadequate to staunch the wounds caused by the Depression, he departed sufficiently from his faith in voluntarism to accept (but not to encourage) the resort to state and local taxes to fund unemployment relief. But he remained adamantly opposed to federal aid. "The moment responsibilities of any community," he said, "are shifted ... to Washington, then that community has subjected itself to a remote bureaucracy. ... It has lost a large part of its voice in the control of its destiny,"[19] he added, conveniently forgetting, in this warning, the loss in the control of its destiny the community had sustained by decisions made in executive offices in Wall Street, Detroit, Pittsburgh, Chicago, and Houston.

A relief check drawn on funds deposited by the Community Chest or by the city welfare department was just that—relief; a relief check drawn on an account contaminated even in part by federal money was a dole. "I am opposed," said Hoover, "to any direct or indirect government dole. The breakdown and increased unemployment in Europe is due in part to such practices."[20]

Congress saw things somewhat differently. The Democrats had captured the House in 1930, and although the Senate was still under Republican control, there were enough Republicans with a background in the old Progressive parties of Theodore Roosevelt and Robert LaFollette to join the Democrats in July 1932 in putting through an amendment to the Reconstruction Finance Act that at last made possible federal aid to the unemployed. It authorized $300 million in loans to the states for direct and work-relief; $1.5 billion in loans to states, local governments, and certain private agencies for self-liquidating public works; and $322 million for federal and state public works.[21] Hoover could have vetoed the bill. The pressure on him to let it become law was overwhelming. He signed, but how he felt about signing it was quite clear in his accompanying statement. The money would be passed out, he said, only on evidence of the absolute exhaustion of state and local funds. He meant it. By year's end a mere $30 million had been lent to state relief administrations, even less for state public works projects.

In his economic philosophy, his passivity toward the deterioration of the country's condition, his strictures on the evils of federal action to relieve distress, Hoover proved an easy target for a public fed up with hunger and misery and yearning for some concern in Washington with the subsistence needs of people and not their moral frailties. His name aroused ridicule, was embodied in the derisive metaphors of common speech. It was not just the packingcase shantytown known as Hooverville. The Hoover wagon was a brokendown car pulled by mules; the Hoover blanket, a newspaper; the Hoover hog, a jackrabbit; the Hoover villa, a privy. Franklin Roosevelt ran against him not only in 1932, but again in 1936 and in 1940, long after the great engineer had left public life but not the public's memory of his do-nothing administration.

Chapter 2

An Unprepared Social Work

The rise in applications for assistance at family agencies in the winter of 1929–1930, the newspaper stories of plant closings and other signs of bad times, caught social work by surprise. Social workers shared with the business community and with the administration in Washington and the press the almost universal view that bad times would be only temporary. They took it for granted that the hastily organized emergency relief campaigns they helped launch under voluntary auspices, and whose funds they administered, would be temporary. Spring, it was believed, would see a return to higher employment levels and to a restoration of the stable economic order assumed in retrospect to have prevailed until the catastrophic fall in stock prices in the fall of '29 and the business contraction and layoffs which followed.

Social work had every reason for such faith. The twenties were by and large an optimistic decade, characterized by buoyant economic growth, rising stock prices, price stability, and relatively little unemployment.[1] These elements seemed to sustain and strengthen the triumph of conservatism in politics, conformity in cultural values, and the emergence of the enterprising businessman as the archetypal American. Campaigning for the presidency in the fall of 1928, Republican candidate Herbert Hoover sounded persuasive when he said that the American experiment in human welfare had brought the United States closer to the disappearance of the poorhouse and the abolition of poverty and the fear of want than humanity had ever before attained. The "experiment in human welfare" was a catchy metaphor for the belief that the nation's standard of living was an automatic by-product of the operation of a largely laissez-faire economy.

In social work, the twenties were marked by the reaffirmation of voluntarism in the funding and control of social services for most people in need, and the well-nigh universal acceptance of the individualized approach in their dispensation. Public welfare departments existed, to be sure, in all the states and in most larger cities; but the public responsibility they represented was confined largely to what was deemed the irreducible minimum of persons with long-term conditions who lacked resources: the poor widow with young children and the aged poor in some states, and the poor who required institutionalization because of a severe disability—the mentally ill, the mentally subnormal, the blind, the chronically ill, the crippled. With some exceptions, the profession of social work turned its eyes away from such people as too hopeless to work with, preferring instead to pursue a dream of solving via social casework the needs of people whose problems were presumably of a short-term nature.

The Triumph of Social Casework

The basic social work texts of the twenties were three. There was Mary Richmond's *Social Diagnosis*, originally published in 1917, which set the tone of the decade by its declaration that in an early stage of democracy doing the same thing for everybody seems best, "but later we learn to do different things for and with different people." Her short book, *What is Social Case Work*, issued in 1922, defined social work as consisting "of those processes which develop personality through adjustments consciously effected, individual by individual, between men and their social environment." And then there was the Milford Conference Report of the American Association of Social Workers, published in 1929, and entitled *Social Case Work, Generic and Specific*. The product of the best minds in the profession, it characterized social casework as dealing "with the human being whose capacity to organize his own normal social activities may be impaired by one or more deviations from accepted standards of normal social life." Such deviations included alcoholism, bigamy, vagrancy, etc., nearly all of which referred to some aspect of personal behavior; a few, such as bad housing, reflected a nodding recognition of problems in the environment rather than in the individual.

All three books took for granted the existence of a rational, stable social order and of standard social norms. All three viewed the individual with problems as either at odds with the social order or in a state of nonconformity with its social norms, and therefore impaired in coping with life. It was the task of social casework to promote his capacity to deal with his impairments; its ultimate goal was to "develop in the individual the fullest possible capacity for self-maintenance in a social group." "It has made its highest contribution when its client no longer needs the social case worker."[2]

When attention is called to the importance of these three books in the thinking of social workers in the twenties, it is not being suggested that social casework was the only service offered by social work in that decade. Money was given by both public and private agencies to people in need of money; medical, rehabilitative, and recreation services were either provided or arranged for as needed; children from broken or disturbed homes were placed in foster homes or placed out for adoption. Little new was written on these subjects, however. What was called the growing edge of social work in the twenties was social casework. It was social casework which preempted the interest of the leaders of the field in the twenties, which loomed large in the literature of the day, which dominated the teaching in the schools of social work; and it was into agencies stressing social casework as their basic technique that most graduates of such schools moved when they got their first jobs.

The triumph of social casework in the twenties may be linked to the parallel rise in importance of psychiatry as a specialty in American medicine, and to the popularity within psychiatry of the psychoanalytic theories of Freud, Jung, and Rank. It was contemporary, too, with the general acceptance in psychology and along the frontiers of literature of the importance of the individual psyche in human affairs (Proust, Joyce, D.H. Lawrence, among other celebrants of the private man, were the culture heroes of the avant-garde writers of the decade). With the sanctions of traditional religion and morality in decay, persons who held advanced ideas—and such persons were to be found in intellectual circles cutting across many disciplines and interests—sought understanding of the affliction and distress of others and salvation for themselves in the exploration of the inner needs of the individual and in their fulfillment. Personality disorders, neurasthenia, the passive-aggressive syndrome, and other neuroses and psychoneuroses, tended to replace social and economic phenomena as causes of the troubles people experienced. The triumph of values which placed a high priority on individual enterprise in the business world provided a hospitable environment for these developments.

The twenties saw psychiatrists added to the faculties of schools of social work to familiarize students with the theoretical basis for social casework; and agencies wishing to be considered progressive took to employing psychiatrists as consultants on difficult cases.

A typical growth organization in the twenties was the National Committee for Mental Hygiene. It had been organized in 1909 by Clifford Beers, whose *A Mind That Found Itself*, based on his experiences as a mentally ill patient, had shocked the public a year earlier by its exposure of the inhuman treatment patients in mental institutions received, and whose proposals for reform via individualized treatment provided the basis for the national committee's program. But it was not until the decade after the war that the organization got off the ground and became a national movement. The title of Beers' book breathed faith and challenge; if my mind found itself, it seemed to say, yours can too.

The National Committee for Mental Hygiene was a lay organization. It stressed public education and public recognition of the need for professionally adequate hospital and clinic care, which meant at the least the use in such facilities of more psychiatrists. But psychiatrists were few in number, too few to meet the demand for their services in institutions and by private patients, and their fees were beyond the reach of most potential clients. Into this void there stepped, among others, social casework agencies. Provided the problems they encountered were not so severe as to require the ministrations of a psychiatrist, social caseworkers were persuaded their training prepared them to provide appropriate treatment. Acceptance of such a responsibility made it possible for them to deal, they believed, with most of the emotional needs presented by the people who came to them for help. In this context, it was not too farfetched to view social pathology—juvenile delinquency, crime, poor health, poverty, even poor housing—as an aggregate of individual pathologies, and the reduction of social pathology as possible only on a case-by-case basis. The environment was transformed in the process to little more than a fixed backdrop against which the therapeutic miracles of social casework were enacted; of little more importance than the neutral theatre curtain before which a skilled monologist displayed his talents.

Not all social workers, to be sure, went so far. Some looked at the role of social casework rather more modestly, as growing out of the distinction between what they called large-order and small-order problems, a differentiation allied conceptually to Mary Richmond's earlier dictum that social work was in the retail not the wholsesale business. Large-order problems, such as unemployment, inadequate education, bad housing, race discrimination, a lopsided income distribution, to name a few, belonged to the economic and political realm. Their solution was the job of government, of politics, and of industry, making use of economists, sociologists, political and other social scientists. Social work was concerned with small-order, manageable problems—manageable, that is, if they were the result of fairly obvious inadequacies or impairments in the individual or in family relationships, and therefore within the capacity of social casework to treat.

For all their differences about its role in the cure of the ills of society as a whole, both groups of social workers shared a common conviction of the supreme value of social casework for the families they served. Money was given, to be sure, to pay the rent and to buy groceries; but this was viewed as of minor value in comparison with the casework services rendered. Few asked by what right caseworkers took it upon themselves not only to dispense money as a gift—as though it were theirs for the giving—but to assume a parental or at least a guardianship, role toward the wretched who came to the agency's doors; to tell them, if not directly, then by implication what was wrong with the way they lived, to prescribe remedies, to order their lives. If such services had universal value, how could their limitation to the poor be justified? Money was the bridge over which the casework services flowed. If the bridge were removed, would the poor still clamor for the services?

To such questions the profession's answer was that the value of case-work services could be judged only on an individual basis. Numerous illustrations of success could be cited to demonstrate the value of the services rendered. There were some failures, of course, as there were in the practice of medicine. The connection between poverty and the need for casework services was an accident of history. Some members of the middle class were in need of casework services and were beginning to request such help at child guidance clinics and family agencies; perhaps they should be charged fees. Historically, hospitals began as dumping grounds for the sick poor; in time they began serving other income classes in the commu-nity and began to charge fees.

The question of the caseworker's right to counsel people in trouble, the argument continued, was too abstract to be more than theoretical, or philosophical at best. Social caseworkers were not philosophers. They were technicians, concerned only with facilitating the process of emotional growth, emotional maturation, and the attainment of emotional health. They were healers. The analogy with medicine was made again. Doctors treated the body's ills. Social caseworkers treated behavioral ills as mani-fested in parent-child or husband-wife conflict, individual failure, asocial activities. Neither kind of therapist had any need to justify what he was doing. Or to be concerned, except as a citizen and a voter, with the conditions some people said created or aggravated the pathology being treated.

The practice of casework, finally, had a clinical basis in experience. Just as physicians worked with a verified body of knowledge concerning the human organism, so social caseworkers in their ministrations drew upon a large fund of information about human behavior derived from the observations of psychologists, psychiatrists, and caseworkers. This infor-mation met the test of scientific truth by being verifiable; by the same token it was technical, arcane, and beyond the understanding of the lay person.

The Rise of Professionalism

Related to the emphasis on social casework and making it the fashionable field to get into was the growth in the professionalization of social work.

Professionalism came rather late to social work. Physicians had orga-nized the American Medical Association in 1847; the American Bar

Association dates from 1878; the American Society of Civil Engineers from 1852; and the National Education Association (1870) had its beginnings in the National Teachers Association formed in 1857. These nineteenth-century origins reflected the growth of public demand for specialized services, provided by trained practitioners, usually based on a university education, in a rapidly expanding industrial and technological society. A parallel demand (if that is the right term) for social work was not sensed by its leadership until the turn of the century because the necessary preconditions did not exist. These were, briefly, the emergence of a sizable body of poor people in American cities, associated with the rapid industrial growth of the country in the post-Civil War period and with large-scale immigration; recognition of the presence of poor people on the part of churches and philanthropic organizations; the increasing use of salaried rather than volunteer workers in the latter; and the growth among salaried workers of a belief that the work they were doing in helping the poor meet the demands of life beyond their own capacity, required a specialized knowledge, and that such knowledge had become sufficiently standardized to be transmissible, that is to say teachable via textbook and classroom.

The New York School of Social Work, founded in 1904, the first in the country, began as a six-week summer training program sponsored by the New York Charity Organization Society in 1898. By 1919, when the Association of Training Schools for Professional Social Work was organized, there were seventeen schools, of which twelve met the accreditation standards of the association. Another seven schools came into existence in the twenties. In 1929, twenty-nine schools qualified for membership in the association, whose name had been changed to the Association of Professional Schools of Social Work. Training for social work was also offered by ten universities and two independent schools not meeting association standards. More than half the schools in 1929 required an undergraduate degree for admission; all but a few, however, admitted some students lacking a degree. The Bryn Mawr School, established in 1915, was the first to limit admission to college graduates.[3]

A second major development in progess toward professionalism was the establishment of the American Association of Social Workers in 1921. The association opened its membership to trained social workers only, as that term was then defined; it required "competent experience" in an agency of "recognized standing." Despite the association's low admisstion standards—as late as 1933 applicants were still required to have only a high school education plus "competent" experience in an agency of "recognized standing"; only a minority were graduates of schools of social work—no one can examine the literature of the twenties without being struck by the insistence that social work was a profession, and by the barely-concealed envious attitude toward the established, status-laden professions.

For all its minimal requirements, the AASW in 1930 had a membership of fewer than 5,000. Perhaps another 2,000 belonged to separate organizations for hospital and psychiatric social workers. All told, the three professional associations accounted for about 18 percent of the 36,000 social and welfare workers and probation officers counted in the decennial census that year.[4] This 18 percent, largely employed in private agencies, considered itself the elite of the profession. From it came the experts who gave papers at social work conferences, who wrote the articles in social work journals and the social work books, and from it were drawn, with some exceptions, the faculties of schools of social work. To these people the theory and practice of social casework was the principal achievement of the profession in the twenties.

The Great Depression came as a shock to the field because social casework had nothing to say on the subject. Its theorists, its practitioners were the first to affirm this. The difficulty they ran into was getting the public to understand it—particularly the businessmen who sat on the boards of social agencies, central welfare councils, and community chests, the writers of newspaper editorials, radio commentators, and government officials from the federal level down, all of whom had always looked to social work to meet need. And need they defined in its conventional sense—lack of food, shelter, clothing, and the other physical aspects of existence. By this definition need was widespread in the winter of 1929–30, when millions were out of work and hundreds of thousands of families quickly exhausted such savings as they had to tide them over emergencies. The private family agencies they largely applied to for assistance were the very agencies in which social casework had had its strongest development in the twenties; herein lay the difficulty. In social casework, need had come to be quite differently defined; largely, as noted earlier, the need for professional counseling in overcoming individual and family blocks to self-sufficiency.

The disparity in the interpretation of need illustrated again, but under very trying circumstances for the field, the growing gap, lamented periodically in the professional press and at conferences, between the true function of social work and the public's understanding of it. For years the profession had been trying to get away from the popular image of social work as the dumping ground for society's failures, not only the incompetent, the disabled, and the behavioral deviates whose deviation was not so gross as to bring them into police stations and the courts, but the poor as well. The expectation of the public that it was social work's job to take care of the new poor in the winter of '29–'30, with emergency funds the same public had organized itself to raise and had turned over to the family agencies, demonstrated, as no earlier confrontation had, the failure of communication between the community, which provided social work with both the money and the social sanction it needed to operate, and the professionals, who determined social agency policy and were responsible for administration.

There was no time for confrontation now. Family agencies couldn't afford selective intake when applications for aid flooded intake desks. Agency boards, government officials and makers of public opinion demanded that the agencies do what was expected of them. They did. As caseloads mounted, additional staff, hastily trained, was added; the concept of "protected caseloads" for social casework practitioners was all but abandoned, and the agencies' main function became the relief of material distress via money grants.

They bowed under public pressure, but with misgivings. This is not our job, they said. We pick up and take care of the unemployed person whose lack of a job is traceable to some deficiency in his personality. We are not, however, the appropriate vehicle for meeting the bread-and-butter needs of the unemployed when they number in the millions and consist in the main of "normal" persons. This is to put social work in the wholesale business, where it doesn't belong.

The Abandoned Ethos of the Progressive Era

Such an attitude would have been foreign to social work not too many years earlier. Poverty, said Edward T. Devine, executive director in the first decade of the century of the New York Charity Organization Society, the largest family agency in the country, was communicable, curable, preventable. In his 1906 presidential address at the National Conference of Charities and Corrections (it didn't change its name to the National Conference of Social Work until 1919) he defined the task of the age as the destruction of the social causes of poverty. And he saw social work as an active force in that destruction. It was a view shared by nearly all leaders in the field during the Progressive Era in America's history, the years from the turn of the century to the outbreak of World War I in 1914. Never before had the profession been so responsive to the values popular in advanced political circles in both the Republican and Democratic parties.

The Progressive Era[5] merits more than passing mention in this account because in its general aspects and in its influence on social work thinking it offers a number of resemblances as well as many contrasts to the thirties.[5] Both were periods of reform, of agitation for greater democratization in American political life, a more equalitarian distribution of the wealth created by the country's industrial growth, and an increased role for government in the attainment of these goals. Both were episodes in the alternating rhythm of progress and reaction (as viewed by liberals), radical innovation and stability (as viewed by conservatives) that has marked American history from its beginnings. Triumphs and failures marked both. Their legacies, the imprint they left on American life differed, for reasons related to differences in the basic problems troubling the country, in the nation's industrial development, America's role in the world, political groupings and their expression within the country as affected by perception of socioeconomic class identity, and the degree to which dissent was felt and manifested. The two periods were akin, however, in their concern with basic issues, their receptivity to new ideas, and the receptivity of social work in both to the most generous impulses of the age.

The Progressive Era was a reaction to the evil aspects of the country's unprecedented industrial growth in the post–Civil War period, a period characterized by an enormous expansion in corporate wealth, in the economic power of the few rapacious men on top, in the size of individual family fortunes; by the popular acceptance of Social Darwinism as a rationale for the general belief that in a competitive world the fittest survive and that the fittest are the best; by the political corruption sustaining the whole system; by the open marriage of money and politics, and the vulgar ostentatious display of wealth captured in the term "the Gilded Age." Little of the new wealth trickled down to wage earners, their ranks constantly replenished by the millions of impoverished immigrants flooding into the country from Europe, their claims to a fairer share frustrated by laws against "combinations in restraint of trade" and employer-encouraged competition for jobs between native and immigrant newcomer, their lives made mean by poor food and bad housing and shortened by excessive disease. In the Progressive Era, a conscience-stricken nation, its eyes on an earlier America of unlimited opportunities for all, sought to put a brake on the concentration of economic power; to end the politics on which it fed and to redress the neglect which permitted the growth of slums, the lack of pure water and sewage treatment plants in big cities responsible for the spread of communicable disease, and the prevalence of quackery in medical care and in the touting of medical cure-alls.

It was the fashion to denounce the rich (the criminal rich and malefactors of great wealth, President Theodore Roosevelt called them), to champion the poor, to expose the dishonest and the wicked, and to document and publicize exploitation and misery. The country seemed eager to end corruption in politics; monopolistic practices in industry and finance; the plunder and chicanery behind the accumulation of great American fortunes; the fleecing of small investors by Wall Street swindlers;

the prevalence of low wages, long hours, and hazardous working conditions in many industries; the evils associated with the employment of women and children in mine, mill, and factory; the unrestricted sale of tainted food and dangerous and useless patent medicines; collusion between police and criminals; and the excessively high disease, infant mortality, and crime rates associated with the overcrowded unsanitary slums of big cities.

These wrongs were amply documented in such government reports as the nineteen-volume U.S. Bureau of Labor study on the employment of women and children, 1910–13; the largely social work-inspired and produced *Pittsburgh Survey*, whose results appeared in six volumes between 1909 and 1914; and in books by social workers, journalists, economists, sociologists, and others, bearing such arresting titles as John Spargo's *The Bitter Cry of the Children* (1903), Robert Woods' *The City Wilderness* (1899), Ernest Poole's *The Plague in its Stronghold* (1903) and *The Street, Its Child Workers* (1903), Robert Hunter's *Poverty* (1904), Jacob Hollander's *The Abolition of Poverty* (1914), Edward T. Devine's *Misery and its Causes* (1909), and *The History of Great American Fortunes* (1910) by Gustavus Myers. A larger reading public for exposés of the seamy side of American life was captured in the short stories and novels of Upton Sinclair, Frank Norris, Stephen Crane, Theodore Dreiser, and Robert Herrick; and in the muckraking articles appearing in *McClures, Collier's, Everybody's* and *Cosmopolitan*, by such writers as Lincoln Steffens, Samuel Hopkins Adams, David Graham Phillips, Theodore W. Lawson, Ray Stannard Baker, Ida Tarbell, and Charles Edward Russell.

Little social or economic analysis accompanied the reporting, whether in government documents, study commission findings, books, or magazine articles. Progressive Era writers tended to see the evils they exposed as the result largely of the greed of individuals in positions of power in industry or politics, the indifference of such persons to the social consequences of their activities, and the failure of the social order to translate into twentieth century terms the promises of liberty, equality of treatment, equality of opportunity, justice and government as the promoter of the general welfare enshrined in the Declaration of Independence and the Constitution. The remedy, for most reformers, was the enactment of laws to restrain the greedy, to end corruption in politics, to ensure the purity of food and drugs, to raise the wages of workers in industry, to restrict, and, if possible, to eliminate child labor, and to improve housing and public health standards.

Identifying with such other great crusades in American history as the abolition of slavery, the repeal of property ownership as a condition for voting, free compulsory public education for children, and free land on the frontier, Progressive Era leaders appealed to the conscience of America. The means employed were public education and persuasion—public education to enlighten the people on the evils afflicting the nation; and persuasion directed by reformers and an aroused public towards Congress and state legislatures to pass laws to put an end to the evils described.

Among these evils, of greatest concern to social workers active in the Progressive Era was poverty. Considerable thought was given to its causes and its cure. The causes were found in unemployment and irregular employment, in low wages, in the interruptions to earnings caused by illness or disability, particularly as associated with hazardous conditions in industry. They were located in state laws which permitted children to work at an early age, which allowed industry and agriculture to pay them miserable wages and to work them unconscionably long hours, and which denied them the education necessary for better jobs.

A similar indictment was made of the failure to protect women in industry. State governments were criticized also for their failure to replace loss of income resulting from work-related illness or disability, old age, and death of the wage earner in families with young children.

When it came to remedies, social workers and other activists of the Progressive Era, with the exception of the few who were socialists, never addressed themselves to the fundamental issue examined by most analysts of the social and economic order ushered in by the Industrial Revolution: how to distribute the wealth it created. In nineteenth-century America, as in Europe, the rewards of the system went mostly to the owners of the resources and productive facilities of the nation. The only restraints were those resulting from the wage and hour demands of labor unions, and state and national legislation designed to curb the most glaring abuses of the system, particularly those which seemed to violate the sacred principles of freedom of competition, the free movement of labor, or which imposed degrading conditions on the laborer. Such restraints had only a minimal effect on the operations of a voracious enterpreneurial economy, dedicated to growth and to high profits, goals viewed as quintessentially American in character.

Socialists advocated distributing the wealth created by the Industrial Revolution on the basis of the labor contributed by each worker, a change which could be effected only by replacing the system, which they called capitalism, by the socialist commonwealth. Under socialism, private ownership of the industry and the resources of the country would be superseded by public ownership. They hoped to accomplish the transformation democratically, although there were some socialists who said the capitalists and the government they controlled would not peacefully surrender their property and that a revolution would be necessary.

Such concepts were foreign to the fundamental ethos of the Progressive Era, which rejected the socialist notion of economic classes and of class conflict, believed in the validity of the American dream of a classless, equalitarian society, saw in reform via legislation the means by which the major social evils could be corrected, and in an appeal to the conscience of the owners of industry the path to a better life for America's wage earners. Industry was asked to pay a "living wage," but the term was never too clearly defined and the means by which it was to be attained were left unexplored. Although sympathetic to the aims of the labor movement, reformers—social workers and others—typically never found a place for it in their proposals.

It was a social work group which articulated in its most comprehensive form the aspirations of Progressive Era reformers concerned with poverty, and the underlying philosophy and measures proposed for its eradication.

The group was the Committee on Standards of Living and Labor of the National Conference of Charities and Corrections, whose chairman, Owen Lovejoy, was secretary of the National Child Labor Committee. The declared purpose of its landmark report, presented to the 1912 meeting, was "to lay the sub-basement floor" under living standards, the "lowest stratum that should be tolerated by a community interested in self-preservation."

It recommended that society set as its goal for a minimum living standard "such food, clothing, housing conditions, and other necessities and comforts of life as will secure and maintain physical, mental and moral health." Where not available, the standards should be attained by "governmental action and control, in the same way as subnormal sanitary conditions are subject to public regulation, and for the same reason— because they threaten the general welfare."

Specifically the report called for:

> A living wage, varying according to local conditions, but enough to secure the elements of a "normal"standard of living, to provide for education and recreation, to care for children in the family, to maintain the family during sickness of the wage earner, and to permit reasonable saving for old age. Advocated were the establishment of state minimum-wage commissions, payment of wages in cash(some companies paid in scrip) and payment at least once every two weeks (some companies paid wages monthly).

> Hours of work limited to an eight-hour day and a six-day week, the prohibition of night work for children, and restrictions on night work for adults, particularly women.

> Federal standards for safety and health in places of employment, enforced by periodic inspection, governing fire hazards; injury due to inadequately safeguarded machinery, equipment, or surrounding

environment; poor sanitation; poor ventilation; poisonous materials or products handled; excessive heat or cold; excessive noise.

Prohibition of child labor, defined as the employment of children under age 16.

Protection of women at work; specifically, banning the employment of women on jobs that required constant standing, and of pregnant women eight or fewer weeks prior to giving birth.

A government program of vocational training for young persons and for unemployable persons.

Social insurance: the enactment of state workmen's compensation and old age insurance laws, and the establishment of unemployment insurance programs under either state, municipal, or private auspices.

Tenement housing standards setting the following minimums: pure running water in every house, inside toilets in every house, adequate sunshine and ventilation in all rooms, privacy, rooms sufficient in number in relation to family size, freedom from dampness, the regular collection of garbage and other solid waste, a rental not to exceed 20 percent of income, the prohibition of home work (work engaged in at home).[6]

The parallel drawn in the introductory paragraphs of the report between poverty and an unsafe municipal water system emphasized not only a public stake in elimination of both, but a recognition, as well, of the dangers to society as a whole of their continued neglect. Rich and poor alike, the report seemed to say, were threatened by bacteria in the common water system, and by the presence of misery in the slums. The parallel illustrated also the assumption, characteristic of Progressive Era thinking, that the two issues were comparable. In the thinking of the writers of the report, the interests threatened by governmental action on wages, hours of work, child labor, tenement house standards, etc., would be no more effective in resisting the recommended reforms than were the so-called taxpayer federations in opposing the spending of money on a safe public water supply. A corollary assumption was that such selfish interests were not represented in government, a government deemed by the report to be some impartial authority, sword in hand, committed to putting to rout the forces of social injustice. At the very least, legislators, employers, and landlords were men of good will, who needed only to have their eyes opened to the wrongs for which they were responsible to agree to their correction.

The Report of the Committee on Standards of Living and Labor was widely circulated among political parties, labor federations, manufacturers' associations, church organizations, and women's clubs. It received its most cordial reception in the Progressive Party, the breakaway Republican group built around the candidacy of Theodore Roosevelt, which incorporated most of its recommendations in the section of its platform devoted to social and industrial justice.[7] The Declaration of Social Faith of the Federal Council of Churches of Christ in America echoed the call for the abolition of child labor, the wage earner's right to a living wage, labor's right to organize, and social insurance against the risks of unemployment, old age, and disability.

The year 1912 proved to be the high water mark of the Progressive Era in general and in social work. Conservative William H. Taft, the Republican party candidate, ran third in the presidential race, drawing only 23 percent of the popular vote and a mere eight electoral votes. Two out of three voters marked their ballots for either Woodrow Wilson, the Democractic party winner, exponent of the new democracy in American life, or trust-buster Theodore Roosevelt. Despite its disavowal of radicalism in politics, the Progressive Era provided favorable ground for the growth of the Socialist party, whose candidate in 1912, Eugene V. Debs, drew almost a million votes.[8] Socialists had elected 56 mayors, 160 city councilmen, and 145 city alderman by 1912.[9]

The Legacy of the Progressive Era

Some of the achievements of the Progressive Era left their permanent imprint on American life: the Sixteenth and Seventeenth Amendments to the Constitution, ratified in 1913, providing for a federal income tax, and for the election of senators by popular vote; the Pure Food and Drug Acts of 1906; the creation of the Department of Labor in 1913; reforms in a number of states in the selection of candidates for political office, and in the use of the initiative, referendum, and recall to strengthen the democratic process; workmen's compensation in most states. The Federal Reserve Act put the country's banking and credit system under public control. The Clayton Act and the creation of the Federal Trade Commission provided more effective regulation of big business than the toothless Sherman Antitrust Act. Labor unions were exempted from antitrust suits and an eight-hour day was instituted for railroad workers.

By 1912 tenement house reform laws had been enacted by almost a dozen states, and tenement house codes and sanitary regulations adopted by some fifty cities. The country seemed ready also to correct the exploitation of women in industry by preparing legislation regulating their night employment and hours of work. The National Child Labor Committee, founded in 1904, largely by social workers, succeeded in getting the worst abuses curbed in a number of states by new laws prohibiting the employment of children in hazardous occupations, setting higher age requirements, and limiting their hours of work.[10]

For social work the principal achievement of the Progressive Era was the creation in that *annus mirabilis* 1912 of the federal Children's Bureau, dedicated to the advancement of the health and welfare of all children, and whose etablishment was one of the more important recommendations of the first White House Conference on the Care of Dependent Children in 1909. Under the leadership of Julia Lathrop and Grace Abbott, the reports and recommendations of the Children's Bureau set new standards for programs in the areas of maternal and child health and welfare services, juvenile courts, visiting nurse services, and free lunch programs in the schools.

The principle of public responsibility for meeting economic need achieved a notable victory in the passage by Missouri in 1911 of a widows' pension or mothers' aid law, the first in the nation. It was limited, however, to Kansas City and the surrounding county. In the same year Illinois enacted a statewide law, and by 1913 twenty states had public aid programs for families containing dependent children with deceased or deserting fathers.[11] This Progressive Era initiative, unlike most, won only lukewarm support from social workers, many of whom opposed mothers' aid laws because of the traditional preference of the field for private rather than public assistance. The 1909 White House Conference had in fact recommended the use of voluntary funds and voluntary agencies for the care of needy children in homes lacking a father. Another ground for social work coldness toward mothers' aid programs was the fixed size of the grant, a feature wholly at variance with the maxim that the amount of aid should be related to need, which was affected by particular circumstances and differed therefore from one family to another.

The principle of social insurance, however, had general support among some leading social workers, despite the fixed-grant feature. The difference in attitude on their part represented an acknowledgement of the distinction they saw between payments based on need, and payments based on a replacement of wage loss, the distinguishing characteristic of social insurance. Receptiveness to social insurance reflected one of the major changes in social work thinking in the Progressive Era, linked directly to the new ideas on the causes of poverty, and to the realization that most of the families receiving aid from charitable organizations were in need because of factors beyond their own control. That families lacked income when the wage earner lost his job, became disabled, or died; that old age and destitution seemed to go together; that families lived in overcrowded, poorly lit, poorly ventilated, vermin-infested and unheated flats; that their children were undereducated, neglected, and that their health needs were slighted; that illness was unattended—these phenomena now spoke not of individual incapacity to overcome difficulties, the traditional moralistic view of nineteenth-century philanthrophy, but of breakdowns in social provision.

In Britain and in most countries on the continent, social insurance had, in Winston Churchill's phrase when arguing for Britain's first Old Age Pension Act in 1908, brought the magic of the average to the rescue of the millions. The idea went back at least to the eighties, when Bismarck, as part of his campaign to detach wage earners from the Marxist Social Democratic Party, introduced compulsory insurance in Germany against wage loss due to accidents, sickness, and old age. It was time, reformers urged, to apply the same remedy to America.

By 1912, study commissions in more than half the states were proposing workmen's compensation for income lost because of work-related injury or illness, and the outlook for enactment seemed favorable in most.[12] Attention was turning to the possibility of extending the principle to cover sickness and disability of all types, in brief, to health insurance.[13] And if health insurance could be considered, why not other forms of social insurance? They had in common the desirable goal of meeting, in part at least, loss of earnings whatever the reason, whether disability, illness, unemployment, old age, or death of the family wage earner.

Here the New World turned to the Old for guidance. A spate of books appeared on European experience with social insurance. In 1910 the Russell Sage Foundation published *Workingmen's Insurance in Europe*, by Lee K. Frankel and Miles M. Dawson; and in the same year Henry M. Seager's *Social Insurance, A Program of Social Reform*, appeared, based on lectures given at the New York School of Philanthropy, as the New York School of Social Work was then called. In 1911 Louis Brandeis, the progressive Boston attorney, spoke at the National Conference of Charities and Corrections on "Workingmen's Insurance—The Road to Social Efficiency"; and Isaac Rubinow, a pioneer student of the subject, came out with *Studies in Workmen's Insurance: Italy, Russia, Spain.*

Implicit in the treatment of the subject, in book, lecture, and conference paper, was the contrast between benefits granted as of right under social insurance, and the demeaning experience of charity when wage income was cut off under circumstances beyond the capacity of the earner to affect. So keenly did some social workers feel on the subject that they found it necessary to denounce the charity they dispensed. Lee K. Frenkel, director of the United Hebrew Charities of New York, called it in 1906 a blot on civilization.[14]

The Twenties: The Progressive Era as Past

The Progressive Era and the hopes it aroused were buried in the convulsions of World War I and the conservative political atmosphere of the postwar years. By the end of the twenties the Child Labor Amendment, passed by Congress in 1924, when the Supreme Court declared the federal law on the subject unconstitutional, was all but moribund; for lack of state support, housing reform was dead; and no further progress seemed possible in consumer protection, safety in industry, wage-and-hour legislation, or social insurance.

Mothers' aid laws were on the books of all but a handful of states by the end of the twenties, and ten states (beginning with Montana and Nevada in 1923) and the Territory of Alaska (whose law went back to 1915) had adopted old age pension laws, but for most social workers their imperfections were painfully obvious.[15] They were limited in geographic coverage (many states had county option laws which were in effect in a few of the wealthier counties only); restrictive in eligibility; penny-pinching in the amount of aid offered (in old age pensions, the highest maximum available was a dollar a day); drew only the most meager state support. For social caseworkers in the twenties there was something repugnant, too, in the idea that giving money to people without services solved any of their problems, problems probably present among most elderly persons and surely among widows and deserted women with young children. In the caste-ridden social work republic of the day, marked by a snobbery and elitism which assigned different rankings of professional esteem to the many welfare services available in the community, mothers' aid and old age pension programs were second-class citizens. Social caseworkers in particular found it hard to accept money as an answer to anything.

Only a minority of social work leaders thought such programs worth supporting for the principle they symbolized of public responsibility for meeting public need, and thought it worth fighting for their improvement. Notable in this minority were the two principle figures associated with the University of Chicago's School of Social Service Administration, Edith Abbott and Sophonisba Breckinridge.

For social work veterans of the Progressive Era the twenties were bleak years indeed. Many of the great figures associated with the period, members of that remarkable generation born about the time of the Civil War—Jane Addams, Julia Lathrop, Owen Lovejoy, Florence Kelley, Edward Devine—were still living in 1929, but they were no longer looked to for leadership by the younger people in the field. It was as though the passions felt in the first decade of the century, the concern with social issues, the passionate commitment to end poverty, were perceived as illusions, so many cobwebs that had to be swept away, using Freud's broom, Rank's, or Jung's, before the true condition in which we lived could be seen in all its nakedness.

There were dissidents, of course, from the prevailing temper of the times in addition to Edith Abbott and Sophonisba Breckinridge. At the 1924 National Conference of Social Work, Mary van Kleeck, director of the Division of Industrial Studies of the Russell Sage Foundation, asserted that little progress had been made toward the realization of the goals set out in the 1912 report of the Committee on Standards of Living and Labor and attributed the lack of success to the failure of social workers to understand how fundamental change in society is effected. The most powerful impetus to change today, she went on, were the efforts of wage workers to win security of employment, which she termed "industrial democracy." The limitations to the understanding by social workers of the true nature of American society lay in their identification with the values of the large givers who dominated the boards of social agencies, and their blindness to the needs of wage earners and the aspirations of the labor movement.

Her remarks, printed in the conference proceedings under the arresting title "Sources of Power for Industrial Freedom," were introductory to a thesis expounded more fully by Roger Baldwin, director of the American Civil Liberties Union and a former social worker, who in a paper titled "The Challenge to Social Work of the Changing Control of Industry," called the Russian Revolution of 1917, the emergence of a Labor party government in Britain in 1924, and the continuing Mexican Revolution, manifestations of the coming struggle for power between the profit-economy system—capitalism—and a new system—the "cooperative commonwealth"—which would abolish "economic classes, poverty, privilege." He identified the steps for achieving the latter goal in the United States as the development of a labor party, public control of natural resources and public utilities, public control of money and credit, the reform of the judiciary, which had been guilty of defeating efforts at raising living standards by declaring unconstitutional minimum wage laws and related legislation, the development of producer and consumer cooperatives, and international cooperation in the "struggle against war and imperialism."

Since social work, Baldwin asserted, had been brought into being by charitable agencies created by the monied classes, its thinking was influenced by their conservative philosophy. Hence the suspicion labor entertained of social work. The central thrust of social work was, however, greater freedom for the individual, from which it followed that social work should seek ways and means of cooperation with organized labor. "If social workers are to be participants in the essential struggle for larger human freedom in this generation, they can achieve it only by identification with the cause of labor." Had van Kleeck or Baldwin been addressing a local chamber of commerce they would have been attacked as socialists or Communists, dangerous enemies of the republic. To the social workers who listened to them they seemed odd rather than dangerous. There was polite applause, a mild rejoinder by Paul Kellogg, editor of the *Survey*, the leading social work journal of the day, then silence.

The subject did not come up again in the twenties. Social workers were interested in other things.

Ignored, too, were the handful of social insurance advocates, who saw in European experience with such systems a guide for America toward a treatment of poverty superior to assistance based on need. Rubinow continued to write on social insurance all through the twenties. Abraham Epstein made himself a champion of the cause of public pensions for the aged by organizing the American Association for Old Age Security in 1927 (the name was changed to the American Association for Social Security in 1932 and its scope broadened) and writing two books on the subject in the twenties, *Facing Old Age* (1922) and *The Challenge of the Aged* (1928), as well as a host of magazine articles and conference papers. John B. Andrews of the American Association for Labor Legislation issued a stream of pamphlets on needed improvements in workmen's compensation acts, and on the values of unemployment insurance and health insurance. They had few readers among social workers, to many of whom they seemed visionaries, if not crackpots.

Little wonder, then, that the winter of 1929-30 came as a shock to social work, that it saw the demands put on it as alien to its true function, and that its initial response was a dazed compliance with what the public expected it to do, but no acceptance of responsibility for locating the sources from which leadership in the development of programs adequate to the crisis should be expected.

Chapter 3

Social Work in Dissent

Porter Lee, director of the New York School of Social Work, was in Washington in 1930 as a member of the Woods Emergency Committee for Unemployment, but the committee itself aroused little enthusiasm in social work as a whole. The profession had rebounded from the initial shock of the winter of '29-'30 and had acquired enough self-confidence to offer the country counsel. In part this reflected delayed remembrance of the expertise its experience in the depression years of '21, '14, and '93 had given it, in part it was a natural response to the almost blind trust the community in its desperation placed in social work to meet the crisis. Counsel came easy because so elementary: don't demoralize the new poor by resorting to hastily organized and humiliating forms of relief such as breadlines and breadbaskets; have the needs of the jobless lacking resources met by established agencies with trained staff experienced in dealing with the poor.

With 1930 and no signs of improvement in the economy had come second thoughts. Late that year the executive committee of the American Association of Social Workers issued a statement, "The Responsibility and Contribution of Social Workers in Unemployment Crises," which marked a distinct departure in outlook. The statement made three basic points:

1. Social work was under an obligation as never before "to bear witness."
2. More information was needed on the extent and characteristics of unemployment. This was an obligation primarily of government.
3. Mass unemployment and the resultant privation had created a national emergency, to cope with which was beyond the capacity of voluntary agencies; it required action by government and industry.[1]

Bearing Witness

"To bear witness" was a familiar term in the profession, carrying with it the solemn sanction of tradition. Taken over originally from religion—the martyrs, by dying for their faith, bore witness to its truth—the phrase meant, in social work, making known to the world the somewhat lesser trauma of the sufferings of the poor, on the theory that the poor, being inarticulate and lacking access to the press, the radio, and other media, could not do their own witness-bearing. In 1930 the injunction to bear witness connoted to the informed person the obligation of social agencies to apprise the public, via newspaper releases, special studies, and testimony before legislative committees, of the detrimental effects of destitution on the health, education, family life, morale, and employability of the jobless.

But while paying lip service to the principle, social work invested few resources in bearing witness. Family agencies, their case records a mine of human-interest stories on the unemployed and their needs, would have seemed the most logical choice for the task, but little of the vast amount of documentation in their files leaked to the public. Perhaps they were too busy to find the time. Or they may have been blocked psychologically by an unsuccessful effort to reconcile their commitment to the values of social casework with its virtual abandonment in the overwhelming obligation thrust upon them by the community's insistence that their first job was to meet the needs of the unemployed. Their national organization, the Family Welfare Association of America, made no appreciable effort at witness-bearing. It was the National Federation of Settlements (NFS), closer all through the twenties to the social vision of the Progressive Era, which undertook the task in its 1930 study of the "human cost" of unemployment, based on interviews with the families known to settlement houses from neighborhood contacts.[2]

A better job of witness-bearing, but called instead reportage, was done by such liberal journals as the *New Republic* and the *Nation* in their articles on local aspects of the Depression. Their vivid reports, which reached a larger public than the NFS study, included stories on deprivation and suffering among the jobless, the reduction to penury of the tenant farmer and the sharecropper by the fall in farm prices, their protests and the often brutal manner in which such protests were repressed by the authorities; and articles as well on the indifference, the ineptitude, the hollow optimism, the astonishing absence of ideas on how to meet the crisis of the men in high places, both in Washington and in the citadels of finance and industry.

Perhaps the best of such accounts were the pieces written by Edmund Wilson for the *New Republic* and published in book form in 1932, under the title *The American Jitters.* Here, with the immediacy of impressions put to paper the same day or the day after, but with the extra perspective permitted by not having to meet the deadlines of the daily newspaper, and sharpened by the skill of the gifted writer, were on-the-scenes reports of the hunger march on New York's city hall January 20, 1931, which ended with a charge by club-wielding mounted police on the demonstrators, who fled or fell, some with broken arms or fractured skulls; Detroit flat on its back in the spring of '31, auto production almost at a standstill, and the primary concern of the jobless Ford worker the source of his next meal and how to keep from being evicted; dead and dying coal towns in the mountain hollows of West Virginia and Kentucky, their mine shafts closed for lack of orders, operated by scabs, since the miners, betrayed by union officials who had signed agreements with the operators for reduced wage rates, had gone on strike under the leadership of an independent union, a strike characterized by armed confrontations between desperate, starving miners and sheriff's deputies at the beck and call of the operators.

Wilson also did a series of articles on the textile workers of Lawrence, Massachusetts, who were driven to strike after a 10 percent general wage cut at a time when four out of five operatives were getting less than $20 a week, and were so poor they kept their children out of school for lack of shoes. Another account dealt with life in a gutted, abandoned, apartment house in Chicago's South Side, once a fashionable hotel, occupied now by squatters, black families evicted from their own homes; everything that made it a house gone except the walls, the floors, and the roof; lacking electricity, gas, heat, and water; doors, windows, plumbing, and lighting fixtures stripped to be sold for food and cheap liquor.[3]

More Data

The second basic point made by the AASW executive committee in its December 1930 statement concerned the lack of informaton on the size and nature of the unemployment problem. In calling for more facts on the subject, the executive committee echoed remarks increasingly heard in liberal and radical circles and among economists of different political persuasions. For a country as big and as industrialized as the United States, it was incredible that so few data existed on both employment and unemployment, official figures for which were collected only once every ten years, as part of the decennial census. Needed, said many economists, social workers and others concerned with the problem, was a continuing reading of the nation's economic pulse, as registered at least in counts of the numbers at work and the numbers idle and seeking work. (The beginning of data-gathering on the labor force and its components and on national income and wealth still lay in the future, one of the many contributions to better social and economic accounting made under the New Deal.)

The absence of such information was a measure of the government's unwillingness to become too involved in the subject. There were national data on hog and corn prices, on wheat, oats, and rice crops, on tons of copper mined and steel produced, on the volume of goods hauled by rail or water, on exports and imports, but none on the numbers employed and unemployed, on duration of unemployment, on differences by city, by region, by industry and occupation, and by age and sex. How was it possible to know whether conditions were getting better or worse? How was it possible to plan?

Instead of data there were guesses, which varied wildly. As if to minimize the whole issue, the national government ignored until 1932 so relatively simple a task as the collection of basic statistics on the number of persons on relief and the amount of relief expenditures. It had the resources in the Children's Bureau and in the Bureau of Labor Statistics, but to collect such statistics was to risk calling attention to the size of the unemployment problem. To help close the gap in information, the statistics department of the Russell Sage Foundation under Ralph Hurlin, beginning in 1929, undertook the collection and publication of a monthly series on relief expenditures in eighty-one large cities, including a few in Canada, based on voluntary reporting and covering both public and private agencies. The series, which eventually embraced 120 urban areas, was taken over by the Children's Bureau in 1932, and constituted the only national index of relief expenditures and recipients until the Federal Emergency Relief Administration came into being following Roosevelt's election and established its own machinery for that purpose.[4]

In time Hurlin's figures demonstrated the important shift that was taking place in the funding of relief, from major reliance on voluntary sources to public aid, despite the heroic efforts of the Woods and Gifford committees named by Hoover to rev up the exhausted giving machinery by annual fall mobilization campaigns. The shift had a significance, of course, going beyond the availability or nonavailability of data. Its dimensions are worth giving here because they illustrate one of the profounder mutations in national life taking place in the early years of the Depression and effectively concealed from public view by the administration's policy of slighting its quantitative aspects.

Contributions by the public for assistance to needy families quintupled between '29 and '32, the peak year for giving.[5] But it was not enough. As voluntary agencies proved unequal to the task of meeting need on the scale required, state constitutional prohibitions against what was called in the nineteenth century "outdoor relief" were rewritten to permit grants in their own homes to needy families who fell outside the special categories of the aged and the widowed with dependent children, for whom there were separate programs. History of a kind was made when New York's Governor Franklin D. Roosevelt set up the state Emergency Relief Administration late in 1931 under Harry Hopkins, funded by an appropriation of $20 million voted by the state legislature, and New York City voted money for home relief in December 1931.[6] Slowly, then with a rush, the barriers to publicly funded general relief, as it came to be called, collapsed in almost all state and local jurisdictions.

Local and state governments increased their appropriations to public welfare departments; converted them in places from agencies limited to the operation of such institutions as poorhouses, shelters for the homeless, hospitals for the chronically ill, to agencies whose largest function quickly became dispensing allowances to the needy in their own homes; and created emergency relief departments where none existed before.

Figures developed later indicate that by 1932 public aid outlays, including work relief, had risen from $60 million in 1929 (approximately half of which consisted of state mothers' aid pensions) to $256 million, accounting for at least 80 percent of all assistance dispensed in that third depression year.[7] The fourfold increase looks impressive, but in operation the public aid program had many limitations. Relief payments generally provided bare subsistence only (in the winter of '31–'32 relief payments averaged $2.39 per week per family in relatively generous New York City[8]), were cut back when funds ran low, here and there ceased altogether for shorter or longer periods. Cities, counties, and states ran out of money, skipped paydays for their employees, borrowed, sold tax-anticipation warrants at discount. To make the money stretch, harsh eligibility requirements were instituted; only about one-fourth the unemployed qualified for assistance.

In asking for more data on unemployment in December 1930, the AASW executive committee was calling attention to a larger question than a deficiency in government statistics. It was, as time proved, throwing a spotlight on the unwillingness of the Hoover administration to document the failure of voluntary social work to meet the needs of the unemployed, and the burden that failure was placing on limited state and local tax resources.

Whose Responsibility?

That point was made more explicit in the third of the three propositions advanced in the AASW's 1930 statement. It represented a recognition by social work that the dimensions of the problem facing the nation were beyond the resources of philanthropy and that voluntarism, which had stood the country in good stead on other occasions, was not the answer, as Hoover contended. Philanthropy, said the executive committee, could not replace payrolls. The national emergency called for jobs, a product voluntarism could neither create nor command. Unsigned articles in the AASW journal, the *Compass,* presumably reflecting staff thinking, elaborated on the subject. Making jobs available was the responsibility of industry. If industry couldn't, government must. This meant in effect a publicly financed work program, whether provided directly in the form of work-relief projects, with city, state or federal government meeting the payroll, or long-range public works using private contractors. The latter, because of the time it took for planning, bid advertising, and contract letting, was no substitute for direct work-relief, which had the advantage of putting people to work almost immediately. Both were required, since every sign pointed to a prolonged depression and it was not too soon to design a long-range public works program.

A similar concern for the long-run aspects of the crisis gripping the nation dictated the other elements in the association's third recommendation. Some states in the twenties had established public employment exchanges to bring together job-seekers and employers seeking to fill jobs. It was high time all states had such programs, possible only under a national system, as mandated, for example, in the Wagner bill, introduced by the senator from New York. There was, to be sure, a U.S. Employment Service, but its responsibilities were limited to "cooperating" with the states. It made no financial contribution to state systems, and it did nothing to fill the gap in states with no employment exchanges. The Wagner bill proposed the conversion of the USES into a truly national system by expanding the scope of its services, authorizing it to make grants to states with state systems, and directing it to operate employment exchanges in states with none.

Similar in its emphasis on public solutions for public problems was the suggestion, voiced in an unsigned article in the November 1930 issue of the *Compass,* which could be taken as speaking for staff, that social workers take a closer look at social insurance. Linked with a public works program and a national employment exchange system, social insurance would serve to complete a program triad making unnecessary, ever again, said the article, the hasty emergency measures in which social agencies now found themselves up to their knees. The unheard voices crying in the wilderness of the twenties, Isaac Rubinow, Abraham Epstein, and John Andrews, now acquired the status of prophets and were listened to eagerly.

It was in a sense a return of social work to the wider social horizons of the Progressive Era. The January 1931 issue of the *Compass* featured an article by Dorothea de Schweinitz reporting on the annual meeting of the American Academy of Political and Social Science, at which the main issue was security in industry. A pointed contrast was drawn between the social insurance approach to unemployment in Europe, and the resort in the United States to what was called the dole. An adequately funded, operating unemployment insurance system, said one of the conference speakers, would reduce the country's relief problem by half or more overnight. Fleshed out by measures to cover the risks of loss of earnings resulting from disability, illness, death of the family earner, and old age, a comprehensive social insurance program, others at the conference asserted, would meet the economic needs of almost all families on assistance.

Such a fundamental change in dealing with mass destitution appealed to social workers because it would not only preserve the dignity of the family by substituting benefits based on right for relief based on a means test, it would also have the merit of restoring social work to its true function of meeting needs having their origin in personal inadequacies, poor familial relationships, and the other problems in which social work had developed expertise. On this issue most social workers were in agreement, both the therapists inclined to see in every individual a potential patient, and the pragmatists for whom the neighborhood, the city, the nation, the social and economic order, was the patient. Social agencies, said the AASW executive committee in its December 1930 statement, cannot administer a large relief program, not only because it is not their job, but also because it would destroy their regular function of fostering the mental and physical health, and the educational and social adjustment of families.

Developments in 1931 accelerated the estrangement between the administration in Washington and social work as expressed in the views of the AASW. The Census Bureau released its count of unemployment in April 1930—6 million—a figure immediately criticized as an undercount because the Bureau missed the hundreds of thousands, possibly millions, on the move in search of jobs. To judge by reports in the newspapers of further layoffs and of plant closings, the situation in '31 was worse than in '30; Hurlin's data from eighty-plus cities indicated relief outlays were double their level in '30,[9] four times higher than they were in '29; recovery seemed further away than ever. Hoover's veto of the Wagner bill for a national employment service prompted a scathing attack by Mary van Kleeck in the April issue of the *Survey*. At its annual meeting in June the AASW appointed a Committee on Unemployment to collect and make public information on the subject from local chapters, to give further thought to the need for unemployment insurance, and to examine and report on proposals for more adequate funding of relief, including the possibility of a federal contribution.[10]

The Need for Federal Aid

Thus gingerly introduced, the hitherto forbidden subject of federal aid was now out in the open, its urgency more evident to an increasing number of association chapters as the months passed. In October 1931, a Social Work Conference on Federal Action was convened by a steering committee consisting, among others, of Walter West, executive secretary of the AASW; Frank Bane, director of the American Association of Public Welfare Officials; Paul U. Kellogg, editor of the *Survey*; Harry Lurie, director of the National Bureau of Jewish Social Research; and other social workers of national prominence. The conference recommended federal grants to the states for unemployment relief, to be administered at the federal level by the Children's Bureau, and at the local level by both public and private agencies making assistance payments, as well as a separately operated, federally aided program for transients.[11] (A special study by the Children's Bureau, issued in '32, called attention to the large number of older, unattached children on the road, living on handouts and odd jobs, the lack of trained staff and facilities for their care, and the callous tendency of local authorities to pass them on to the next town.[12])

That fall of '31 Senators Costigan of Colorado and LaFollette of Wisconsin introduced bills providing for federal aid. The bills were endorsed by the AASW's Committee on Unemployment, by the National Catholic Welfare Conference and by the American Federation of Labor. At the hearings in December, West of the AASW marshalled an impressive array of social work witnesses in support, including William Hodson, executive director of New York City's Welfare Council, and Dorothy Kahn, director of the Philadelphia public welfare department. The Costigan bill went down to defeat when it came to a vote in the largely Republican Senate in February 1932. New bills on federal aid and on federal public works programs were introduced and endorsed by an increasing number of AASW chapters.[13]

On the surface, there was a smooth facade of cooperation between social work and the President's Organization on Unemployment Relief, appointed as noted in 1931 and headed by Walter S. Gifford. He had asked for and received a promise of assistance from the principal national organizations in the field. The Family Welfare Association of America had been requested to prepare a handbook on the organization and administration of public relief agencies, and another on community organization for the care of the homeless. The National Association of Travelers Aid Societies had been invited to coordinate the efforts of local communities to care for transients in need; and the Association of Community Chests and Councils had been charged with making estimates of the relief needs of cities of 25,000 or more.[14]

But when social workers got together, they voiced unhappiness with congressional failure to face up to the nation's problems, and particularly with the obdurate refusal of Hoover to abandon his opposition to any form of meaningful federal responsibility. In January 1932, the AASW Committee on Unemployment held a two-day meeting in New York, in the course of which it said that distress was at its highest level in a century, that the income of millions of families on and off relief was below the essentials for the maintenance of health, and that a national program to raise living standards was acutely necessary. The committee endorsed pending federal aid bills because mass need, national in origin and national in scope, was beyond the capacity of local communities to meet, and constituted a primary federal responsibility. However new and unprecedented, the committee added, federal aid for relief programs was to be viewed as a temporary expedient only, not because such aid was wrong in principle, as the administration contended, or because the Depression would soon be over, but because more permanent and constructive measures were needed to meet mass unemployment, i.e., unemployment insurance, a national employment exchange, and so on.[15]

At the national delegate assembly in June 1932, the AASW officially endorsed the principle of federal responsibility by supporting the new Costigan-LaFollette bill making grants to the states for unemployment relief.[16] About the same time, the American Association of Public Welfare Officials was told by its executive director, Frank Bane, that federal relief was not only necessary but inevitable.[17] The organization itself took no stand on the question, however, reflecting the attitude of its membership, which consisted in the main of state and local welfare directors, concerned largely with administrative and personnel problems, and being accustomed to taking its cue on public policy issues from city councils and state legislatures. Few had the forthrightness of William Hodson, who wrote Hoover that cities and states had exhausted their ability to raise relief funds via taxes and bond issues and that federal grants were necessary. Hoover's reply—that the country was about to launch its annual Community Chest drive and that the need for Hodson's remedy would not be known until the results were in[18]—only served to exacerbate the repugnance with which the social work leadership now regarded the administration in Washington.

At the 1932 National Conference of Social Work that June, social workers heard themselves praised by Walter Lippmann for their patience, their courage, and their resourcefulness; they were told that when the history of the times came to be written, it would be said that they deserved well of their country. This may have come as balm to some of the tired, frustrated social workers present, but to others it must not only have sounded trite but seemed an insulting avoidance of the real issues at stake by 1932. More bracing to them perhaps than the syrupy words of Lippmann was the note struck by Rabbi Abba Hillel Silver, who said that social workers shared responsibility for the Depression because they had not thrown themselves into the struggle for a radical reconstruction of society as zealously as they had given themselves to the perfection of their techniques.[19]

The breakthrough on federal aid came with the amendment to the Reconstruction Finance Act Congress passed in July, which became law when reluctantly signed by Hoover. It authorized, as noted in chapter 1, loans to the states for direct and work-relief and public works, and a separate federal public works program. Writing in the *Compass* for July, Harry Lurie hailed the measure as an act of vital significance for public welfare and social work, but expressed regret that the aid took the form of loans rather than grants, a factor he thought likely to inhibit applications from states already overburdened with debts and with tax resources strained to the limit. He was critical also of the discretionary power given the RFC to accept or reject applications for aid.

Lurie spoke prophetically. By year's end only one-tenth of the sum authorized under the amendment had been passed out to state relief administrations. The trickle of federal funds had little effect on the abysmally low relief standards in many areas and the practice of reducing grants to meet chronic budgeting crises. When this happened in such a relatively wealthy state as Illinois, the Chicago chapter of the AASW was moved to protest to the state relief commission.[20]

Reflecting the national association's concern with the issue, the executive committee appointed a Committee on Federal Action on Unemployment to monitor developments under the new federal program.[21] At hearings in January 1933 on a new Costigan-LaFollette bill providing direct federal grants to states, the association provided twenty-five witnesses who reported on conditions in forty-four cities from data submitted by local chapters. Their testimony yielded a "sorry picture," the *Compass* noted, "of chaotic administration of relief, steadily decreasing relief standards, increasing numbers of people . . . whose needs are not being met," and "the disastrous results of appropriations for relief on a month-to-month basis."[22]

Meeting in the same month, the executive committee reendorsed the need for a federal direct grant program, with grants proportional to the size of the relief requirements and the state's resources for meeting them. Its statement called attention to the "unduly humiliating conditions" under which public assistance was being given in many parts of the country, the "famine rations" level of the assistance granted, and the failure of many local offices to take account of the shelter, clothing, heat, light, medical care, and other essential needs of the families granted assistance.[23]

What the executive committee said was largely a reaffirmation of positions taken earlier. It was also a reminder to the new administration elected the previous November of the expectations aroused by the Democratic victory. The atmosphere was charged with hope.

II The First New Deal, 1933–35

Chapter 4

In the Promised Land

Honeymoon

When Harry Hopkins, social worker, member of the American Association of Social Workers, FDR intimate, and newly appointed Federal Emergency Relief Administrator, appeared before the 1933 National Conference of Social Work, he was given a hero's welcome. It was a climactic moment in the history of American social work. Detroit, the conference city, its auto plants closed or operating on half time, its chimneys smokeless, its assembly lines silent, its traffic almost at a standstill, stretched in desolation for miles about, the visible symbol of the devastation wrought by the Great Depression. Within the conference halls, however, the general mood was one of elation, triumph, bedazzlement. The ship of state had weathered every rack, the port stood at hand, the prize sought was won, but unlike the image pictured in Whitman's threnody, there was a living not a dead captain on deck—sanguine, even cocky, and with a sure hand on the tiller.

Called into special session by the new President only five days after his inauguration, not to adjourn until June 15, Congress had enacted during what came to be known as the Hundred Days a trunkful of new laws, to get the country moving again, in the President's phrase. But what gladdened the hearts of the several thousand social workers who met that June to cheer Hopkins and other representatives of the new administration were the new federal work and assistance programs: a Federal Emergency Relief Administration (FERA) to make outright grants, not loans, to the states for relief purposes, under legislation passed by House and Senate by huge majorities, signed by the President May 12, and backed by an authorization to spend up to half a billion dollars; and the Civilian Conservation Corps, designed to put several hundred thousand of jobless young men from eighteen to twenty-five to work in the national parks and forests on reforestation, flood control, and related projects. The Civilian Conservation Corps had become law with the President's signature March 31 and had moved so rapidly that some 1,300 camps holding over 200,000 youngsters, had been set up even as the National Conference of Social Work was meeting. Except for a job program for the still idle fathers of these boys, the goals social workers had been fighting for during the late unlamented Hoover administration seemed attained. Further gains could be expected. The aims of the new administration looked good in the eyes of most social workers; and social workers were members of its inner councils. There was not only Hopkins. Frances Perkins, Secretary of Labor, was an AASW member, as was Frank W. Persons, Director of the U.S. Employment Service (USES).

In his brief talk, frequently interrupted by applause, Hopkins outlined the new federal program, as made known to him in the few weeks he had been on his new job (until May 22 he had stayed on as head of the New York state Temporary Emergency Relief Administration). Federal aid was not just for the traditional charity cases, but for the families of all needy unemployed; the program was to be an example of federal-state-local cooperation, administratively and financially; eligible local agencies were to be public, terminating the use of private agencies to spend tax funds for unemployment relief; programs for transients would be 100 percent federally financed; FERA funds could not be used to subsidize substandard wages. He ended on a thrilling note: under the new Public Works Administration (PWA), established that June as authorized by Title II of the National Industrial Recovery Act and given a $3.3 billion appropriation, he expected to see 2 million unemployed put to work by October.[1]

During the honeymoon New Deal year of '33–34, most social workers were enthusiastic supporters of the administration and its program. The May 1933 issue of the *Public Welfare News* of the American Public Welfare Association (APWA) hailed the recognition of unemployment as a national problem and its resultant distress as a national obligation. The *News* also found praiseworthy the special features of the FERA called attention to by Hopkins in his national conference address, particularly the channeling of federal funds to public agencies only and the inclusion of the costs of medical care in federally supported public assistance. The requirements state and local public welfare agencies had to meet to qualify for federal aid, noted the *News*, would deal a welcome death-blow to poor-law practices in some states, which went back to colonial days and whose demise no one would mourn except a few troglodytes in state legislatures and county courthouses. As an organization dedicated to the modernization of public welfare programs, the APWA saw in federal standards powerful leverage to accelerate the realization of the association's program of a strong, nonpartisan, well-administered public welfare department in every state and county in the country, manned by trained, experienced, or appropriately educated personnel, selected and promoted solely on a merit basis. An association resolution passed at the 1935 meeting hailed Hopkins for his accomplishments and his success in eliminating partisan politics in relief.

The *Compass* of the American Association of Social Workers observed with some satisfaction that FERA policy made strikers eligible for relief, a radical departure from existing practice and a challenge to exploiting employers, particularly in such low-wage areas of the country as the South.[2]

Social workers were cheered also by the Civil Works Administration (CWA), a crash job program for the unemployed inaugurated by Hopkins in November 1933, when it became apparent that the Public Works Administration in the Department of the Interior could not move fast enough to absorb any appreciable number of jobless.[3]

Addressing himself to the larger picture, Ewan Clague, director of research of Philadelphia's Community Council, saw in the New Deal the nation's best hope for the restoration of a stable and orderly economic system, with something positive in it for all major economic interests— industry, agriculture, labor—and he found especially gratifying the family security implicit in the collective bargaining section (7a) of the National Industrial Recovery Act and in the underpinning provided by the FERA when jobs were not available.[4]

The 1932 Election: A Political Upheaval

The outlook for the country had been transformed not only for social workers but for almost everybody. The '32 election represented a political upheaval as decisive as the rejection twelve years earlier of Wilsonism and the Democratic party and the triumph of old-fashioned Republicanism in the overwhelming election of Warren Gamaliel Harding. The election reversed the balance of political strength that had emerged from the election in 1928, held at the height of the boom of the twenties. The Democratic party's vote rose from 15 to 23 million, that of the Republican party fell from 21 to 16 million.[5] The Democrats' triumph was more a vote against Herbert Hoover as a person and a symbol than a vote for Franklin Roosevelt, or for the Democratic party platform. Roosevelt was a largely unknown quantity at the time of his nomination, a man with a mildly progressive record as governor of New York (he had established a state Temporary Emergency Relief Administration as early as the fall of '31), but hardly the charismatic figure he would become later and certainly lacking the national recognition the name Hoover evoked. And to compare the Democratic and Republican platforms adopted in the '32 conventions was to call attention to their likenesses, which were more evident than their differences. Both emphasized the need for a reduction in government spending, a balanced federal budget, a "sound" currency, higher protective tariffs, and laissez-faire economics in the relation of government and business. Both called for federal loans to the states for unemployment relief, rather than outright grants or a federal relief program.

The major differences in the Democratic party platform were an endorsement of state unemployment and old age insurance laws; federal regulation of holding companies, interstate utilities, and securities and commodities exchanges; refinancing of farm mortgages at lower interest rates; the development of the nation's water power in the public interest; and, most popular of all the planks with the convention delegates, a call for repeal of the Eighteenth (Prohibition) Amendment.[6] It was, the times considered, a moderate platform, which assumed that the poor, the jobless, and the insecure wage earner who had suffered several cuts in pay, would not vote for Hoover, and which sought to reassure the average middle-class American, dismayed by the events of '29–'32 but fearful of innovation, that he had nothing to fear from a Democratic victory.

First New Deal Achievements

The image of Roosevelt as a bold new leader, optimistic about the country's future and in full command of events, and of a Democratic Congress willing and anxious to enact his legislative program, was brilliantly etched in the public imagination in the first three months of his presidency. With almost all banks closed, Roosevelt declared a four-day bank holiday and called Congress into special session. The Hundred Days' sitting produced, among other relief and recovery measures, not only the FERA and the CCC, but also the Tennessee Valley Authority (TVA), empowered to build dams to control floods and produce and sell electricity and fertilizer, and to develop the agricultural and recreational resources of the region for the benefit of the people living in it; the National Industrial Recovery Act, authorizing the establishment of industrial fair-trade codes, with its corollary of exemption of participating businesses from antitrust laws and regulations, guaranteeing labor's right to collective bargaining, and setting up a Public Works Administration for the planning and construction of permanent job-producing, materials-consuming federal buildings, dams, and other projects; the Agricultural Adjustment Act, to raise farm income by paying farmers to take land out of production, authorizing government purchase and storage of surplus crops, and subsidizing farm exports; the Farm Credit Act, reorganizing farm credit conditions; the Railroad Coordination Act, establishing a federal role in the coordination of the nation's rail systems; and a whole series of fiscal measures to refinance home-owners' and farm mortgages, provide a federal guarantee for savings accounts up to $5,000, require full information on new stock issues to prospective purchasers, and to divorce commercial from investment banking.[7]

The pace of New Deal legislation slackened after the Hundred Days, but by the end of 1935 Congress had enacted the Social Security Act, establishing the country's first national social insurance system for older retired workers and for the unemployed, and making a permanent commitment of federal aid to the states for public assistance to needy aged and blind persons and to needy children in families with a dead, absent, or permanently disabled father; the Railroad Retirement Act, providing benefits to retired railroad workers; the National Youth Administration Act, offering part-time employment to needy students; federal job programs for the unemployed (Civil Works Administration, 1934; Works Progress Administration—later the Work Projects Administration—1935, and renewed annually); the National Housing Act, establishing the Federal Housing Authority (FHA) to guarantee mortgages for the purpose of encouraging home construction and ownership; the National Labor Relations Act (1935), making permanent labor's right to collective bargaining and outlawing antiunion activities by industry; a series of acts to help the farmer, establishing the Commodity Credit Corporation, the Resettlement Administration, the Soil Conservation Service, and the Rural Electrification Administration; the Federal Communications Act, to regulate the radio, telegraph, and cable industries. Other legislation sought to reorganize or reform practices in banking, the stock market, the operation of the Federal Reserve System, business bankruptcy proceedings, public utility holding companies, the merchant marine, coal mining, and other areas of economic activity. A beginning was made in righting the century-old wrongs committed against Indians, with the appointment as Commissioner of Indian Affairs of John Collier, executive secretary of the Indian Defense Association, whose program included restoration of land and self-government to Indians, encouragement of native cultures, and abandonment of all efforts to remake the Indian in the image of the white man.[8]

Not all of the new laws survived the test of time or constitutional challenge; in the main, however, they comprised some of the more innovative legislation of the century. It was not until the civil rights and antipoverty acts of the sixties that statutes of comparable importance were made part of the corpus of federal law.

The economic centerpieces of the first New Deal of 1933–35 were the National Industrial Recovery Act (NIRA), and the Agricultural Adjustment Act (AAA). They were basically an American version of the managed economy, with government, business, labor, and agriculture viewed as partners in a cooperative enterprise to restore the nation's economic health. A harmony of interests was assumed, an abadonment of laissez-faire, dog-eat-dog capitalism, but no venture into the dangerous waters of socialism. Under the NIRA business was freed from the shackles of antitrust legislation by authorizing the establishment of trade associations to promulgate codes of "fair competition," which set minimum prices, a maximum work week, and a minimum hourly wage rate. To win organized labor's support, the act, in section 7a, required employers to recognize their workers' right to join trade unions and to engage with them in collective bargaining.[9]

Agricultural revival in the first New Deal was to be attained by paying farmers to take some of their land out of production: reduced output, it was hoped, would in turn cut the "glut" and raise farm prices. As embodied in the AAA and administered by the Agricultural Adjustment Administration and the Commodity Credit Corporation, the program achieved its intended aims: farm "surpluses" were reduced, among other ways, by making payments to farmers to plow under standing crops and to slaughter young livestock, and by moving food crops into relief channels; loans were made to farmers on future crops to tide them over from one year to the next; and, most important of all, farm prices rose.[10] Net income of farm operators from farming doubled from 1933 to 1935; the relation of prices received by farmers to prices paid by farmers (the so-called parity ratio) rose from 64 to 88 percent; and farm mortgage debt fell.[11]

By most economic indicators, the bottom of the depression was reached in '32–'33. As a result, in part, of the measures undertaken by the new administration, the climb out of the pit began, moving more rapidly in some areas than in others, but advancing over a broad front. From its low in 1933 of $56 billion, Gross National Product, which measures the total output of goods and services, moved up to $65 billion in current prices in 1934 and to $72 billion in 1935. The ranks of the unemployed fell over 2 million in the same period. The numbers at work actually rose about 3.5 million, a difference accounted for by the growth of the labor force.[12]

A Disquieting Turn

In March 1934 Hopkins abruptly terminated the CWA job program. It was a disquieting turn of events for social workers, accustomed after twelve months of the new administration to glad tidings only in the news from Washington. The CWA, said Hopkins, had broken the back of the terrible winter of '33–'34; it was no longer needed. Oh no, groaned the social workers running the local relief offices. The four million unemployed who had been on CWA were pretty much back where they had been the preceding fall, out of work and out of money. They were now at the doors of the relief offices, filing applications for public assistance. The AASW's Division of Government and Social Work protested CWA's liquidation in a letter to the President, in which it affirmed the continued need of a federal work program. "We urge careful consideration of this plea for the liberalization and strengthening of your unemployment relief program, in the spirit which we believe has actuated your administration," it concluded.[13]

Some of the bite of CWA's discontinuance was softened by the administration's announcement that FERA funds could be used for local work projects, not only for the unemployed in large cities but for two groups traditionally neglected—stranded populations in single-industry communities with no hope for future reemployment, and distressed families in rural areas, particularly sharecroppers and tenant farmers in drought-stricken regions and subsistence farmers living on submarginal land. These initiatives lifted a little the spirits of social workers made unhappy by the abandonment of CWA. The American Public Welfare Association (APWA) found encouragement in the new rural rehabilitation programs.[14]

By and large, however, the profession was not happy with the turn the administration's relief program had taken by 1934. At the National Conference of Social Work that year, it listened with skepticism to the use by Aubrey Williams, who had been assistant CWA administrator, of the broken-back metaphor, so inappropriate when estimates of unemployment still ran from 10 to 12 million or so. Commissioner of Labor Statistics Isador Lubin noted gloomily at one of the conference sessions that even if industrial production returned to 1929 levels, a goal beyond the expectations of the most optimistic New Deal planners, only half the unemployed would be absorbed by the new jobs.

If the New Deal's work and relief programs impressed some social workers as indicative of an imaginative administration in Washington, open to suggestions, willing to break the crust of tradition and to experiment, they confused and dissatisfied others by their somewhat erratic and seemingly improvised character. The difficulties encountered in reading the administration's intent were if anything intensified by the almost schizophrenic contrast between a performance marked often by abrupt changes in program scope and direction, and the stress put on the need for permanent, long-term planning by its spokesmen when talking to social workers. At the same 1934 conference at which Williams and Lubin gave their papers, Rexford Tugwell, undersecretary for Agriculture and reputed to be a principal member of FDR's Brain Trust, talked of the breakdown of the old social order, said business recovery and relief for the unemployed, two major goals of the New Deal, were not enough, called for large scale social engineering and big thinking, defined the New Deal as the remaking of the institutions of the country to serve the many rather than the few. Social workers were enraptured by his incantatory, almost evangelical phrases, flattered when he ended by calling on them to help achieve the goals he had outlined.

And Harry Hopkins, in a paper sanguinely entitled "Social Planning for the Future," assured his listeners that basic changes were coming, some of them to be sure in the next 20 years, but others more immediately. The latter embraced a shift from the relief rolls to a pension program for the needy aged, the totally disabled, and the widowed. He also came out for universal compulsory health insurance, unemployment insurance, and a permanent public works program to provide jobs for those unemployed who had exhausted benefits and could not find employment in private industry.[15]

For these cheering visions Tugwell and Hopkins drew applause in the APWA story on the national conference.[16]

Chapter 5

The Critical Eye

Gaps Seen: Promise and Performance

Major doubts concerning the administration's program for meeting the needs of the unemployed developed even before CWA was shut down. At the Conference on Governmental Objectives for Social Work, held by the AASW in Washington in February 1934, resolutions were adopted opposing the abandonment of the work program and calling for the establishment of a large federally financed scheme based not on need but solely on unemployment and job qualifications. Tribute was paid to what was termed the courageous and ingenious social thinking represented by such New Deal programs as the National Recovery Administration (NRA), FERA, CCC, and CWA; but the administration was urged to give thought to the need for a permanent, comprehensive, well-coordinated, and adequately financed system of welfare services, with provision for federal, state, and local cooperation in administration, and the employment of a trained staff on a merit basis. Specific recommendations were made for a federal relief appropriation sufficient to meet the direct assistance needs of the country; continuation and improvement of the wholly federally financed program for transients; decent public assistance levels; relief in cash not kind; related to the latter, a surplus-commodities distribution program completely separate from public aid; "fair" wage rates in the public works program; expansion of the federal employment service and related state programs; a public housing program; adoption of the Child Labor Amendment.[1]

In advance of the Government Objectives Conference, the association distributed a series of bulletins which informed its members that unemployment as estimated by the American Federation of Labor was still in excess of 10 million, and that 3 million families were on public assistance in December 1933. A bulletin prepared by Harry Lurie under the title "Future Coordination of the Federal Dependency Relief Programs," proposed as basic principles recognition by the federal government of responsibility for a nationally integrated program of economic recovery, a national minimum-wage and maximum-hour law; acceptance by the government of responsibility for guaranteeing full employment by providing public service jobs for workers in excess of private industry's requirements; the development of a job-training and placement program for youth; a comprehensive federal public welfare program, embracing direct assistance and welfare services, and resting on a minimum national standard; the establishment of a social insurance program covering all risks to income.[2]

When the National Conference of Social Work convened in June, it heard New York City Welfare Commissioner William Hodson in his presidential address term the closing down of CWA a tragedy, affirm social worker sympathy with the dissatisfaction of the unemployed, and describe relief levels as intolerably inadequate—strong words for the man who headed the country's largest social public welfare department and might have been expected to take a more "responsible" attitude toward the administration's problems in reconciling needs and resources and in satisfying the different interest groups affected. It was absolutely necessary for the government to recognize relief as a permanent responsibility, he said, and to put its financing on a stable, dependable basis. He urged the adoption as well of a national social insurance system.[3]

At the conference, the AASW's Committee on Current Relief Programs registered its discontent with these aspects of the new FERA program: the return to relief in kind in rural areas, a policy in conflict with the principle of cash relief; the proposed stranded populations program, which would, the committee feared, move people against their wishes; the proposed abandonment of federal responsibility for transients, persons ineligible for public assistance by state and local agencies because they lacked "settlement," i.e. , residence requirements; the low levels of assistance standards in some areas; the lack of sufficient attention by FERA to the need for trained staff in state and local agencies. The committee voiced criticism also of the restrictive policies announced for the local work projects that would replace CWA: lay-off after six months on the project, for example, the limitation of an individual's employment to twenty-four hours a week, the absence of workmen's compensation for job-related injuries, the lack of coordination with the program of the U.S. Employment Service, the requirement of certification on the basis of verified need as against the use of simple affidavit, the use of work-relief to discipline or punish "noncooperative" members of families on public assistance.

The committee proposed the replacement of FERA work projects by a public jobs program incorporating minimum NRA standards, separated completely from the relief program and paying wages which would not have to be supplemented by public assistance. The committee concluded its report by calling attention to the need for abandoning the illusion that the Depression was temporary in character. The establishment of a permanent public service job program for workers not absorbed by private industry, it said, would symbolize recognition for the long-range planning needed.[4]

Criticism also emanated from the U.S. Conference of Mayors, whose recommendation for a permanent public works program paying prevailing wages differed very little from that of the AASW.[5]

The APWA, inclined to be more circumspect than the AASW, reprinted in the *Public Welfare News* a syndicated column by Walter Lippmann, characterizing direct relief for the unemployed as demoralizing, but voicing disapproval at the same time of a permanent public works program because it would compete with private industry when recovery got under way, and would require a large capital investment. Lippmann favored what he called a demountable work-relief program for the short run, labor-intensive, with minimal capital requirements, capable of being quickly put in place and just as quickly disassembled, with a wage-scale low enough not to discourage persons working in it from taking jobs in private industry, a fault he found to have been present in the CWA program.[6]

Quitting the Relief Business

Social-work disagreement with the administration reached a new high in January 1935 when the President, in another 180-degree turn, announced in an address to Congress that the government "must and shall quit this business of relief," a responsibility he now proposed to turn over completely to the states and localities, including the hitherto 100 percent federally financed program for transients. To sweeten this bitter pill, he announced his intention to create a vast new job program for the employable unemployed under a new agency, the Works Progress Administration—promptly dubbed WPA to conform with the craze for identifying by letters of the alphabet the names of the new agencies and programs the administration spawned almost weekly. The WPA, he estimated, would reduce the relief rolls by 70 percent. The remaining 30 percent, he said, could easily be picked up by state and local welfare departments, particularly when the aged, the blind, and the dependent children in the relief population were absorbed by the categorical aid programs to be set up under the proposed social security legislation.

Roosevelt asked Congress for a little less than $1 billion to close out FERA and $4 billion to finance WPA. The bill embodying the President's recommendations, introduced later that month, provided for the continuation of CCC, and specified that WPA projects would include slum clearance; construction of rural housing; expansion of the rural electrification program; soil erosion control; blighted area and submarginal land reclamation; improvement of existing road systems; construction of national highways; and the development of special projects for white-collar and professional persons. The objective of the new work program, as specified in the bill which became law in April, was to create 3.5 million jobs, or one million more than were available on FERA work projects. Criteria for project approval included usefulness, the promise of permanent improvement in living conditions or future wealth of the country, the absence of competition with private industry, a local contribution where possible, and a relatively large ratio of direct labor costs. Wage rates, varying by region, size of community, and type of work, were to be higher than the "dole" (FERA relief), but not so high as to reduce the incentive to take private employment; this was to be effected by limiting hours per week to permit a monthly wage within the range of $19–94. The nationwide monthly average aimed at was $50.[7]

Since the number of persons on public aid of all kinds, including work programs, was put that June by Hopkins himself at about 20 million, or one in six in the population, many social workers said the end of FERA would throw an intolerable burden on state and local resources, and regarded with a critical eye Hopkins's brave talk about direct relief to employables as a "miserable business," and his assertion that for the first time in American history the philosophy of the government was the improvement of the people's welfare. He was speaking in the relatively friendly atmosphere of the APWA, whose views were dominated by public welfare officials inclined to be receptive to the federal establishment's outlook and hesitant about appearing at odds with the source of so large a part of the funds they spent. By formal resolution, the APWA commended Hopkins for his accomplishments, in particular his effectiveness in eliminating politics in relief. The association said nothing officially that could be interpreted in the least as disapproving of the abandonment by the federal government of grants for direct relief, as it had made no comment on the ending of CWA earlier that year; the one faintly critical note in the resolution passed was the fear expressed that WPA wages in some localities could possibly fall below the budgetary needs of some families; Hopkins was urged to give careful attention to the problems that might arise in such circumstances.[8]

Social Work Takes Exception

The reaction of the AASW was somewhat different. The *Compass* welcomed the promise that categorical aid programs for the aged, the blind, and dependent children were to be included in the social security program. It expressed concern, however, that the states and localities lacked the resources, the administrative machinery, even in some states the constitutional authority and necessary legislation to take on the "tremendous burden" of supporting the needy not picked up by WPA, CCC, or social security. Countering the President's optimistic estimate that 70 percent of the families on relief would be absorbed by WPA, it put the percentage at less than 50—because many families either lacked earners or had earners who were too old, too young, or with too many health problems to qualify for WPA employment. Despite Roosevelt's assurance in his message to Congress, the first batch of projects proposed for WPA had little place for persons with work experience in service, clerical, professional, and related white-collar occupations. FERA experience demonstrated, furthermore, that one family in six on relief required aid to supplement earnings in private employment, and a similar ratio could be expected under WPA. It was essential, the *Compass* concluded, that a general relief or general assistance title be added to the proposed social security act to provide for the families that fell between the WPA and categorical assistance stools.[9]

These views found ample scope for expression at the 1935 delegate conference of the association in February. At the AASW's Conference on Governmental Objectives for Social Work, held exactly a year earlier, tributes had been paid the administration and Congress, and references to the government's relief program had been generally approving. Hopkins. had dropped in; his appearance had evoked applause. The only dissenting note sounded had concerned the administration's announcement of the demobilization of CWA. Such consensus, such good will, was perceptibly absent at the '35 meeting. No member of the administration was at hand in an official capacity; the few who showed up briefly were observers only.

The notion of a federally financed job program for the unemployed had general support, but the kind the delegates favored was not quite what Roosevelt or Hopkins had in mind in their plans for WPA. For one thing, employment should not require a means test and should be open to all persons lacking jobs. Employment in the program furthermore, was not to be made compulsory for earners in relief families under the threat of a cutoff in aid if the job was refused. Wage rates were not to be set below prevailing rates. While in agreement with the administration that projects should be useful, delegates urged that projects not be limited to the standard construction types—roads, bridges, dams, soil erosion control, floor control, etc.—and that provision be made for employment in the arts, in education, recreation, and other services, to help preserve the skills of jobless persons with training or experience in these areas.

Belief was affirmed in the continued need for a federally-aided relief program and for the preservation of the federal program for transients. The categories that would get federal grants under the proposed social security act would absorb only half the families on relief, leaving the other half to the inadequate financing, restrictive eligibility conditions and low assistance standards of the state and local programs of pre-FERA days.

With federal aid gone, hope of reform in the nation's crazy-quilt pattern of public assistance standards would be lost, delegates feared. Only a modest beginning in that directon had been made under FERA, which limited itself to such one-shot deals as making strikers eligible for relief, but left the old rules for the most part unchanged. FERA field representatives reported what many social workers had long known, but not in such graphic detail, that persons in need were being treated unequally depending on where they lived. The two principal conditions affecting eligibility were income and assets. In the larger cities, particularly in the industrial states in the North, public assistance could be used to supplement inadequate wages, but in some local jurisdictions, most commonly in the South, any income, as little as one dollar a week, made one ineligible for public aid.

Variations in the treatment of assets could fill a small book. If you owned your own home, which could be a miserable shack with an outdoor privy, no running water, and heated by a wood stove in winter, you had to sell it to qualify for aid in some places, and not only sell it but exhaust the money you got. In other places you were eligible if the assessed value of your home was below a fixed dollar maximum—often as high as $1,000 or more. Possession of a burial policy worth as little as $75 rendered a family ineligible in one county; in another, life policies of $1,000 or more did not affect a recipient's right to assistance. Other kinds of assets which affected eligibility included ownership of a car, tools, a radio, burial plots, livestock, farm acreage if you farmed for a living, and so on. A welfare applicant with a jalopy worth $25 would be turned down in county A; in county B, if it was needed to look for a job or for transportation when working, a car worth several hundred dollars was considered a necessity and no more made you ineligible than possession of a pair of shoes. Rules on livestock ownership were defined in terms of numbers of cows, sheep, pigs, and horses the farmer could own and still qualify for assistance. In some counties you could own one cow only, provided it gave milk and there were children home. Some rural welfare departments even set a maximum on the number of weeks' supply of hay and grain on hand to feed livestock.

Second thoughts on the categorical public assistance provisions of the proposed social security program erased for most participants at the AASW '35 delegate conference the favorable impression the administration's advance announcement had created a year earlier, with its promise of a permanent federal commitment to selected groups among the needy. Categorical aid, based on such special conditions of eligibility as age, blindness, or the presence at home of dependent children with a dead, absent, or permanently disabled father, now seemed wrong in principle because it made distinctions irrelevant to what should have been recognized as the primary condition for public assistance eligibility, namely, need. Categorical aid had been useful in the past (the reference here was to state old age pensions and mothers' aid programs) in helping break up the old "shameless" poor laws inherited from colonial days. It had served its purpose; it was time now to progress beyond it. The conference voted approval for a single public assistance title in the proposed social security act, one which would cover all persons in need, irrespective of age, disability, or family composition.

It was in essence a reaffirmation of the position on relief standards adopted by the executive committee of the association almost two years earlier, on the occasion of the launching of FERA, under legislation which put into the hands of the administering authority broad discretion in the management of the new program. The standards suggested by the executive committee had been offered as guides in the drafting of FERA rules and regulations. They undoubtedly had exercised some influence, since the FERA guidelines issued reflected an intent to establish a program embodying the best in social work thinking on the subject. But to what extent the guidelines determined practice was a matter of some dispute, for reasons having to do with the haste characterizing the introduction of federal grants, the broad language of the regulations, the relatively small field staff at FERA's command to monitor compliance, and the tendency of local administrators to continue traditional practices.

That the recommendations of the association's executive committee in those hectic May 1933 days aimed high was clear from the shortcomings in local programs, alluded to a few pages earlier, that had come to light in '33–'35. And now, in '35, when FERA was about to be dismantled, they possessed the special appeal which attaches to all brave standards whose adoption is suddenly seen as less and less likely. Who could deny their validity? In '29, '33 or '35? Relief sufficient to assure the maintenance of health and a minimum social life, including food, shelter, fuel, light, clothing, medical supplies, recreation, transportation, replacement of household furnishings and clothing? Payment in cash and continuing in character as long as eligibility was maintained? Dispensed on a regular basis, so that the family could plan its expenditures? And so on. Nothing new. Long-recognized canons of good social work practice.[10]

Quitting: Some Consequences

WPA was inaugurated in the fall of 1935 and FERA grants were simultaneously phased out. The transition was rough and some of the worst fears of the AASW were realized. Hundreds of thousands of families suffered a reduction in income, in some places were cut off from assistance altogether when federal funds ran out. Detailed information on the subject was not available for the several years it took the WPA's research division to make the necessary studies on the effects of the withdrawal of federal aid from what came to be known as general assistance, to distinguish such aid from the categories under the Social Security Act.

Newspaper headlines told the story in capsule form; "Penniless Relief Agency To Take Over FERA Functions in Duval County" (Jacksonville, Florida, *Journal*); "10,000 Will Starve, Social Workers Say in Drive for New Orleans Help" (New Orleans *Tribune*); "4000 Wheeling Unemployable Face Crisis as U.S. Dole Ends—County Unable to Shoulder Huge Relief Load" (Wheeling, West Virginia, *News Register*). The Englewood, New Jersey *News* commented editorially on the "spectacle of a hundred poor families eating garbage from the public dump," called it a "revolting practice"; recommended the replacement of the dump by an incinerator.[11]

A summary prepared by the national office of the AASW in January 1936, based on reports from twenty-five state and thirty-eight local relief administrators, revealed that the reduction in FERA grants proceeded at a faster pace than transfers to WPA; that the states and localities were unable to take up the slack because of fiscal, legal, and constitutional obstacles; that in some places the ability to finance general assistance was impaired by the need to put up part of the cost of WPA projects; that budget cuts for families on relief were common (in New York City, with one of the highest relief standards in the country, the per-person meal allowance was reduced below the March 1935 level of 8 cents); that staffs were cut to conserve dwindling funds; that many families were worse off financially under WPA than under FERA, and required relief supplementation as well as continuing help in obtaining medical care, nursing care and other services.[12]

AASW chapters in dozens of cities held protest meetings in the fall of 1935 and fired off telegrams to Washington requesting a restoration of federal grants for general assistance, climaxed by a telegram to the President in November by Walter West, AASW executive secretary, which said in part, "Only solution is continuing federal grants to states . . . otherwise . . . this will be worst of all depression years for unemployed and others in need." At the suggestion of the Division on Government and Social Work, the executive committee of the association adopted a resolution calling on the federal government to resume responsibility for grants to the states for general assistance, to be administered by the newly appointed Social Security Board running the programs established under the Social Security Act.[13]

Social Security:
What Social Workers Wanted and Got

Since the Social Security Act has been mentioned several times, it may be useful at this point to outline briefly social work's position on the characteristics of a desirable social insurance program, and what it got in the act Congress adopted. As noted in the preceding chapter, a favorable position on the need for such a program had developed among social workers during the Hoover years. Although the Democratic party platform for the '32 election said nothing on the subject except to endorse a state-by-state approach to unemployment and old age insurance, prospects for the enactment of a federal program brightened with Roosevelt's victory and seemed confirmed by his special message to Congress in June 1934, urging consideration of the issues to be faced in the establishment of a national program. By executive order he established the President's Committee on Economic Security, to which he appointed, reflecting the importance he attached to its recommendations, the secretaries of Labor, Agriculture, and Treasury, the attorney general, and the FERA administrator.

In the same month, the American Public Welfare Association endorsed the principle of a national program to cover the risks of unemployment, old age, poor health, and the death, absence, or disability of the father in families with dependent children.[14] The AASW also addressed itself to the subject, but it was in terms of social work rather than social insurance concepts. The Conference on Governmental Objectives for Social Work, held in Washington in February 1934, adopted a platform which included the need for what was described as a permanent, comprehensive, and well-coordinated system of welfare services, to "insure" people against the common hazards of unemployment, old age, widowhood, sickness, and other threats to self-maintenance. The program proposed would provide for financial and administrative participation by federal, state, and local units of government on an "equitable" basis. This was not a social insurance approach as commonly understood, but a hybrid with ancestral roots in a century of social work history dominated by voluntary agencies and the development of individualized service programs, and in a lingering distrust of fixed benefits as a device for meeting need. The conference did, however, endorse the administration-supported Wagner-Lewis unemployment insurance bill then before Congress, urging an increase in the minimum benefit payable under the bill and in the eligibility period.[15]

The President's Committee on Economic Security reported in January 1935. It recommended the creation of a federal old age benefit program, to be financed by a payroll tax divided equally between employer and

employee; a state-administered but federally guided unemployment insurance program, financed by an employer payroll tax, forced into being, in
a sense, by a federal payroll tax against which the state tax would be an
offset; federally aided public assistance programs for needy aged and for
dependent children in families with a missing or incapacitated father; and
federal grants to the states for expanded child and maternal health services
and for public health services. Administration was to be divided between
the Department of Labor and the FERA.[16]

The program as a whole was fairly modest in scope, and to some social
workers rather disappointing in the light of the hopes aroused by the
administration officials who had spoken at the National Conference of
Social Work the previous June. Could this be all there was to the major
social planning for the future Hopkins had said was under way in the
White House; or all the fruits of the social engineering and big thinking
Tugwell had asserted the times called for?

Bills incorporating the committee's recommendations were introduced
by Wagner of New York in the Senate and Lewis of Maryland in the
House, accompanied by a presidential message urging early passage. Their
only rival was the Lundeen bill, introduced in the House by Ernest
Lundeen, Farmer-Labor party, Minnesota, which was supported by a
coalition of left-wing unemployed worker groups, some labor unions,
radicalized liberals, and the Communist party. In its 1935 version (it was
first introduced in February 1934) the Lundeen bill's few pages provided
for unemployment insurance for all jobless persons eighteen years of age
and older, with benefits equal to average local wages but in no case less
than $10 a week plus $3 for each dependent. The program was to be
administered by commissions elected by workers' and farmers' organizations under rules and regulations prescribed by the secretary of Labor.
These commissions would also be responsible for developing social insurance programs (coverage, benefits, administration not specified in the bill)
to cover the risks of sickness, old age, maternity, industrial injury, and
other disabling conditions. Costs for all programs established under the
bill would be borne by the federal government out of taxes on individual
and corporate income in excess of $5,000 per annum and inheritance and
gift taxes.[17] To nearly all members of Congress, to commentators on
public affairs in press and radio, most economists and social insurance
experts, the Lundeen Bill, in its lack of detail, its basic incongruities with
the economics of the labor market, its defiance of "reality," was little more
than a pipe-dream, pie in the sky, a ticket to Utopia. To its fervent
supporters, these seeming deficiences, symbolic of labor's aspirations,
were its virtues.

The Wagner-Lewis bill was endorsed by the American Public Welfare

Association, but within the AASW dissenting views blocked endorsement or rejection of either the Wagner-Lewis or Lundeen bills.

The Wagner-Lewis bill, after undergoing a number of minor changes in committee, was passed in the summer of '35 and became law with the President's signature August 14.[18] The basic recommendations of the Committee on Economic Security remained intact, but the Social Security Act included three categories of needy to receive federal aid, the blind, as well as the aged and families with dependent children and no able-bodied father; and administration was put in the hands of an independent three-member Social Security Board, appointed by the President with the consent of the Senate. The board was responsible for the operation of all the titles except those dealing with maternal and child health services, services for crippled children, and child welfare services, responsibility for which was given the Children's Bureau in the Labor Department; those dealing with public health services, entrusted to the Public Health Service in the Treasury Department; and those concerning the collection of taxes for the support of the old age and unemployment insurance programs, assigned to the Bureau of Internal Revenue in Treasury.[19]

Given $76 million by the House to get under way, the country's first social insurance system had to mark time until January 1936 because a filibuster in the Senate killed the companion appropriation. The delay contributed to the distress which accompanied the transition from FERA to WPA that fall.[20]

Chapter 6

The Emergence of a Left Wing in Social Work

The inability of the AASW early in '35 to agree on a position on pending social insurance legislation arose out of fundamental disagreement within the delegate conference in February on the position the association should take on major governmental policy toward unemployment, poverty, and related issues. According to the account presented in the association's *Compass*[1], three viewpoints emerged, none persuasive enough to engage the support of a majority of the delegates.

The first was committed to the support of the administration. It hailed the New Deal as a great advance in popular democracy and in economic reconstruction, applauded the federal work programs for the unemployed, and approved the Wagner-Lewis bill as the initial step toward a broad comprehensive program of social insurance.

The second could be said to be proadministration but with reservations. It called attention to the shortcomings of the government's public aid programs, particularly the go-and-stop character of FERA and CWA, and to what it deemed the faulty thinking involved in the decision to confine federal responsibility to work programs for the employable, leaving the socalled unemployables and their families, less the categories to be aided under the Wagner-Lewis bill, to the states and localities. Representative of this viewpoint was Kenneth L. Pray, dean of the Pennsylvania School of Social Work, who said, "We are not any of us satisfied with the Administration's program for security and public welfare. We are far from satisfied with the insurance features; we are dissatisfied, decidedly dissatisfied, highly critical, of the work provisions; we are gravely concerned about the relief features and we are perhaps most of all troubled by the lack of cohesion and symmetry in the whole program."

The Third Viewpoint

The third viewpoint was critical not only of the government's relief and work programs, but of the New Deal as a whole and of the moral validity of the prevailing economic order. Its two leading figures were Mary van Kleeck, director of the Division of Industrial Studies of the Russell Sage Foundation, and Harry Lurie, executive director of the Council of Jewish Federations and Welfare Funds. Identifying themselves with van Kleeck and Lurie were some younger delegates who called themselves Rank-and-Filers, members of a group whose philosophy and activities are discussed in chapters 8 to 11.

Van Kleeck and Lurie were knowledgeable, articulate, persuasive, personable. But a greater contrast between two individuals in background and personality could hardly be imagined.

Mary van Kleeck, who had the patrician carriage and speech, the imperious presence and the grande dame manner of the mistress of a nineteenth-century salon, traced her ancestry to the Dutch settlers who came here in the seventeenth century, and was a member of the Colonial Dames of America. (She did not take her affiliation too seriously; I suspect she joined the Colonial Dames to upstage members of the Daughters of the American Revolution, an organization whose views she detested and which she dismissed as beneath contempt.) You could see her in twentieth-century America as chairman of the board of the American Red Cross, or as president general of the DAR, but hardly as a serious student of the lives of women in industry, a job which occupied her for five years after graduating from Smith in 1904, or as the head of the Sage Foundation's Industrial Studies Division, a position to which she was appointed in 1909, and which she held for thirty-nine years. She served as a member of the War Labor Policies Board in the 1917–18 War, as chairman of the program committee of the World Social Economic Conference in 1931, and as president of the Second International Conference of Social Work in 1932. She fitted neither the popular image of the social worker nor the specialized technician image evoked by that term among members of the AASW. She possessed wide-ranging interests. At one time or another, she was a member of the board of directors of the Encyclopedia of the Social Sciences, a vice-president of the American Statistical Association, a fellow of the American Association for the Advancement of Science, the first woman member of the Taylor Society, founded in 1911 to advance the ideas of Frederick W. Taylor on scientific management in industry, and the author of numerous bulletins and books on women in industry, and on labor relations, particularly in coal mining.

Her studies in depth of some of the country's basic industries and of labor relations, her government service, made her partial to a critical view of the economy and the political order. She was a lone voice in the twenties in her dissent from the bland conforming optimism of that decade, as noted in the reference in chapter 2 to the paper she gave at the 1924 National Conference of Social Work; but she found a more responsive hearing with the coming of the Depression. In 1934 she addressed an open letter to a number of journals in social work and other professions, inviting their readers to cooperate with industrial workers in the adoption by Congress of a comprehensive social security program for wage earners and their dependents. She may have had in mind the example of Britain's Fabian Society, which enlisted some of the leading intellectuals of the day in research and propaganda on behalf of socialism in the decades before and after the 1914–18 war; but as it turned out her appeal attracted only such radicalized groups as the National Lawyers Guild, the Federation of Architects, Engineers, Chemists and Technicians, and in social work, the National Coordinating Committee of Rank-and-File groups, described in chapter 9. They joined with her in launching the Inter-Professional Association for Social Insurance, or IPA, as it became known in that decade of acronyms. Its activities were limited fairly closely to promoting advocacy of the Lundeen bill; obtaining expert help among lawyers in making more explicit some of the vaguer elements in the original draft of the bill; and in securing sponsorship for a companion measure in the Senate. The IPA also favored the unionization of professionals and the eventual affiliation of their unions with the labor movement, but found little time to promote this aspect of its program. Mary van Kleeck was elected chairman; Dr. Frankwood E. Williams, the noted psychiatrist, treasurer; and the present writer served as secretary.

Harry Lurie came to the United States from his native Latvia in 1898 as a boy of six. His first social work job was with the Federated Jewish Charities of Buffalo in 1913-14. He became research director of the Associated Charities of Detroit in 1915, and from 1920 to 1922 served as head of the Relief and Social Service Department of the Detroit Department of Public Welfare. While employed in the latter capacity he completed the requirements for graduation from the University of Michigan in '21 and for an M.A. in '22. Between 1925 and 1930 he directed the Jewish family agency in Chicago, and in his last year there served as a member of the state Public Welfare Commission. In 1930 he moved to New York to take the directorship of the Bureau of Jewish Social Research, which became in '35 the Council of Jewish Federations and Welfare Funds, the central body of Jewish philanthropic organizations in the United States, including agencies engaged in rescue, education, vocational training, medical care, and direct assistance on behalf of Jews overseas.

Lurie possessed what one social-work journal described as a corrosive intellect. He had indeed a mind which saw through the conventional pieties on public issues, social and economic, and must at times have puzzled some of the more conformist members of his board. Now and then you caught a saturnine look on his wide expressive mouth, as though he was amused at the sluggish thinking of those he had to deal with, but he was essentially a modest person, diffident in manner, uninterested in promoting a cause or a following. Nevertheless, by sheer intellectual acuity he usually dominated committees of which he was a member, and he was often requested to prepare their reports, since he was adept at articulating and resolving conflicting points of view and was a master in the preparation of a carefully thought-through, integrated analysis of the subject assigned the committee.

Lurie was easy of access; he had none of the inhibitions and suspicions with which most social workers in his position regarded labor unions, organizations of the unemployed, and leftist political groups; he readily engaged in correspondence when they wrote him and he accepted invitations to speak to their members. In 1932 he addressed a Sunday evening forum on emergency relief under the auspices of the New Workers School (dedicated to "Training for the Class Struggle"). He did not hesitate to accept an invitation to join a committee of the New York Social Workers Discussion Club, which met in 1934 with William Hodson, director of the city's welfare department, to present a report sharply critical of its relief practices. At the request of the club he wrote Governor Lehman later that year about the hunger march on Albany the Workers Unemployment Council was planning; he noted that most social workers believed increases in relief budget food and clothing allowances were necessary, and suggested the governor give the council delegation a full opportunity to present their case. Lurie was one of the few nationally prominent social workers to send greetings to the first convention of Rank-and-File Groups in Social Work in 1935. He readily accepted an invitation by the Interprofessional Association for Social Insurance that same year to serve on a committee to seek Senate sponsorship of the Lundeen bill.

To return to the 1935 delegate conference of the AASW.

The position identified in the reports on the assembly as the "third viewpoint" was most forcefully presented perhaps by Mary van Kleeck. The government's measures in the areas of relief, work, and social insurance, in effect and proposed, were, she said, inadequate in scope, in degree of federal participation, and in their failure to provide the unified and permanent federal public welfare authority for which the continuing crisis in the economy called. They were designed to maintain the status quo, to quiet discontent, and to put forward promises which could not be fulfilled. The President's rationale for the Wagner-Lewis bill, she went on, did not constitute "genuine acceptance of any [new] principle of governmental responsibility." It appeared, rather, "to be the reaction of embarrassed political leaders" who preferred treating symptoms to causes. "For social workers to endorse promises under these circumstances as a great step forward is to encourage the American public in a delusion." Approval of the Wagner-Lewis bill was "politically naive, postponing effective action and stimulating false hopes." She saw the Lundeen bill as a better answer to the nation's need for an adequate social insurance program.

Lurie argued the merits of the Lundeen bill on similar grounds.

Another supporter of the Lundeen bill, challenged by a delegate who said that it was not feasible except under "a complete system of state socialism or communism," denied the charge, replying that while the bill "radically departs from our present philosophy concerning the poor and labor," social workers "can do no less than depart from a philosophy which has been so unsatisfactory and so undesirable in the past. . . . We do not believe," he concluded, "that it really means a radical change of our organized economic structure."

Pro and con positions on the two bills were not always identified with political philosophy. Sympathetic laughter, for example, greeted the remark that "we are all to the left of the administration." And one participant in the discussion said that more important than the Lundeen bill was "something far worthier—a socialized system in place of a competitive profit-motivated system."

To Kenneth Pray, however, supporters of the Lundeen bill were "a radical minority seeking immediate Utopias." While critical of the all- out supporters of the administration as a "complacent minority willing to accept almost anything labeled progress," he reserved his severest strictures for the "radical minority." "I think there is a great danger that the association, by its unwillingness to indicate any confidence in the administration, will play into the hands of the reactionary group opposed to the principle of governmental responsibility."

When it came to the showdown, the Communist-tagged Lundeen bill had the support of only a handful of delegates, but sufficient doubts were fostered by Lurie and van Kleeck about the Wagner-Lewis bill to drain off the approval of many who had a month earlier been impressed by the report of the Committee on Economic Security and the President's backing of the bill. In the end it failed to muster the necessary majority for endorsement.

The debate on the merits of the two bills expressed in acute form delegate differences on the specific issues involved. Less noticeable at the time, but more significant in the long run, was the exposure of those present to the leftward drift in the thinking of the two leading exponents of the Lundeen bill on basic social and economic issues, both at the conference itself and in the pages of the *Compass*, which printed a detailed report on the two-day meeting and summarized a memorandum by Lurie, giving his and van Kleeck's views a national audience.

Events proved Pray's warning needlessly alarming, but the concern he expressed was not atypical of the large middle-of-the-road group in the AASW which looked with mingled apprehension and fascination at the emergence within the ranks of social work and the AASW itself of a radical wing. Middle-roaders comprised the great majority of social workers and readers of the *Survey*, whose editor, Paul U. Kellogg, was an ardent New Dealer. Kellogg, however, as a good editor, presented not only laudatory articles on the New Deal's relief and job programs, but news reports and articles reflecting what was referred to a few pages back as the second viewpoint at the '35 delegate assembly of the AASW, a viewpoint committed to the general goals of the administration but critical of features violative of the profession's commitment to adequate relief standards, federal support of the direct relief program, etc.

A Just Social Order

The emergence of a left wing in social work had been foreshadowed by earlier developments.

The annual Milford Conference, a more or less informal gathering of leading social workers sponsored by the AASW to review the profession's basic concepts, adopted as part of its 1932–33 report an affirmation of its belief that "the future of social work is bound up with the coming of a sounder social order." The report went on to say that "the members of this profession have not only the obligation to work for justice . . . but the professional duty to make real the conditions under which their service can be given."[2]

The AASW Committee on Federal Action on Unemployment, appointed by the executive committee in 1932, whose chairman was Linton Swift, executive secretary of the Family Welfare Association of America, and whose members included Harry Lurie, Frank Bane of the American Public Welfare Association, Joanna Colcord and Ralph Hurlin of the Russell Sage Foundation, the *Survey*'s Paul Kellogg, Stanley Davies of the New York Charity Organization Society, and the association's executive director Walter West, presented a report on "National Economic Objectives for Social Work" at an all-day meeting of interested association members in April 1933. A summary, prepared by Lurie, who prefaced it with a statement that the Depression had opened the eyes of social workers to the undesirable features of the prevailing social and economic order, affirmed support for three general principles: 1. The social order had an obligation to provide a minimum standard of living for all persons in the population. 2. Social and economic planning was necessary. The blind forces of individual competition and individual incentive for private gain had to be curbed. 3. Social workers would do well to interest themselves in measures for social reform. In the absence of an active reform movement, groups benefiting from the maintenance of the status quo would use force to suppress dissent and stay in power.

Specific measures endorsed by the committee, reminiscent of the concern with basic issues animating the Progressive Era in social work, dealt with labor standards, relief, public works, social insurance, employment exchanges, and taxation. With respect to labor standards, the committee proposed a nationwide minimum wage, administered by a joint board representing management, labor, and the public, and the prohibition of child labor, i.e., the employment of children under the age of sixteen. A federally aided national relief program was necessary, with minimum standards of assistance and specific provision for transients. To meet the needs of the unemployed, the federal government was urged to launch a public works program large enough to absorb all the jobless, emphasizing conservation, water power, flood control, slum clearance and public housing. A national system of employment exchanges was essential to coordinate existing state programs with the new federal program. Economic security for wage earners required a contributory social insurance system with federal participation, covering the risks of unemployment, old age, and sickness. The committee's tax reform program condemned as regressive in character the increasing use by states of sales taxes to finance relief and favored basic reliance by state and federal governments on income and inheritance taxes, with rates proportionate to income.[3]

Speaking on behalf of the committee, Lurie presented a paper with the same title and making the same points at the 1933 National Conference of Social Work.[4]

Critical questioning of the basic rationale of the existing order emerged in the most respectable places. At the 1933 national conference, at which Lurie spoke, Frank Bruno's presidential address, "Social Work Objectives in the New Era," referred to the "cultural lag" (a concept popular among social scientists of the time to "explain" paradoxes in the social and economic order) responsible for the country's failure to solve the problem of an equitable distribution of the wealth produced by industrial and technological growth. He advocated a huge public works program to absorb the unemployed, and endorsed the principle of social insurance.[5] Touching on the same theme, Harold Moulton, president of the Brookings Institution, in a paper on the sources of poverty, attributed it to the lack of purchasing power to absorb the nation's productive capacity. Moulton declined to discuss the reasons for the lack of purchasing power on the ground that they were highly technical. He did however affirm his belief that a redistribution of income was necessary and was hopeful it would be achieved.[6]

And at the 1933 conference so solid and even conservative a social worker as Homer Folks, secretary of the New York State Charities Aid Association, the very citadel of the nineteenth century tradition of good-works philanthropy, called for the enactment of a social insurance program paid for largely by government, since its cost would be beyond the means of the average person.[7]

"A Planned Economy as a National Economic Objective for Social Work," was the title Mary van Kleeck gave the paper she presented at the April 1933 meeting of the AASW on "National Economic Objectives for Social Work." Printed in full in the May issue of the *Compass*, the paper ascribed the breakdown of the economy to lack of national planning and the maldistribution of income. Such planning as existed was designed to maximize profits and only exacerbated income differences in the population. The agricultural policy of the new administration was planning of the same character, since it was designed to raise prices, not feed the hungry. Because it organized scarcity not plenty, it was basically irrational. She contrasted such planning with the planning in the U.S.S.R., whose goal was to maximize resources, raise production, and distribute increased yields in industry and agriculture to all segments of the population, raising the national standard of living. True, this involved the abolition of private ownership of the country's resources, she continued, but in pursuit of its objectives, wasn't the U.S.S.R. fulfilling the goals held up as desirable by a recent encyclical of the pope on the reconstruction of the social order, which quoted from the encyclical on the same subject by Leo XIII some forty years earlier? Van Kleeck stressed that her favorable reference to the Soviet Union was not designed "to convert any of you to communism. I am trying to emphasize," she said, "the need for objective study of the new economic system of the Soviet Union . . . . I use it as illustrative of the need for studying the basic problem of organization in the economic system in relation to a declared objective." National planning, rather than such piecemeal reforms as the minimum wage, better employment exchanges, and so on, should command central attention.

That fall the executive committee of the AASW changed the name of its Committee on Federal Action on Unemployment to the Committee on Federal Action on Social Welfare, and gave it a broader scope.[8] The renamed committee played an important role at the association's Conference on Governmental Objectives for Social Work in February 1934, to which reference was made at the beginning of chapter 5. Its members, who included Harry Lurie, were largely responsible for the program adopted by the conference, which dealt primarily with the need for a permanent comprehensive federal public welfare program, but included a little-noticed yet significant section which said that social problems arise out of a faulty distribution of wealth and proposed changes in income tax laws that, in combination with the underpinning of the income of the poor provided by public relief, would result in a more equitable distribution of income in the population as a whole.

It was perhaps the first appearance in social work of a concept, to be called "transfer payments" by economists, the application of which, it was hoped, would ease the harsher aspects of an economic order in which income flows were determined largely by the ownership of property or other assets, or by employment, and little provision was made for rechanneling some of the income to persons with neither assets nor jobs.

Among the bulletins issued to delegates in advance of the '34 conference was the memorandum by Lurie, "Future Coordination of the Federal Dependency Relief Programs," in which he voiced "grave doubts concerning the effectiveness of the present capitalistic system for the economic well-being of the population." He looked with a skeptical eye on the programs—FERA, CCC, CWA, Interior's Public Works Administration, TVA, and the proposed Subsistence Homesteads Program—all of them bearing a good image in the Democratic-leaning press and among most social workers, and dismissed them as failing to meet economic realities. The realities were, in Lurie's words, the consequences of the malfunctioning of the economic system. Their correction required more fundamental measures than those put forward by the administration.

Later that year the Committee on Federal Action on Social Welfare became the association's Division of Government and Social Work;[9] the association's Committee on the Coordination of Governmental Services was retitled the Committee to Outline a National Social Welfare Program[10] (in this period of rapid changes in government programs, the AASW seemed compelled to keep up by constantly revising its own committee structure), "aimed at the economic and social security of labor, and the solution of the problems of dependency."

Van Kleeck at the 1934 National Conference

The committee did not meet until fall. Before it convened, the face of social work was changed by the emergence of Mary van Kleeck as a charismatic figure for the younger people in the profession. In June 1934 she electrified the 1934 National Conference of Social Work in Kansas City with two papers, "Our Illusions Regarding Government," and "The Common Goals of Labor and Social Work." She drew jammed halls. "The younger and more volatile rose as to a trumpet call," Gertrude Springer, the *Survey's* reporter at the conference, said in her account, "the soberest were shaken."[11] The applause as she finished reading

"Illusions"was so prolonged, conferees who had not been present demanded a second reading, held this time in a larger hall, again to standing room only.[12]

Kansas City papers put the story on the front page the next day and sent reporters to interview conference president William Hodson. New York's welfare commissioner felt compelled to issue a statement saying America faced three choices: the Hoover do-nothing program, the Roosevelt do-something program, and revolution. He indicated clearly his preference for the second. A day later, according to the account in *Social Work Today*, the organ of the Rank-and-Filers (see chapter 10), one thousand attendees at the conference met and voted to censure Hodson for "attacking" van Kleeck.

"Our Illusions" was given one of the two Pugsley Awards, presented by the editorial committee of the conference when selecting papers for publication in the *Proceedings*, for having "made the most important contribution to the subject matter of social work." (The other went to Eduard Lindeman of the New York School of Social Work for his paper on "Basic Unities of Social Work.") It was printed in full in the June issue of the *Survey*, and the *Compass* that same month ran excerpts which filled three pages. "Common Goals" had been promised to *Social Work Today* and appeared there in abridged form in October.

"Our Illusions" invited attention to two contrasting theories regarding the nature of government. The first, in which most social workers believed, saw government as independent of the conflicting interests of society, as arbiter in effect among these interests, and dedicated to the greatest good of the greatest number. Van Kleeck regarded this theory as an illusion. She espoused the second view, which viewed government as dominated by the strongest interests and, because of the nature of the American economy, tending to protect property rather than human rights. She was critical of the New Deal's economic policies, which were designed to shore up rather than curb the forces of exploitation in the country—in particular, she criticized the National Industrial Recovery Act, which suspended the antitrust laws and encouraged industry collusion to raise prices; section 7a of the act, added to protect labor's collective bargaining rights, but which was being abused by industry to promote the formation of company unions; and the Agricultural Adjustment Act, which helped big growers, not the small farmer.

She described the government's relief and job programs as inadequate and was critical of social workers who defended them or the New Deal in general. The rise in purchasing power they made possible among the poor was far less than would be available under a planned economy. She called on social workers to redefine their goals, to reexamine their fundamental assumptions, and to ask themselves whether private ownership and profit-making were compatible with the public good, and whether a planned socialized economy would not do a better job of raising the living standards and security of the American people. She appealed to social workers to align themselves with organized labor in pursuit of the objectives common to both groups.

The impact of the paper on a veteran social-work journalist is caught vividly in the note Gertrude Springer dashed off to her boss, Paul Kellogg, the *Survey's* editor. Van Kleeck, she wrote, "takes the hide off the AASW for its naive faith in the government expressed in the resolutions of the February meeting in Washington. Also plumps for the Lundeen bill and knocks Wagner for a goal."[13]

Unhappy at this frank espousal in the pages of the *Survey* of what sounded like socialism and might even be taken by some as communism, Kellogg had David Cushman Coyle, an economist with an engineering background, prepare an article for the July issue entitled "Illusions Regarding Revolution." Revolution, wrote Coyle, ignoring van Kleeck's rejection of violence, was a tempting prospect for persons weary of the long struggle against the inertia and stupidity responsible for the Depression; it yielded only new wrongs, new horrors; intelligence, not bloodshed, was called for.

"Common Goals" developed the last point of "Our Illusions" in greater detail. The common goals of labor and social work were the elimination of unemployment and exploitation and the attainment of security for all. These ends could be realized only in a planned economy devoted to production for use, not profit. To call for a planned economy, said van Kleeck, was not to call for revolution. America had the resources and technology to provide abundance for all. It took only the will to want the result to attain it. She expressed the hope it would be effected peacefully, by majority decision. If violence came, she said, it would be exercised by those who held power and refused to surrender it peacefully.

Van Kleeck gave a third paper at the 1934 conference, "The Effect of the NRA on Labor," a discussion of the mauling the unions were taking under section 7a of the National Industrial Recovery Act. "She skins the NRA alive," Gertrude Springer wrote Kellogg. "The girl is good at skinning."[14]

Van Kleeck was not alone at the 1934 national conference in raising doubts about the adequacy and competence of the prevailing social and economic system. *Social Work Today*, reporting on the meetings in its June issue, described the mood of the conference as one of revolt, citing not only the ovation given van Kleeck, but also the paper read by Eduard Lindeman. "Basic Unities of Social Work" challenged the profession to recognize the need for a "new social order," among whose essential features would be "a high degree of collectivism in economics." *Social Work Today* summarized the paper as saying America faced two choices:

a workers' government or Fascism. And Bertha C. Reynolds, associate director, Smith College School of Social Work, long identified with the teaching and practice of social casework in its classic form, presented a paper on the futility of psychiatric techniques in the prevailing social order.

A Fundamental Disagreement

When the AASW Committee to Outline a National Social Welfare Program assembled in the fall of '34, it had before it as a basis for its report to the 1935 delegate conference two draft memoranda. The first, prepared by Harry Lurie, was identified by him as the *minimum* program the committee could justifiably support. It called for a national Department of Public Welfare, with authority to make grants to the states for public assistance and for public welfare services and to set standards governing eligibility for grants assuring adequacy in levels of assistance, and the use of trained personnel in administration. The *maximum* program was not specified in Lurie's draft, but implied a social insurance approach to the problem of meeting need.

This was spelled out in the second memorandum, drafted by van Kleeck, which proposed primary reliance on social insurance, but would attach to it a supplementary service program to meet needs other than income. The Lundeen bill's approach to social insurance was preferred to that of the Wagner-Lewis bill. Offered for committee consideration also was a federal job program for all the unemployed, and a national system of employment exchanges to coordinate placement of the unemployed in the private and public sectors of the economy. Almost as an afterthought and without any elaboration of the details, the van Kleeck memorandum suggested the desirability of replacing the going economic system with a planned economy.

Discussion of the two memoranda revealed basic differences within the committee, not surprising when one considered its membership. This included not only Lurie and van Kleeck, but such administration supporters as Grace Abbott, chief of the Children's Bureau from 1921 to 1934, who had just retired to become a professor of public welfare at the University of Chicago's School of Social Service Administration; Ewan Clague, of the Pennsylvania School of Social Work, an enthusiastic New Dealer; Dorothy Kahn, head of the Philadelphia Department of Public Welfare, and president that year of the AASW; Frances Taussig, executive director of New York's prestigious Jewish Social Service Administration; and Linton Swift, executive director of the Family Welfare Association of America—all pillars of the social work establishment, all strong personalities and with views on the issues before the committee which varied from barely liberal to middle-liberal, but were ranged along a spectrum still a good distance from the positions staked out by Lurie and van Kleeck.

The basic differences concerned the relative emphasis to be given public welfare and social insurance programs in the committee's recommendations, and the nature of the social insurance program to be supported. There was general agreement, to be sure, on the principle of social insurance, but not on the specific provisions. Other than Lurie and van Kleeck, the Lundeen bill found no supporters among committee members. Clague doubted the economic capacity of the country to pay for it. He called the system envisaged in the bill "socialism"; said he had no objection to a discussion of socialism, but did not approve of the subject's being dragged in "in this backhand fashion." Most committee members thought public welfare should be given first place in the report rather than social insurance, and argued for the adoption of a program strong enough to rally the country's social workers behind it. They could not agree among themselves, however, on public welfare priorities and on the relation of the public welfare and social insurance systems, irrespective of the specific characteristics of the two.

Failing to reconcile their divergent views, the committee agreed to have each member draft a separate statement for transmittal to AASW chapters for the guidance of chapter representatives to the delegate conference scheduled for February 1935.

Two weeks before the conference was to meet, the steering committee of the Division of Government and Social Work, alarmed at the confusion it feared would be created, voted to reject for advance circulation the Lurie and van Kleeck memos as well as the separate statements of each committee member. The decision only encouraged speculation on the nature of the documents, the reasons for the "suppression," the extent of disagreement among committee members, and the relative strength of what were quickly dubbed the "left" and "right" wings of the committee.[15]

Thus incrementally, between 1932 and 1935, were laid the little mines which exploded with such unforeseen results at the 1935 AASW delegate conference.[16] A profession, united on what it thought were first principles, found itself in disarray. It failed to reach common ground on the position it should take vis-a-vis the government's public welfare and social insurance programs. Most alarming of all, perhaps, it discovered within its ranks professed or alleged enemies of the prevailing social and economic system, a discovery made particularly disconcerting to the leadership by the attraction which this view seemed to have for the younger members of the profession, and the appeal to them of the great challenger of the system, Mary van Kleeck.

Skinning the administration or preaching the planned society, van Kleeck played a gadfly role for the rest of the decade. At the 1935 National Conference of Social Work she addressed a general session on "Social Work in the Economic Crisis," in which she called attention to the administration's failure to reduce unemployment significantly, and categorized its economic, relief, and social insurance programs as the stabilization of poverty. The return of direct relief to the states, she said, was the response of an administration grown weary of carrying the burden of such aid and too weak not to succumb to the pressures of big business. She called on social workers to support higher taxes on the well-to-do, whose share of the national income under the New Deal was increasing, she said, and to throw their weight behind the Lundeen bill.

In *Creative America, Its Resources for Social Security,* published in 1936, van Kleeck developed in greater detail than was permitted by national conference papers her views on social security, the role of social work, the labor movement, a planned society, democracy, Fascism, Communism, and the choices facing America. The theme of the book, in essence, was the existence in the United States of the material, technical, and intellectual resources to make possible abundance for all, provided America was unshackled from the social and economic chains binding her under the present system. In the past, social work had been used by the prevailing order to meet the minimum subsistence needs of its victims. Its best thinking, reflected in the 1912 report of the Committee on Standards of Living and Labor, showed a deep concern for social justice, but an inadequate grasp of the forces blocking that goal. Social work believed in 1912, and still did in 1936, that research to uncover the facts about the exploitation of the many by the few, and their airing via research reports and stories in the press, would be sufficient to arouse the public to force government to act to correct the evils exposed. It failed to understand that government was controlled by big business, and failed equally to grasp the concept of the social dynamics behind such control, whose stranglehold could be broken only by a strong labor movement dedicated to altering the rules by which the economy was run.

That such a labor movement was nowhere in sight in the United States did not bother van Kleeck. Even in 1929, at the height of the twenties' boom, the American Federation of Labor had a membership of only 2.9 million, fewer than 10 percent of the nonfarm employed work force that year. Perhaps another half-million were in other unions. By 1933 AFofL membership had declined nearly a third and the federation was almost, if not quite, moribund. A hidebound leadership regarded with suspicion any proposal to take militant action against the wage cuts of the early years of the Depression and cast a jaundiced eye on programs to protect the living standards of wage earners by means other than collective bargaining.

William Green, federation president, said at the 1930 convention that unemployment insurance would make the worker "a ward of the state"; the federation did not endorse unemployment insurance until 1932, and as late as 1933 opposed minimum-wage legislation.

Perhaps van Kleeck, in speaking of a strong labor movement, had in mind the establishment in 1935, by John L. Lewis of the Mine Workers and a handful of other labor union presidents, of the Committee for Industrial Organization (CIO), dedicated to organizing the mass industries which the predominantly craft unions in the AFofL had failed to penetrate. The CIO, to which fuller reference is made later, was only a promise of a strong labor movement. No matter, it was the principle that was important.

There was, then, class conflict in America, as there was in other capitalist countries, van Kleeck continued. The Great Depression, worldwide in scope, revealed the failure of capitalism to solve the problems created by the unequal distribution of wealth and income inevitable under the system. Italy and Germany thought they had the answer in Fascism. Fascism, however, was only the dictatorship of capitalism, and could not succeed because it did not address itself to the basic faults of the system. The correct solution was a planned society, whose essential features were joint union-management operation of the economy, full employment, and full utilization of the material and technological resources of the country, in short, industrial democracy. In the planned society, industrial democracy would be paralleled by political democracy, from which, in 1936 as in earlier years, blacks were excluded in the South, and whose fulfillment in the country as a whole was blocked by control of the two major parties by business interests.

A planned society would be of course a classless society, as in the Soviet Union, which she praised for its economic planning, its abolition of unemployment, and its gains in national income and in living standards. What was good for Russia was not however necessarily good for the United States. Revolution and Communism were not needed in this country to achieve a planned economy, full employment, and a classless society. These goals could be attained democratically. She ended her book on an optimistic note. "What lies ahead is the America of our dreams— collective in its economic basis; democratic in its political control by all who serve society by their work; individualist in the unfettered achievement of its creative workers."

Creative America received a mixed reception. Attacks on the author as a Communist or a Communist sympathizer because of her uniformly favorable comments on the U.S.S.R. and her failure to criticize the repressive aspects of the Soviet regime left her untouched. She had referred in her book to class conflict in the United States but not in orthodox

Marxist terms; she avoided Communist party clichés; and she formulated her ideas in terms of American experience and American democratic traditions. This put her closer to the Socialist than to the Communist party, but she did not espouse either party program, preferring to mark out her own political ground.

The fundamental disagreement within the profession, reflected in the failure of the 1935 AASW delegate assembly to reach a consensus on the position to be taken on government policies, was not limited to the association. The radicalization of some members of the social work community, symbolized by the Pugsley Awards to the van Kleeck and Lindeman papers at the 1934 National Conference of Social Work, and given an organizational form by what was beginning to be known as the Rank-and-File Movement in Social Work, reached into the profession's latest recruits, the largely untrained investigators staffing the vast public aid program, to judge by the attraction the movement had for them. The trend was serious enough to alarm leading members of the social work establishment, who saw in the administration's relief, work, and social insurance programs progress in the attainment of the profession's primary goals, and in the New Deal as a whole, a major effort to overcome basic faults in American society.

The 1935 National Conference of Social Work, at which van Kleeck characterized the government's policies as designed to stabilize poverty, heard Katherine Lenroot, who succeeded Grace Abbot as chief of the Children's Bureau, and was president of the conference that year, stress the important role social work was playing in the enhancement of the objectives of the New Deal and vice versa. AASW president Dorothy Kahn hailed the gains social work had made by 1935, which included, she said, acceptance by the administration of the idea of social security, the incorporation of medical and nursing care in relief programs, the payment of direct relief in cash, the eligibility of strikers for relief, the beginnings of a merit system for personnel selection in public welfare departments, the beginnings of state registration of social workers, and the growing acceptance of the need for trained social workers in relief agencies. Frances Perkins, secretary of Labor, recounted labor's gains under the New Deal, had good words to say about New Deal work programs and the NRA, and called for social work support for the new Social Security Act about to be launched. Aubrey Williams, Hopkins's assistant, gave a preview of the act's main provisions, acknowledged its shortcomings, but dismissed them as almost inevitable in any new program and pretty certain to be corrected later.

And Paul Douglas, professor of economics at the University of Chicago and an old friend of social work, praised the New Deal as a first step in the elimination of America's social and economic evils; the next steps, he hoped, would be a big public works program for the unemployed, a more comprehensive social insurance system, including health insurance, and tax reforms to effect an equitable distribution of income. He warned an appreciative audience against what he termed extremists of the right and left, victory against whom could be achieved by strengthening the forces of democracy. To ensure the defeat of the extremists and the expansion of the New Deal, he called for a consolidation of the progressive forces in the Democratic, Republican and Socialist parties.

Attendees at the 1935 national conference also heard a protest from Grace Marcus against the low esteem into which social casework had fallen among social workers, whose sense of proportion, she thought, was distorted by their obsession with the economic aspects of the Depression. Marcus, whom the *Newsletter* of the Chicago Council of Social Agencies referred to as one of the two "high priestesses" of social work (the other being Mary van Kleeck—"high priestesses of two different religions"), in her paper, "The Status of Social Case Work Today," made a spirited defense of the validity of social casework in good times and bad. She referred, in caustic terms uncharacteristic of her usually moderate, courteous, "professional" manner, to the social workers who had "retreated entirely from any acknowledgement of personal factors in maladjustment . . . into economic dogmas that caricature Marxian theory." "Its fundamental purpose," she said of social casework, "of adjusting the individual to himself, his human relationships and his environment seems trivial and reactionary to some. Case work," she went on, unable to resist the temptation to engage in a little caricaturing herself, was for such social workers, "a sop to the underprivileged, obscures the issues of social justice, imposes on the individual the cruel burden of adapting himself to a psychotic society, and insofar as it succeeds, constitutes a brake on social action. From this point of view case work is not equal to basic problems and bears no more relation to social welfare than the art of cosmetics does to health."

Social casework, Marcus stoutly maintained, recognized "the ineluctable fact that individual lives have to come to terms with reality, however barbarous and unjust these terms may be. Casework does not and cannot impose that necessity for enduring existence. The necessity survives throughout all the developments and disintegrations of economic orders and cultural institutions. Within the restrictions of its functions casework has the unique and indispensable contribution to make to social insight, improvement and change."[17]

Grace Marcus was in the twenties and remained in the thirties, in her capacity as a case supervisor, casework consultant, writer and conference speaker, an eloquent, highly articulate exponent of the individualized approach, the one-to-one relationship of social worker and client, therapist and patient, in treating the ills of the body politic. No, she would never say the body politic, but the body human. Perhaps the body politic, like the public, either didn't exist for her, or was outside her concern, was somewhere else, to be dealt with by politicians, lawyers, legislators. Grace was an appropriate first name. There was grace in her angular frame, the thin face, the luminous eyes. Grace shone from the translucent pale skin, and was conveyed by her nunlike, humble manner. It was part of her charm. Who, once having met her, could fail to see the halo that seemed to hover over her head?

In her 1935 national conference paper she was attacking, many believed, not so much Mary van Kleeck or Harry Lurie, as the Rank-and-File Movement in Social Work. Her remarks on "economic dogmas" were more appropriate, however, to an earlier period in the movement, as will become clear later in this narrative. By 1935 the movement had shed its wholesale dismissal of social casework as charged by Marcus and was trying to work out its own understanding of the contribution which social casework could make even under the trying conditions of low relief standards, uncertain budgets, and an inadequately trained staff.

Chapter 7

The Liberal Connection

In questioning the aims and the achievements of the New Deal, and in their strictures against the prevailing economic order, whose fundamental structure they said the New Deal did not challenge, social workers like van Kleeck, Lurie and their supporters were responding to shifts in the intellectual temper of the times responsible for a profound radicalization among many liberal writers on the political scene.

A Turn to the Left

Their turn to the left began early in the Hoover years. The initial reaction to the stock market crash of '29 was relatively mild. It was not until the failure of 1930 to usher in the expected business revival that liberalism abandoned, one by one, the articles of faith by which it had lived through the twenties, which it had offered as remedies to meet the recessions of '21 and '24, and which it dusted off and put forward in '29–'30 as the answer to what looked like still another downswing in the business cycle. These remedies were government ownership, or at the very least government regulation, of public utilities, reduction of tariff barriers, a national conservation program to provide public service jobs, a government-subsidized housing program to meet the country's housing needs and to create additional employment in the construction industry, a national unemployment insurance system to provide the unemployed with benefits as of right rather than public assistance or private charity, and finally a government guarantee of labor's right to collective bargaining.

   As the recession took on the characteristics of a full-scale depression, an increasing number of liberal writers and journalists saw such proposals as mere palliatives. They seemed now to be based on a shallow analysis of the problems facing the country. They assumed that short-sighted behavior on the part of greedy men in charge of the economy was responsible for the Depression. Such proposals assumed further that bought-and-paid-for hirelings in Congress, in the White House, and in the courts, protected the greedy men running the country; that an awakened public, if properly informed and appealed to, would drive from their seats of power, economic and political, the greedy men and their hirelings, and replace them by good men dedicated to the public weal, in industry and in government.

How superficial this picture was, said those who claimed to have looked a little deeper into things. More fundamental changes were necessary; the economic system itself was at fault and needed replacement, not tinkering. Reforms would not eliminate the paradox of farmers with surplus wheat and corn and consumers with no money to buy food, of crop destruction in the midst of hunger. Neither would they solve the puzzle of how to bring together idle men and idle machinery in a nation with a seeming surplus of both.

In his *Autobiography*, published in 1931 after a lifetime of muckraking journalism, Lincoln Steffens, a veteran of the Progressive Era, said it wasn't bad men who were responsible for political corruption, social injustice, unemployment, uncared-for illness, and poverty, but the economic system itself, called free enterprise by most Americans, called capitalism by socialists and communists since Karl Marx. Change the system and you change the man; change the system and you eliminate political, social, and economic pathology. The system he clearly preferred had been identified by him after a second visit to Russia in 1919, from which he returned with the startling observation, "I have been over to the future and it works."

Farewell to Reform, proclaimed John Chamberlain in 1932, in his book by that arresting title. Efforts to curb the worst evils of capitalism by antitrust legislation and other laws intended to curb combinations in restraint of trade, were mere window dressing; illusions based on the dream of a return to the simplicities of an earlier rural America, the simplicities Jefferson saw in his vision of an America of small independent farmers. To believe in them, asserted Chamberlain, influential book reviewer for the *New York Times*, whose column was seen by a million or more readers, was to be blind to the reality of large-scale industrial and technological development, and the necessity of continued growth for a healthy economy and a high standard of living. The fundamental question concerned control. The system was now controlled by a handful of men sitting on the boards of the big corporations and the banks. Traditional liberalism failed to see reality because of its blind faith in the timeworn political process—electing good men to replace the bad men in office, passing new laws—none of which effected any true change in the stranglehold of big business on the economy. There were no countervailing centers of power. Few men in office, good or bad, questioned the system. Organized labor, as represented in the AF of L, accepted the system, wanting only a slightly larger share of the pie.

Chamberlain left it at that. He didn't advocate socialism or Communism, but many readers of his book drew their own conclusion. After all, what alternatives were there to 1920-style capitalism in the America of 1932?

Economic Planning, U.S. Model

There was another, some liberals insisted: economic planning, U.S. model. "Let's take Communism away from the Communists," Edmund Wilson proposed in the *New Republic* in January 1931, in "An Appeal to Progressives." He meant ownership and direction of the economy by the people for the public good, full employment, and the ideals professed by Communism, but without the repressive features to be found in practice in Russia. The call had little appeal to most liberals.

Neither Communism nor Fascism were applicable to America, argued Stuart Chase in *A New Deal* (1932). He agreed with Steffens, Chamberlain, and Wilson that capitalism was through in the United States, but urged an American brand of collectivism, not fully spelled out, as the next stage in our national life. It was flattering to Chase to see the new administration inaugurated in March 1933 call its program the New Deal, and Chase was an early if critical supporter, hailing the reforms inaugurated under Roosevelt as a major contribution to the development of American democracy.

In *The Modern Corporation and Private Property*, also published in 1932, Gardiner Means and Adolph Berle documented their finding that the ownership and management of the 200 largest nonbanking corporations in the country—controlling almost half the nation's nonbanking corporate wealth—were not the same, and that management ran what could be described as an administered rather than a free market. They proposed that the economy be taken away from the small management group controlling it, deemed dangerous in a democracy, and turned over to technicians for operation in the public interest.

How this could be effected was a political, not an economic problem and hence outside the scope of the book, said the authors, one an economist and the other a liberal lawyer.

Third-party movements run like a scarlet thread through the patchwork fabric of American political history, and it is not surprising that some liberals in the early thirties saw in a third party an appropriate vehicle for mobilizing dissatisfaction with the two old parties and for the promotion of the major changes they believed were needed in the economics and politics of the country. The Progessive Conference of March 1931, John Dewey's People's Lobby, and the December 1931 Conference for Independent Political Action were the more prominent of several efforts to bring together progressive senators, dissatisfied Socialist party members, and forward-looking trade union leaders in a viable alliance. That no third party emerged from the conferences held, and the proposals advanced in magazine and newspaper articles and in books, reflects the wide range of views held by liberals, their stubborn individualism, and their unwilling-ness to accept the kinds of compromises essential to the success of any mass political organization in a democracy, which usually turns out to be a shifting coalition of diverse interests, united on some but not all issues.

When 1932 rolled around, the *Nation* and the *New Republic* supported Norman Thomas, the Socialist party candidate. Lincoln Steffens, novelists Theodore Dreiser, Sherwood Anderson and John Dos Passos, and a number of other well-known liberal and radical writers, critics, journalists, and artists, called for the election of William Z. Foster, the candidate of the Communist party.

The Democratic party victory and the legislative program enacted by Congress threw liberals into disarray. Some became zealous New Dealers; others regarded with skepticism the claim that the New Deal would yield the fundamental changes in the economy the Depression required. Com-mon to all was a belief in the virtues of economic planning.

A number of people, supporters on the whole of the direction America was taking under Roosevelt, offered planning models stamped "Made in U.S.A." George Soule's *The Coming American Revolution* (1934), Alfred Bingham's *Insurgent America* (1935), and John Dewey's *Liberalism and Social Action* (1935) shared a rejection of the answer of some European countries and some prominent European political movements in the Depression (Fascism, Communism); a belief in the absence in America of either a revolutionary situation which could serve as a basis for Commu-nism, or a political tradition of authoritarianism essential for acceptance of either Communism or Fascism; and a faith in the possibility of transforming the reformist impulses of the New Deal into basic changes in the American economy.

They were critical of classic capitalism because it channeled its rewards to the rich and exploited the poor, and because it was wasteful and inefficient. Rejecting revolution or the use of force to effect change, they looked to public enlightenment to achieve the consensus needed to convert the economy into one in which labor, management, and government cooperated for the common good. In this collaborative effort, labor would be represented by the trade unions, government by dedicated public servants responsive to the needs of people, and management by an elite corps of technicians.

In the magazine he edited, *Common Sense*, Bingham envisaged a gradual transition to socialism, to be attained by persuasion not force, ballots not bullets. Force breeds counter-force, and middle-class America, which is how Bingham saw America, detested violence.

Economic planning along socialist (small s) lines, and within the broad framework of traditional American democracy, was advocated also by Reinhold Niebuhr of the Union Theological Seminary; the social critic and historian of ideas, Lewis Mumford; and Robert S. Lynd, the famous author of *Middletown*.

So strong was the tide in liberal circles for national planning that even Oswald Garrison Villard, longtime liberal, owner and editor of the *Nation* until 1932, now older and turned somewhat conservative, favored it, albeit within the confines of the existing economic system. And liberal Charles Beard, maverick historian, also saw national planning and what he denominated a "collectivist democracy" as the answer to the nation's problems. He viewed successful planning as the end-result of a long-time process, however, to be reached only as the growth of science and technology, which obeyed their own laws of development, replaced rule of thumb in the management of the nation's economy.

The more skeptical liberals looked at Roosevelt and the New Deal with a jaundiced eye. The *Nation* could thrill to FDR's inaugural address, call it "a challenge ... a trumpet blast," but it made Edmund Wilson yawn. Reporting the day's events in the *New Republic*, he found the new President's words unctious, the tone inflated, the confidence exuded forced and even phony, and in the call for action and the promise of bold leadership he heard echoes of the rhetoric of Hitler and Mussolini. He described the parade which followed as "abysmally silly," a phrase that could serve as a summary of his view of the entire day's proceedings.

Wilson and liberals like him saw only the conservatives in the cabinet with which Roosevelt surrounded himself, as liberals in the other camp saw only the progressives. There was, for example, William H. Wooding, secretary of the Treasury, an old-fashioned cautious banker. The bank holiday could be viewed as a bank rescue operation. Cordell Hull, the secretary of State, could hardly be classified as a progressive. Former Republican Harold Ickes, secretary of the Interior, whom Congress gave $3 billion for public works, was so concerned with getting value for the dollar, most of the money went unspent that first year (as had the money Congress voted the RFC for relief and public works loans to the states in Hoover's last year in offic, critics noted.)

The First New Deal: Fascism?

For left-leaning liberals, the National Industrial Recovery Act had parallels with some aspects of the Fascism they detested in Europe, particularly the freedom given industry to enter into collusive arrangements on markets and prices. It was recovery for business not the people, recovery sought through monopoly not competition, recovery through higher prices and lower production, scarcity not plenty. The act raised prices for the consumer, said the *Nation* and the *New Republic*, profits for the manufacturer, and failed to meet Roosevelt's promise to reduce unemployment and raise wages. They assailed the President for not raising taxes on corporate profits; and for his failure to nationalize the banks, the public utilities and the railroads when they were flat on their backs and he could have done so. John Dewey, George Soule, Bruce Bliven, and Stuart Chase saw the NRA Blue Eagle parades in all the major cities (250,000 turned out in New York, cheered by 1.5 million spectators, most of whom thought they were celebrating the end of the Depression) as Madison Avenue hoopla, would have preferred the picture of a restored America of humming factories, worker-management cooperation, a new sense of shared community—in other words, democratic socialism, not the New Deal.

An appraisal of like severity was made of the administration's agricultural policy. The benefits of the Agricultural Adjustment Act, designed to reduce surpluses and to raise prices paid farmers, were largely unavailable to the poor farmer, the tenant farmer, or the sharecropper. It was the farmer with the larger acreage and the greater resources, and the million-dollar processors owning or effectively controlling farms through crop contracts, who could afford to take advantage of the program for paying farmers to leave land idle, to plow under evey third row of cotton, to slaughter the little pigs, or who could qualify for the new low-interest federally insured loans. They were also in the best position to profit from the rise in farm prices.

Said Max Lerner in the *New Republic* in 1935, the essential logic of the New Deal is increasingly the naked fist of the capitalist state. Editorially, the *New Republic* asserted in the same year in a rather stark manner that either the nation must put up with the confusion and miseries of an essentially unregulated capitalism, or it must prepare to supersede capitalism with socialism.

When they were not assailing what they termed the near-Fascist aspects of the NIRA and Roosevelt's patch-capitalism philosophy, the *Nation*, the *New Republic* and *Common Sense*, liberal journals all, by no means to be confused with the Communist *New Masses*, were critical of his veering from right to left and left to right in strategy, his vacillation, his improvisation.

The first New Deal died when the Supreme Court ruled that the NIRA (May 1935) and the AAA (January 1936) were unconstitutional.

Some contemporary observers felt its death as early as 1934, with the fading of the splendor of what now seemed to them to have been the false dawn of a new era in American life. They reported experiencing a letdown. The emergency measures passed in the Hundred Days had not ended the Depression. The magic of FDR's appeal for bold new action had been perhaps nothing more than the magic of a stage magician. What next, they asked; does he have any more rabbits in his hat?

To radicalized liberals nothing had been lost in the death of the first New Deal but a near brush with Fascism, American style. Its demise at the hands of a conservative Supreme Court was an irony which delighted the left.[1]

Chapter 8

The Rank-and-File Movement in Social Work: Social Workers Discussion Clubs

The radicalization of social workers during the period 1930–35 went furthest and deepest in what was known as the Rank-and-File Movement in Social Work. Its views were shaped by many influences, among which perhaps the strongest was the attraction of the political left, also felt, as noted, by many liberal writers, critics, columnists, and educators in journalism and in academic life in these years. This attitude, focused most sharply during the Hoover and first New Deal periods, moderated with time, but remained left of center throughout the decade.[1]

The leaders of the Rank-and-File Movement attributed the Depression to the breakdown of the old order. They believed its attendant evils would end only when the old order was replaced by a new order based on public ownership of the nation's resources, and their planned, rational use. They were anticapitalist in the old-fashioned sense of that term, prosocialist with a small s, without committing themselves to either the Socialist party or the Communist party, although in the specific causes supported one saw more the influence of the Communist party than of the Socialist party.

The origin of the term "Rank and File" is obscure, but may be linked to its frequent use by opposition groups in labor unions to identify themselves when challenging the leadership. It implies that the challengers were representatives of the foot soldier in the ranks, of the membership at large in the union, of the powerless silent majority. The term had a special appeal for social workers who viewed sympathetically the aspirations of the labor movement for a better life for wage earners, and who saw parallels between the Establishment in organized labor—a self-perpetuating, small-minded, timid group of union officials, often corrupt, often bought out by management, given in this and other ways to betraying their membership—and the Establishment in social work, not corrupt or bought out, to be sure, but faint-hearted, at times pusillanimous, deferential to the conservative views of the businessman who provided the lay leadership in social work, and committed like them to the preservation of the status quo. A harsh judgment, given the humanity of the great social-work leaders of the past, especially in the Progressive Era, but then Rank-and-

Filers were young, knew little or no social work history, and were given during the early formative years of their movement to sweeping beliefs and unqualified generalizations.

The Rank-and-File Movement comprehended several kinds of activities in the thirties, grouped here under five headings:

1. Social Workers Discussion Clubs, essentially forums for talks on issues of interest to social workers, including some so broad in scope as to be of concern to almost everybody who read a newspaper. First organized in 1931, they were most active during the years 1933 and 1934. They disappeared after 1935, when their functions were absorbed by the newly organized unions in the field and the forums conducted by the journal *Social Work Today*.
2. Practitioner groups in some chapters of the American Association of Social Workers, and caseworker councils in some private family agencies. Relatively few in number and small in membership, they were never very significant in the movement as a whole and are here treated in conjunction with the discussion clubs.
3. Social work unions, whose beginnings may be traced back to protective organizations in private agencies in '31–'32, though they did not take on size until the middle of the decade, when employees of public relief agencies in the larger cities organized themselves into unions and obtained AF of L charters. Most of these unions switched to the CIO later.
4. *Social Work Today*, a journal founded by the Social Workers Discussion Club in New York in 1934, the national news organ of the Rank-and-File Movement and its ideological mouthpiece; published initially as a bimonthly, later put out eight or nine times a year; issued from 1934 to 1942.
5. Involvement by discussion clubs, unions, practitioner groups, and *Social Work Today* in joint activities with other organizations on issues ranging in scope from national social welfare programs to American foreign policy.

These five types of activities are treated here sequentially. The separate treatment is necessary to bring out the distinctive features of each but, as will be evident from the account given, such an approach is purely arbitrary, since membership overlapped and the basic constituency appealed to—persons working in social agencies, professional and non-professional—remained the same.

The initial impetus for the movement came from a small group of trained social workers, graduates for the most part of schools of social work, and many of them members of the AASW. As the movement grew, it attracted support among employees of the new public relief agencies, untrained as a rule, and not inclined to think of themselves as social workers. In time this group constituted more than half the membership of the organizations identified with the movement. Leadership, however, tended to remain with the original organizers, professional social workers who provided the continuity to be traced from '31 to the end of the decade. The same name often appeared as chairman of a discussion club one year, member of the editorial board of *Social Work Today* the next year, officer of a social work union in still another year, member of the executive committee of the Social Workers Committee to aid Spanish Democracy concurrently or a little later, member of the city-wide joint board of the national CIO labor organization the social work union joined, and so on.

Origins

Social workers in the early years of the Depression who felt dissatisfied with the thinking of the social work establishment, unhappy about the political and economic order, and anxious to do something about these two evils, found that a natural first step was a meeting to talk things over. You talked things over to find out how many felt the way you did. When you had a like-minded nucleus, you held a meeting to influence other social workers. In time a following was established.

The normal channels of communication in social work were of course open to the organizers of the first discussion clubs: meetings of the AASW local chapter, the National Conference of Social Work, the annual state conference of social work, and such journals as the *Survey*, the *Family*, and the *Compass*. The subjects the dissidents wanted to talk about, however, and the views they wanted to hear hardly fitted the agenda of the typical AASW chapter meeting. The national conference met only once a year and there were problems about getting on the program. And social work journal editors were not likely to print articles they would consider "extremist," to use a term indicative not only of how far the first self-styled Rank-and-Filers felt alienated from the AASW, the national conference, and the social work journals, but also how they believed their views would be regarded.

The medium chosen, because they could say what they wanted to say, hear what they wanted to hear, and have complete control over organization, was the Social Workers Discussion Club. The first club was established in New York in the spring of 1931 as an "open forum for the analysis of basic social problems and their relation to social work." There was nothing modest about its claim that basic social problems would be analyzed, or about the solutions offered. Subjects discussed at the early meetings, which attracted about a hundred-odd social workers employed in voluntary agencies, included such topics as "Psychiatry and Society," "Social Aspects of Literature," "The Negro and the Crisis," "The Dangers of War," and, coming closer to home, "The Causes and Cure of the Depression," and "Unemployment Relief and Unemployment Insurance."

The issues touched on under these titles invited, of course, a wide range of views. Since it was not considered by the club's leadership its responsibility to illustrate how wide the range could be, but rather to persuade the audience that there was only one position—the correct position—that one could take on a given issue, it invited as speakers members of the editorial board of the *Daily Worker* and the *New Masses*, writers and critics inclined to be sympathetic to the outlook on national and international questions expressed in these Communist party publications, and leaders of unions and of organizations of the unemployed treated with respect in their columns.

Some conservative social workers at the time, and Red-hunters two decades later, regarded such one-sidedness as evidence of Communist party influence in the organization and program of the Social Workers Discussion Clubs. They were not far from the truth in their attribution, but how these things are perceived and the significance to be attached to them varies from one decade to another, as the history of the past twenty years illustrates. To the persons attending the meetings of the New York Social Workers Discussion Club in 1931 and 1932, few of whom were Communist party members, the charge of "Communist thinking" in what the speakers had to say about a given topic was irrelevant. Disillusioned for the most part by Hoover and his policies and doubtful of the ability of social work leaders to come up with a worthwhile plan to meet the needs of the unemployed, they found the "Communist thinking" expressed by the speakers a novel and refreshing experience. For these social workers and for other middle-class professionals in the early thirties, as the preceding section indicates, Communism had a fascination a later more sophisticated generation found difficult to understand. It combined several elements: the attraction of the new and strange at a time when the old and familiar was being rejected wholesale by thoughtful people; the association of Communism with far-off Russia, which had no depression and no unemployment; and the intellectual thrill that came with being in contact with the latest fashion in political ideas in advanced circles.

Most of the social workers who came to the meetings were employed in Jewish agencies, where the urge to identify as caseworkers, that is to say as bottom-rank professionals, rather than as social workers who perforce included agency executives who made policy, was felt with particular keenness. A caseworkers group at the National Conference of Jewish Social Service was established as early as 1931, presented papers at the '32 and '33 meetings, and was made a constituent section of the conference in 1933. The '32 papers said low salaries in social agencies and insecurity of tenure gave caseworkers a sense of kinship with industrial workers, and asserted that the overwhelming lesson of the Depression was the short shrift given casework techniques by the more powerful forces in society making for poverty and maladjustment. These were identified as central to a social and economic order based on exploitation. Social workers could be most useful, said the authors, as supporters of labor's struggle for higher wages and unemployment insurance.

The papers at the '33 Jewish conference dealt with protective aspects of the AASW program, which were found wanting; with the experience of the Association of Federation Workers in New York, the first union in social work; and with the feasibility of a national protective organization for social workers. Abridged versions of all three papers appeared in the *Jewish Social Service Quarterly*.

In an article in *Labor History*, winter 1975, "The 'Rank-and-File Movement' in Private Social Work," John Earl Haynes associates the appeal of the discussion clubs to workers in Jewish agencies with the "deep tradition of Jewish labor radicalism in the United States." He is less than persuasive on the point. To begin with, "Jewish labor radicalism" was mostly Socialist party in inspiration and leadership; its Communist wing was small and was fought bitterly and on the whole successfully by the Socialist party group in the twenties, a development described most recently by Irving Howe in *World of Our Fathers* (1976). In the second place, social workers in Jewish agencies, like most social workers, had a middle-class background; very few were of working-class origin or came from families with parents who were members of labor unions.

The predominance at New York Social Workers Discussion Club meetings of workers from Jewish agencies may be related to the fact that the discussion club's organizing group consisted largely of caseworkers and supervisors in Jewish agencies; and to the more receptive attitude among Jewish agency workers to noncomformist ideas, as compared, for example, with workers in the Catholic Charities, or on the staffs of the principal nonsectarian (read Protestant) agencies, such as the Charity Organization Society (COS), the Association for Improving the Condition of the Poor (AICP)—yes, it was still around in the early thirties and it still clung to the name it had started with in the middle of the last century— and the Brooklyn Bureau of Charities. Why Jewish social workers were more open to unconventional notions is a complex subject whose exploration would take us far afield from the main themes pursued in this narrative.[2]

It is somewhat easier to identify the reasons for the emergence of the first discussion club in New York. New York was the center of liberal and radical ideas in the country. Here were the headquarters of the Socialist party and the Communist party. Here were located the Rand School (Socialist), the Workers School (Communist), and the publishing enterprises which, under one name or another, turned out the Marxist classics and the Marxist tracts of the day. The *Nation*, the *New Republic*, and the *Modern Monthly*, the leading liberal journals, were published in New York, as was the *New Masses*, the principal Communist journal. The big mass meetings (Madison Square Garden, Mecca Temple, the Manhattan Lyceum, Webster Hall) were held here. New York was the city with the largest May Day parade in the country. It was the first stop for speakers on the American lecture circuit, who came here to report on radical political developments in Europe, not only Russia, but Germany, France, Britain, Spain, Italy—reports of developments above and below ground in countries with a long history of trade union and revolutionary movements.

That New York was not alone in being hospitable to leftist views among social workers became evident in the organization of Social Workers Discussion Clubs in Chicago, Boston, and Philadelphia in 1932, and in St. Louis and Cleveland in 1933. By '35 there were discussion clubs as well in Kansas City, Pittsburgh, Los Angeles, and San Francisco. With time, forum subjects came to include the more immediate issues of the day: relief policy and practice, the federal job programs, organizations of the unemployed and relief recipients. Social insurance meetings argued the pros and cons of the Wagner-Lewis and Lundeen bills and the Townsend plan for curing the Depression by making fixed monthly payments to persons sixty and over, provided the money was spent within a month. Broader social issues were considered under such heads as "The Social Worker and the Labor Movement," and "The Rights of Labor Under the NRA." The international scene was assessed in meetings devoted to "Social Work Abroad," "Social Workers and War," "Can the League of Nations Prevent War," "War and Fascism," "New Social Orders." As the clubs became better known, attendance increased; in New York the discussion club could count on 500 or more on a really burning issue, and on one occasion attendance exceeded 1,000.

Issues, Activities

The clubs were not content with airing issues. They wanted, within their capacity, to take action. The New York club endorsed the march of the unemployed on city hall in '32, contributed funds to the national hunger march on Washington that same year, endorsed the Lundeen bill. Following a report by Margaret Schlauch of New York University on the Amsterdam Congress Against War, to which she had been a delegate, the club voted to send delegates to the U.S. Congress Against War in September 1933, and issued a flier urging congress attendance and financial support by social workers. The Philadelphia club elected delegates to a joint committee of farmers, milk drivers, and consumers with a program of government purchase of milk from dairy farmers for free distribution to the unemployed and low-price sale to families with working members. The Chicago club contributed funds for the defense of Tom Mooney and the Scottsboro Boys, two *causes célèbres* of the time in liberal and radical circles, as victims of miscarriages of justice motivated by antiunion and racist sentiments respectively; issued a statement in support of a dressmakers' strike; and protested Nazi excesses in a telegram to the German ambassador.

Some clubs involved their members in the development of more information on the topics discussed at meetings; research committees were established to prepare reports on relief standards, personnel standards—a sore issue in the new public relief agencies—unemployment insurance, and other subjects of interest.

An account of one activity engaged in by the Social Workers Discussion Club of New York in 1934 may be taken as illustrative of the issues seen as important, the approach taken, and the tactics used by the club considered the pacesetter for the others in the country. The New York group established a committee to examine the administration of the local public relief program. It came up with findings and recommendations which were presented to William Hodson, director of the city's welfare department. To lend the occasion more authority, the club delegation was accompanied by two nationally known social workers, Harry Lurie and John Slawson, executive director of the Jewish Board of Guardians, who had read the report and presumably had approved it. The report was highly critical of the agency's public assistance standards, described as below a health and decency minimum; the rental scale, for example, forced families to live in substandard housing. It made a series of recommendations which Hodson, who had interrupted the reading of the agency's deficiencies several times to say he was well aware of them, pronounced impossible to effect because of agency budgetary limitations, city-state-federal relationships, and the agreement with the banks meeting the city's annual deficit. Only massive public pressure would help change the difficulties the agency was in, said Hodson, who rejected the delegation's offer to help promote pressure.

When the delegation reported back to the discussion club, the members present voted to send an Open Letter to Hodson, with a copy to the mayor, censuring him for his attitude and for "encouraging police violence" against the unemployed seeking more adequate relief. The Open Letter was published in *Social Work Today*.[3]

Since relief standards were wanting everywhere, Social Workers Discussion Clubs in other cities also found the subject deserving of examination and critical comment. Local chapters of the AASW were doing the same thing. Relief retrenchments that accompanied the inauguration of CWA (Civil Works Administration) in '33 and WPA in '35 were the subject of protests by a number of clubs. The Cleveland club organized a conference, which attracted wide participation from the social work community, to dramatize the county's failure to raise sufficient funds to finance the mothers' aid and child welfare programs, managing at the same time to bring within the scope of the conference such issues as the inadequacy of unemployment relief and of salary levels in the public relief agency, proposed social security legislation pending in Congress, and the financing of private social work.

Endorsements were voted by Social Workers Discussion Clubs of the Lundeen bill and delegates were sent to the Congress for Unemployment and Social Insurance, held in Washington in January 1935 under the initiative of the Unemployed Councils of America. Measures supported by discussion clubs were not limited to social welfare and social insurance. They included proposed legislation on the subjects of birth control, food and drugs, lynching, and other issues of general interest. Concern with the grievances of public welfare workers led the New York, Chicago and Cleveland clubs to encourage their efforts to organize unions.

Meeting a real need, the unions underwent rapid growth in number and size. It was this growth, and the launching of *Social Work Today* in 1934, which put in question the necessity for the continued existence of the discussion clubs. The journal provided a forum for the examination of ideas in which the clubs were interested, and the unions—socially-conscious unions concerned with more than bread-and-butter issues—offered an opportunity for the promotion of activities in which the clubs had been interested and for which the unions were now a more appropriate vehicle. Some clubs converted themselves into unions, others simply ceased calling meetings.

By the end of 1935 Social Workers Discussion Clubs had disappeared from the scene.

With some exceptions, notably Harry Lurie and Mary van Kleeck, nationally known social workers were either indifferent to, or looked askance on the activities of the Social Workers Discussion Clubs. Another exception was Walter West, executive secretary of the AASW, who was principally responsible for such publicity in the *Compass* as the clubs received. An early instance was "The Practitioners' Movement" in the July 1933 issue, really a misnomer as a title since the author, Joseph Levy of the caseworkers group of the Chicago chapter of the association, devoted the article largely to the activities of the local discussion club. The invitation to write the article was consistent with West's concern with poor personnel practices in public relief agencies. His concern was also expressed in the telegram he sent Hugh Johnson, director of the NRA, protesting the exemption of social agencies from the maximum-hour and minimum-wage provisions of the act, and asserting that social work, of all professions, could be expected to support the government in its efforts to establish fair personnel standards (social work language for what unions called hours, wages, and working conditions.)

Practitioner groups were of relatively minor importance in the Rank-and-File Movement as a whole, in terms of size, activities, influence. They were encouraged by the leadership of the movement because of the entrée they provided to social workers frightened off by the radicalism of the discussion clubs, uptight about the idea of unionism in social work, but sufficiently conscious of their difference from the executives who dominated the typical AASW chapter, and of their identity as employees of the agencies in which they worked, to want to meet separately to talk about problems special to them.

There was another factor in the friendly attitude of the movement toward practitioner groups. They provided a link with the AASW. The adversary stance the movement took in its early years toward the association was in part play-acting, reflecting the need to attract attention to itself by castigating in over-severe terms what it deemed the cooptation of the profession by the Establishment, its timidity, its amiability in the face of Hoover's outrageous disregard of the needs of the unemployed, its acceptance at face value of the early claims made for the New Deal by the administration and its supporters. At the same time, the movement's leadership recognized that within the top councils of the AASW there were people like van Kleeck and Lurie, who could influence the association to take a more "progressive" position on relief, social insurance, and jobs for the unemployed, and that cooperation was possible and even useful on specific issues. The existence of practitioner groups would facilitate such cooperation.

The first practitioner group was organized in the Chicago chapter of the association in January 1933 and grew out of the discontent of some of the younger members at the chapter's failure to make a more vigorous fight against salary cuts in social agencies. It concerned itself not only with economic security for the social worker, but such professional topics as practices in public agencies affecting relief recipients and staff members, staff-recipient relationships, community provisions for homeless men. Recommendations emerging from its meetings were reported to the chapter as a whole and generally accepted.

The Chicago practitioners group presented a paper descriptive of this experience at the 1933 National Conference of Social Work in one of the meetings under AASW auspices. It urged the creation of similar groups in other chapters. The inital response was from members of the New York chapter active in the Social Workers Discussion Club. Upon their request, the chapter appointed a committee of caseworkers to consider the advisability of sponsoring a practitioners group. The committee's favorable report in December was approved by the executive committee and a group was organized early in 1934. Publicity for its philosophy and activities was promoted by a one-and-a-half page article in the October issue of the *Compass*, "The Case for the Practitioner Movement."

A third group was established in the St. Louis chapter, also in 1934. That June members of practitioner groups at the 1934 National Conference of Social Work attended an AASW luncheon meeting at which short papers were read on practitioner activities in the three chapters with groups. Members of groups and of Social Workers Discussion Clubs, fired up by the excitement van Kleeck's papers had created at the conference, held three informal meetings, of which the one that drew the largest audience passed resolutions in support of the Lundeen bill, called on conference delegates to leave a hotel at which a strike of stationary engineers was in progress, and condemned the discrimination against Negroes reported at some of the conference hotels.

The impetus behind the whole development of practitioner groups, which had touched only three of the seventy-odd chapters of the AASW, petered out in 1934. The reasons for the lack of growth, and for the disappearance after 1935 of the three groups that were formed, may lie in the more active role of chapters in the issues of primary concern to the groups, the greater attraction of social work unions for dissident association members and their increasing absorption in union activities, and the appearance on the scene of *Social Work Today*, in whose pages and in the forums which it sponsored, the issues of interest to them as social workers and as citizens were more effectively presented.

Related to the practitioner groups in AASW chapters in membership and interests were the caseworkers councils established in private family agencies in the twenties under the auspices of the Family Welfare Association of America. Their history in the thirties provides another illustration of the radicalization of social workers in response to the intellectual pressures felt in all the liberal professions. The dominant motive for the organization of the councils had been self-improvement, and at meetings in their first few years the topics discussed ran the gamut of accepted subjects, from the essence of supervision to social work ethics. A national visitors' council was established in 1926.

In 1934 the name of the national organization was changed to the

Caseworkers Council and the publication of a *Caseworkers Council Bulletin* was authorized. The first issue carried an appeal to caseworkers to face "the present social dilemma—even at the expense of individual techniques which adjust the client to an environment which is awry." In the same issue, readers found a list of Rank-and-File groups then in existence and a notice which referred them to *Social Work Today* for information on program and activities. Representatives of the Chicago and St. Louis councils attended the National Convention of Rank-and-File Groups in Social Work in Pittsburgh, in February 1935, fuller reference to which is made in the next chapter. When the national organization met at the 1935 National Conference of Social Work, it was addressed by Mary van Kleeck and Harry Lurie; at its business meeting it recommended that member councils affiliate with the National Coordinating Committee of Rank-and-File Groups in Social Work.

Chapter 9

The Rank-and-File Movement: Social Work Unions

Social work unions, or more accurately, unions in social agencies, consti-tuted the largest component of the Rank-and-File Movement by the end of the decade in terms of numbers and activities. When issued charters by the AF of L, and later by the CIO, they symbolized for the movement the attainment of one of its most cherished goals, identification with and acceptance by organized labor. The affiliation provided living expression of the movement's belief that social work employees, as wage and salary earners, were members of the working class, and its hope that it would prove to be the bridge for linking the broad social objectives of social work and the labor movement.[1]

The beginnings were modest. In 1926 a number of caseworkers and supervisors in family, childcare and protective agencies, and in the social service departments of hospitals funded by the Federation of Jewish Philanthropies of New York, dissatisfied with the lack of standardization in professional position requirements in federation agencies, the minimal role of financial incentives in the improvement of professional skills, and excessive job turnover, organized the Association of Federation Social Workers (AFSW). Its objectives were the standardization of requirements for appointment to professional positions; a salary scale related to train-ing, experience, and position requirements; regular increases in salary to ensure retention of experienced workers; caseload standardization; and an employee health insurance program.

The association met at infrequent intervals and limited its activities pretty much to the preparation of reports on the desirability of its program goals. The AFSW had the tacit approval of both federation and agency executives, who saw little in the program, except perhaps health insurance, inconsistent with the personnel practice standards that had been advo-cated for years by the AASW itself. Such minimal progress as was made by 1929 in their attainment could hardly be attributed to AFSW efforts.

In the winter of 1931-32 the federation instituted a salary cut in all agencies which shared in its allocations. Galvanized into action by the more or less radicalized members who had been instrumental in the organization of the Social Workers Discussion Club only a few months earlier, the AFSW redefined its primary purpose as the protection of the economic security of federation employees, and opened membership to clerical, maintenance, and other nonprofessional workers. A new program was adopted, emphasizing the importance of the employer-employee relationship in social agencies and calling for recognition of the renamed Association of Federation Workers (AFW) as the collective bargaining agent for federation agency employees on salaries, hours, and working conditions. A negotiating committee was named to meet with the federation board of trustees to demand the rescinding of the salary cut and acceptance of the AFW as the organization to speak on behalf of all federation agency workers.

What is Collective Bargaining?

Since this development was unique in the annals of social work history, the initial experience of the negotiating committee is of some interest, particularly because it was typical of other first encounters between the organized employees of a private agency and the executive director.

The members of the committee had had no trade union experience, had never engaged in collective bargaining, knew the term only from reading about it and hearing it talked about. They were so confident, however, of the justice of their cause and the reasonableness of their demands that they didn't bother to seek help on strategy and tactics from persons in trade unions expert in these matters, or arrange to bring along to the meeting with federation representatives a consultant experienced in negotiations. They felt buoyed up, furthermore, by the militancy aroused in those days by the thought of a face-to-face meeting with the enemy, the enemy not only of federation workers but of all the exploited in the country, for the typical board member was a banker, an industrialist, Mr. Money Bags himself.

To its dismay, the committee encountered difficulties getting an appointment with the executive director of the federation, much less one with an appropriate committee of that remote body, the federation's board of trustees. Why did the committee want to see him? asked the executive director, a message transmitted by his secretary since he himself was too busy to take the call. The committee's answer, relayed by the secretary, evoked an impatient response, again at second hand, to the effect that committee members seemed unaware that the country was in a depression, that money to support federation activities was more difficult than ever to raise, and that the increase in unemployment had placed a greater burden on the federation's budget than ever before. Didn't committee members read the newspapers?

The committee persisted, and in the end the executive director reluctantly agreed to an appointment, provided it was short. The meeting, which lasted longer than the half-hour agreed to, hardly followed the scenario envisaged by committee members. Collective bargaining? The executive director had never heard of anything so outrageous. The purpose of the federation was to succor the poor and to heal the sick, not to bargain with employees about salaries. To restore salaries to the '29 level, said the executive director, whose salary was rumored to be five or ten times that of an average supervisor in a federation agency, would reduce the amount of money available to help the poor and the sick. Surely you don't want that, he went on, not waiting for an answer. How could the committee members reconcile their demand for collective bargaining with their sense of professional responsibility? Unions had no place in nonprofit organizations such as social agencies and hospitals, whose primary responsibility was the welfare of their clients and patients, not that of their employees. If committee members were dissatisfied with their salaries, they didn't belong in social work but in the world of commerce and industry, where profits were or used to be made, and unions could advance a claim for a larger share of the firm's net income. There were no profits in philanthropy.

The committee said in response that federation workers were not high earners and that a reduction in their income lowered what was only a modest standard of living to begin with; that the federation had a responsibility to educate its contributors to the need for funds both to meet the requirements of the poor and the sick, and to engage a staff qualified by education and experience to serve client and patient, entitled to compensation matching the skills their positions required; that there was no conflict between the two objectives; that as a philanthropic organization the federation had an obligation to the community to set an example for industry by maintaining compensation levels at a time when every wage and salary cut reduced purchasing power and accelerated descent into a worse depression.

The executive director could hardly conceal his restlessness during this exposition. He repeated his initial statement, seemingly unimpressed by the committee's arguments.

After an hour of fruitless exchanges, the executive director excused himself; he had another appointment.

Was this collective bargaining? The committee left the meeting stunned.

In industry, refusal by management to engage in collective bargaining often led to a strike. There was no sentiment for a strike among AFW members, as the negotiating committee quickly sensed when it reported back at the next membership meeting. The discussion on tactics appropriate to social work was heated. A number of steps were agreed upon—publicity arraigning the federation for cutting wages and salaries and for denying AFW recognition; a letter to all members of the board of trustees setting out the AFW position and inviting support; the backing of trade unions, particularly those federated in the United Hebrew Trades.

The letter to federation board members went out; appeals for union support were effected by direct contact and by mail. Response was perfunctory at best; there was none from board members. Publicity releases were printed only in the *Daily Worker* and in the left-wing union press. There were greater troubles stalking the country. It was difficult to get people excited about a small group of workers who still had jobs and whose major complaint was a salary reduction at a time when wage cuts of a far more sweeping character were commonplace.

Such were the inauspicious beginnings of unionism in social work.

What saved the AFW from going under at this point was the faith of the leadership in the principle of unionism and the loyal support of the membership. That September (1932), the federation, alleging a shortfall in campaign contributions, again reduced allotments to constituent agencies, leading in some to a second round of wage and salary cuts. The AFW forwarded protests to federation board members and to the boards of the agencies. A meeting was finally effected with a committee of the federation's board. Although it had no immediate results, morale among AFW members was boosted by the experience. A petition for salary restoration was circulated among federation agency employees, drew 500 signatures, and was forwarded to the federation's board. When a partial restoration of wages and salaries was instituted following a successful fall campaign, AFW claimed partial credit. It could also claim 400 members, not small as organizations of that type went those days; in some agencies members comprised a majority of the employees.

The caseworkers section papers given at the 1932 National Conference of Jewish Social Service, alluded to in chapter 8, were prepared by AFW members and found a sympathetic response among caseworkers in attendance from other cities. Within a year organizations modeled on the AFW were established in Philadelphia, Boston, and Detroit. As in New York, their appeal was primarily to workers in Jewish agencies. Efforts to attract members in Catholic and nonsectarian private agencies in the four cities met with indifferent success. Not that their employees had no grievances. A study by the Association of Community Chests and Councils reported that because of failure to meet campaign goals pro-rata cuts were common in most cities. Between '32 and '33 one or more agencies were discontinued altogether in twenty-seven communities. Salary reductions in agencies ranged from 5 to 25 percent or more. Payless vacations were instituted in some agencies and new workers were being hired at a 10 percent reduction from the salary the position formerly paid. The Family Welfare Association of America studied family agencies in twelve representative cities and found that between '30 and '32 the ratio of caseworkers to total staff had dropped from 73 to 5 percent; the explanation was their replacement by emergency workers and trainees—at lower salaries, of course.[2]

Initiative and leadership in organization in the private field remained with the New York AFW. To dramatize its demand for full restoration of the '32 salary scale, a two-hour stoppage was held in February 1934, marked by a meeting attended by 500 federation employees from 48 agencies and representatives of students in attendance at the New York School of Social Work and the Graduate School of Jewish Social Work. Whether influenced by this expression of worker dissatisfaction or by an improvement in income resulting from better economic conditions, higher federation grants made possible that spring a return in most agencies to the '32 salary scale for employees earning up to $2,000 per annum; in some agencies the '31 scale was restored. Clerical workers gained more liberal vacation schedules. By the end of 1934 membership of the AFW had increased to somewhat over 700, employed in 30 of the 90-odd federation agencies, but these 30 included all the major casework agencies, six hospitals, two Y's and several settlement houses.

Most resistant to organizational efforts were the hospitals. Workers in the maintenance, laundry, and kitchen departments of hospitals were among the most exploited groups in nonprofit agencies. Not uncommon among hospitals in the United States in the early thirties was a seven-day week and monthly wages as low as $35 and maintenance. Lebanon Hospital, a federation-supported institution, locked out twenty-six employees for participating in AFW's two-hour stoppage in February 1934. Beth Moses Hospital, a Brooklyn federation affiliate, fired seven employees active in promoting AFW membership. A few days later about one hundred Beth Moses employees held a two-hour stoppage in protest; all were dismissed.

The AFW threw picket lines around both hospitals. The placards read: "Locked out for organizing against yellow-dog contracts, low wages, irregular wage payments, unpaid overtime, forced vacations." Administrators and boards of the two hospitals deemed the picketing insolence; they refused to meet with AFW committees, called in the police, who roughed up the pickets, arresting some who resisted. In 1934 even the minimal guarantee of collective bargaining provided by section 7a of NIRA specifically excluded nonprofit organizations, and there was no state law to appeal to.

Denied legal protection, lacking public support, and discouraged by its failure to engage the sympathy of employees who remained on the job,

AFW discontinued the picket lines after several weeks, silently acknowledging defeat. It would be decades before hospital workers were organized; when organization came it would be under other auspices.

Spreading the Message

Unionization made greater strides in public welfare agencies than in the private field. For one thing, the potential was larger. One estimate put employees in public relief agencies and staff running work-relief programs in the country in January 1935 at 164,000[3]; private agency workers, including nonprofessional staff, numbered perhaps 50,000 to 75,000 at the most when hospitals were excluded. For another, the presumed conflict between the professional obligations of a social worker and membership in a union, an issue troubling caseworkers and supervisors in many private agencies (the Jewish agencies in New York were an exception in this regard), did not exist in the public field. The public emergency relief agencies were staffed in the lower ranks by white-collar employees, often recruited from the relief rolls (need remained a condition of employment for years in some agencies) and with backgrounds in sales and clerical employment, bookkeeping, accountancy, insurance, and other office jobs; many were unemployed teachers, engineers, or recent college graduates with no employment history. Trained and experienced social workers were to be found only in supervisory or administrative positions. Personnel working directly with relief applicants and relief recipients, called investigators, considered themselves lucky to have jobs at all; many of them were conscious, at the same time, of their low salaries, long hours, lack of tenure, large caseloads, the absence of workmen's compensation and sick leave, the minimal character of vacation leaves where available, and the often primitive conditions under which they worked: improvised desks (packingcases in some agencies), improvised filing cabinets (cartons), improvised chairs (fruit boxes), and the poor lighting and limited sanitary facilities in the warehouses, vacant stores, and other inappropriate but rentable space which often housed the relief agencies.

The first effort at organizing public relief workers was undertaken by the Chicago Social Workers Discussion Club, which drafted a code for social workers in the fall of 1933. (Industry-wide agreements under NIRA on prices, wages, working conditions were called "codes;" the word had popular appeal.) Discussion club members employed in the Cook County Department of Public Welfare's Unemployment Relief Services organized the Social Service Workers Union in November to promote acceptance of the code. Membership was open to all employees below the rank of supervisor. The code specified minimum salaries and maximum hours; provided for vacation and sick leave; proposed that working conditions conform to the standards recommended by the Women's Bureau of the Department of Labor; set a ceiling on caseloads; entitled employees to workmen's compensation, to free medical care, and to time off for courses in social work; forbade discrimination based on race or organizational activity; called for a month's notice on discharge.

Announcement of the formation of the union brought almost instant reprisals from the public welfare department. Six active members were summarily dismissed. The chairman of the Illinois Emergency Relief Commission, which funded the county's unemployment relief program which a mixture of state and federal moneys, issued a public statement that the firings were based on membership in, or sympathetic affiliation with, "Communist organizations."

Protests forced the reinstatement of four of the six persons laid off, but the threat of dismissal for mere membership in the union lost it nearly all its adherents. The few who remained reorganized as the Federation of Social Service Employees and undertook an unobtrusive long-range educational program to promote acceptance of the union idea among all social agency workers in Chicago. It made only slow headway in the prevailing atmosphere of intimidation.

More success attended the effort to organize public relief workers in New York. In September 1933 employees of the state Temporary Emergency Relief Administration working on research projects organized the TERA Employees Association to stop a threatened salary cut. They won recognition and the rescinding of the planned salary reduction. About the same time, workers on a Bear Mountain construction project also funded by TERA gained a wage increase and improved working conditions following a demonstration at the site. The two victories prompted workers in New York City's Emergency Home Relief Bureau, also paid out of TERA funds because job eligibility was based on need, to organize the EHRB Employees Association, open to all persons below the rank of supervisor. A little over 100 persons came to the first meeting in December 1933; 400 attended the second meeting; 600 the third; and 1,000 the fourth.

A Success

A delegation from the organization met with the executive director of the TERA and obtained a promise of nondiscrimination for organizational activities. In January 1934 the association's program was presented to the local office of the federal Civil Works Administration, which had taken over the EHRB payroll. CWA officials were impressed by the evidence of association strength that attendance at meetings provided, and agreed to nearly all its proposals. The new union won wage increases ranging from 50 to 80 percent for investigators, case aides, clerks, porters, guards and messengers; extension of the five-day absentee rule (dismissal after five days' absence) to two weeks; termination of need as a condition of employment; and workmen's compensation.

Such gains augured well for the future of the organization in the eyes of agency employees. The association grew rapidly, soon numbered thousands, changed its name to the Association of Workers in Public Relief Agencies (AWPRA) when EHRB became part of the city's welfare department and the union undertook to organize the department as a whole. It remained from the beginning the largest and most effective organization of its kind in the country. Faced with layoffs as a result of cutbacks in FERA in the transition to WPA, for example, AWPRA held a rally at Madison Square Garden in October 1935 which drew 15,000 concerned employees of the agency. The rally and protest led to a reduction in dismissals from 3,000 to 1,200, for most of whom WPA jobs were found.

New York's success prompted similar efforts at organization in other cities. Unions were formed in 1934 in relief agencies in Newark, Philadelphia, Pittsburgh, Cleveland, Cincinnati, and Minneapolis. A second attempt at union organization was made in Chicago and succeeded. In 1935 the movement spread to Baltimore, Washington, St. Louis, St. Paul, Detroit, Milwaukee, Denver, Los Angeles, and Oakland. County associations were established in Ohio and Pennsylvania, based on the organizational structure of the relief administration in these states. Local associations combined to form statewide groups in Michigan, Ohio, and Pennsylvania.

The directory of Rank-and-File organizations in *Social Work Today's* December 1935 issue listed forty-eight organizations, for the most part protective in nature, in twenty-three cities and counties, including the three statewide groups. Most of the organizations followed the industrial union principle, opening membership to all employees; some, however, were confined to so called professional employees (investigators and supervisors). Few called themselves unions or held charters from national trade unions. Their programs, however, were typically those found in unions: increased salaries, compensation for overtime, more liberal vacation and sick leave policies, reduction in the length of the work day, a five-day week, adequate working conditions, workmen's compensation, union recognition. Rejection of the concept of temporary and emergency relief programs, evident in such acronyms as FERA, TERA, SERA, and their local counterparts, was reflected in the demand for civil service status.

A survey made in 1935 indicated that gains won included improved and standardized salary schedules, sick and vacation leave, more holidays with pay, a five-day workweek, elimination of overtime, workmen's compensation, reduced caseloads, improved working conditions, dismissal notice prior to layoff. Two organizations reported reinstatement of discharged workers. The New York union fought for and claimed to have won an end to discrimination against blacks in appointments and promotions. Three agencies formally or informally extended recognition to the association as the collective bargaining agents for their employees. The signed agreement between New York's Home Relief Bureau and AWPRA in August 1935 provided not only for recognition, but for hearings on grievances and consultation on changes in personnel policy.

As noted earlier, social agency unions were criticized by some social-work executives and some deans of social work schools as being concerned solely with the economic interests of their members. This was not quite true. Plans for the reorganization of the state relief administration in Illinois and of New York City's welfare services were drafted by the Chicago and New York unions respectively; the latter was notable for including provisions for legal, economic, medical and casework services. Fourteen Rank-and-File groups, protective organizations in the main, submitted a statement to the FERA in November 1935 calling upon the federal government to continue allocations to the states for direct relief, to raise assistance standards, to resume full responsibility for the transients program, and to set up a federal Department of Social Welfare. The same statement pledged support for a federally financed job program, open to all unemployed persons, with eligibility not conditional on need, and providing work on socially useful projects at trade union hourly rates and an adequate weekly wage.

Representatives of employee organizations offered testimony before committees of city councils and state legislatures on the need for more adequate financing of public assistance programs. The Lundeen bill was endorsed. Bills to make lynching a federal crime were approved, as was the Child Labor Amendment to the Constitution. Sales taxes to provide funds for the state and local shares of public assistance, one of the most pernicious innovations of the Depression, were vigorously opposed.

To demonstrate their solidarity with other unions, some protective organizations contributed funds to chapters of the Newspaper Guild on strike, to strikes organized by department store and taxi unions, and to unions participating in the San Francisco general strike. Contributions were made also by some of the unions to the defense of the Scottsboro boys and Angelo Herndon, a black twenty-year old Young Communist League militant, arrested by the state of Georgia for his efforts to organize an unemployed council in Atlanta, and indicted on a charge of "insurrection" under a law dating back to the 1870s.

Going National

Among the papers presented by the caseworkers section at the National Conference of Jewish Social Service in 1933 was one on the feasibility of a national protective association for social workers. It found the rationale for such an organization in the failure of the AASW and other social work groups to take effective action against salary reductions, or to develop a program to improve the economic security of social workers. The experience of such related occupational groups as teachers, actors, and government workers was cited as indicative of the value of union organization for economic security. The paper concluded with a proposal for the establishment of a national organization, open to all employees in social agencies, whose primary purpose would be to engage in collective bargaining on behalf of its members, and to "contribute to the building of a better social order."

No steps were taken to realize the goal proposed. The growth, however, of Social Workers Discussion Clubs, practitioner groups, and protective organizations, and the launching in the spring of 1934 of *Social Work Today,* which served to publicize their activities and to promote a common philosophy, stimulated sentiment for a national center for activities, to which the term "the Rank and File Movement in Social Work," increasingly became attached. The 1934 National Conference of Social Work provided an opportunity for these groups to exchange experiences. Encouraged by the stir created by Mary van Kleeck's papers and by the élan they felt as part of the new wave in social work, they voted to request *Social Work Today* to issue a call for a meeting to consider the establishment of a national committee "to coordinate and organize practitioners' activities" and "to obtain recognition of the practitioner group as an associate body" of the National Conference.

Social Work Today was then being published by the New York Social Workers Discussion Club. In December 1934, after sounding out sentiment for a national meeting among the thirty-odd groups who were the potential participants, the New York club issued invitations for a conference in Pittsburgh, February 22–24, 1935. The purpose was defined as the promotion of "common thinking and action" against low salaries, poor working conditions, and layoffs in public relief agencies. Only a month earlier the President had announced that the government was "getting out of this business of relief," and the call to the conference took cognizance of the effect this would have on the jobs of people working in direct relief programs. The failure of professional organizations to influence national relief policy or to take steps to correct the grievances of relief agency staffs, the invitation said, made it necessary for employees to take action on their own behalf and to find a voice through which they could speak nationally on both social policy issues and job security.

Answering the call to the conference were delegates or observers from ten cities and two counties, representing seventeen protective organizations, six Social Workers Discussion Clubs, and seven practitioner and miscellaneous groups. Organizations of employees of public relief or public welfare agencies were in the majority; over three-fourths of the delegates listed themselves as caseworkers or case investigators; few were over thirty.

The conference opened with greetings from, among others, Mary van Kleeck, Harry Lurie, and Roger Baldwin, executive director of the American Civil Liberties Union, who wired, "Warmest greetings to those of you who are carrying on a vital job begun by pioneer social workers in the class struggle. We were few those days. You are many and may you be many more."

Sessions were held on personnel practices, professional standards, federal relief, social security, social action, and proposals for national coordination. Before closing, the conference voted to establish a National Coordinating Committee of Rank and File Groups in Social Work and adopted a platform which defined positions in the areas of personnel practices, professional standards, and a national social welfare program.

The goals endorsed in personnel practices embraced the principles to be found in the programs of most of the protective organizations represented: mandatory yearly increases in salary; a shorter workweek, equal remuneration for equal work; compensation for overtime; adequate working conditions; a reduction in worker caseload; abolition of work quotas for clerical workers; sick leave with pay; adequate maternity leave; leaves of absence for study and travel; open hearings for dismissed employees; civil service status; workmen's compensation; a ban on the use of volunteers for work normally performed by salaried persons; abolition of a means test as a condition of employment; an end to discrimination based on sex, race, creed, or political affiliation. Organization was identified as the key to achieving these goals, and collective bargaining as the most effective instrument.

Professional standards were touched on only briefly, reflecting the more immediate concern of the delegates with job security and national social welfare policy. The platform adopted called for a "thorough reevaluation" of the concept of professional service to reflect "our new understanding of the grouping of forces in society," but left unstated the nature of the new understanding. The one specific recommendation made concerned more opportunities for free training.

The national social welfare program endorsed was premised on the belief that "employees in social agencies are members of America's working population and must relate their understanding of their function, their place in society, their desire for better standards of service, of remuneration, and of job security, to the needs, the experiences and the aspirations of American labor." Support was voted for an improved direct relief program under federal auspices; an extended and improved work-relief program and a long-term public works program; adequate maintenance, with federal aid, of other social services, such as child-caring agencies, agencies for the aged and handicapped, and hospitals; a social insurance program along the lines of the Lundeen bill.

The social welfare platform won ready acceptance by the delegates because most of the separate elements had earlier been endorsed by their organizations; the conference version had the appeal of being an updated comprehensive statement that brought together positions on several issues, now seen to be related, concerning the responsibility of government for the welfare of the people of the country. The desirability was affirmed of cooperative action with other groups, such as the Interprofessional Association for Social Insurance, in efforts to obtain adequate relief and social security measures.

More general in character was the endorsement of measures to guarantee freedom of organizaton and collective bargaining for industrial and professional workers in private and government employment, and cooperative action with organized labor to this end. Support was voted for legislation to guarantee civil liberties and "to forbid all repressive activities whether by state legislative bodies, or by organized extra-legal groups (such as socalled 'citizens' committees, 'vigilante committees,' etc.) aimed against any effort to maintain and improve the standard of living of the wage earner."

The National Coordinating Committee of Rank and File Groups in Social Work (NCC), created in Pittsburgh in February 1935, was not the individual membership organization proposed in 1933, but a committee made up of one representative from each affiliated organization and the four officers. Its principal functions were identified as the establishment of a center for information and advice on rank-and-file organizaton; the promotion of organization among unorganized workers in social agencies; the promotion of national action for adequate personnel practices; efforts to win collective bargaining rights for employees in social agencies; mutual assistance among member organizations on specific issues; joint action with other groups on social welfare and social insurance issues; cooperation with organized labor on common objectives. (Omitted, not by design but perhaps because it seemed not of sufficient importance to mention, was any reference to cooperation with the AASW or other professional social work bodies.) The NCC was authorized to call annual delegate meetings, establish committees to develop activities in furtherance of the platform adopted, issue discussion materials, organize a speakers' service, make public statements on behalf of member organizations, support social legislation, and arrange for participation in the National Conference of Social Work.

The present writer was elected chairman; David Kanes, of the Philadelphia County Relief Board Employees Association, eastern regional vice-chairman; Joseph Levy, of the Chicago Federation of Social Service Employees, midwestern regional vice-chairman; and Bernard Riback, president of the New York EHRB Employees Association, secretary.

Eighteen organizations representing about 12,000 members joined the NCC in the twelve months following the conference in Pittsburgh. There were no dues, neither was there an office or a budget, and all officers and committee members volunteered their time. The extent of such volunteer activity is reflected in the work undertaken by the NCC in its first year. Counsel was given to new organizations and to established groups in nine cities visited weekends by NCC officers. In a year marked by relief contractions, mass layoffs of staff in public agencies, and administrative chaos, twenty-one new Rank-and-File groups were formed and statewide organization was effected among relief-workers' protective organizations in three states. They welcomed NCC assistance offered in correspondence and by visit, on structure, strategy, and tactics.

Well-attended sessions were organized by the NCC at the 1935 National Conference of Social Work on the subjects of "Sources of Power for the Social Work Program" (a paper given by Mary van Kleeck); "The Role of the Unemployed Movement and its Relation to Social Work" (the speaker was Herbert Benjamin, national organizer of the Unemployed Councils of America); "Standards of Employment in Social Agencies"; "Social Work and Political Action"; "Social Work and Fascism"; "The Negro in Social Work"; "Security for the Social Worker"; "Mental Hygiene in a Changing World." Round tables on organizational methods were conducted. An NCC booth provided information and consultation service. Daily bulletins publicized NCC sessions and services and NCC views on issues raised by conference papers.

At the close of the conference the NCC issued an Open Letter to the Social Workers of America, published in full in the July issue of *Social Work Today,* exhorting them to build organizations supportive of a "decent standard of living" for social agency employees, to advocate a "genuine" social insurance program and an "adequate" social welfare program. It urged social workers to take a stand with the labor movement against developments threatening the standard of living, to combat racial discrimination, attacks on civil liberties, and other "tendencies toward fascism." The concluding paragraphs encouraged promotion of these objectives in all organizations of which social workers were members, not only unions, but AASW chapters as well, and state and local conferences of social work, so that a "common front" could be forged "against the forces of reaction and despair."

NCC activities at the National Conference of Social Work encouraged similar efforts by Rank-and-File groups at state social work conferences in New York, Ohio, Pennsylvania, California, Michigan, New Jersey, Minnesota, and Colorado.

The Social Work Establishment and the First Unions

The response of the social work Establishment to the emergence of unionism in social agencies was mixed, but on the whole sympathetic when not neutral.

Beginning at least with the Progressive Era in the early years of the century, social work leaders saw themselves as liberals on social issues, embracing in their credo the right of wage earners to form trade unions and to campaign for higher wages, shorter hours, and better working conditions. The famous *Pittsburgh Survey* of 1907–08 included an extensive examination of wage levels, working conditions and labor relations in the steel industry and their bearing on poverty among steelworkers' families; it was only one of several such studies undertaken under social work auspices in the first two decades of the century. Social settlements opened their doors to union meetings; in some cities they provided the only hall available to unions.

It seemed consistent with this tradition for the *Compass*, the AASW journal, to publish the first accounts of organizational efforts by private agency workers to identify themselves as employees and to protect their economic security. The editor's introduction to an article in the issue of April 1930 on the history and objectives of the New York Association of Federation Social Workers, by Isidor Gandel, its chairman, asked, "To what extent do executives dominate the staff members in social agencies and to what extent does the American Association of Social Workers represent the executives among social workers rather than the practitioners?" The question implied that there might be differences of opinion on the subject and invited readers to consider the "other" side. When the Association of Federation Social Workers became the Association of Federation Workers in 1932 and opened its membership, as noted earlier, to all federation employees, the *Compass* ran an account in its December 1932 issue of the reasons behind the change, under the title "Other Forms of Security," prepared by Lillian Shapiro, chairman of the AFW.

An attitude of open-minded inquiry, one may guess, also lay behind the

1934 decision of the New York chapter of the AASW to study new forms of organization among workers in social agencies, and the decision of the committee responsible for developing information on the subject to request the present writer, a member of the chapter, to prepare a discussion outline on the theory and aims of protective organization and the factors accounting for the growth of protective groups in social work. In 1935 the chapter's Committee on Personnel Practices endorsed the principle of collective bargaining for social agency employees.

Recognition by the National Conference of Social Work that the subject merited attention came in 1934, when Joseph Levy of the Chicago Social Workers Discussion Club was invited to give a paper on "New Forms of Organization Among Social Workers."

Prominent figures who took an affirmative position on union organization in social work included not only Mary van Kleeck and Harry Lurie, but also John Fitch, who taught labor relations at the New York School; Elizabeth Dutcher, secretary of the Family Welfare Division of the Brooklyn Bureau of Charities; and Marion Hathway of the Pittsburgh School. In her presidential address at the 1935 National Conference of Social Work, Katherine Lenroot, Children's Bureau chief, acclaimed the Rank-and-File Movement as "one of the most significant developments in social work in the last two years." Kenneth Pray, director of the Pennsylvania School, in an article prepared for the 1935 *Social Work Year Book*, referred to the "divisive effects the development of this radical faction" had on social work; nevertheless he welcomed its coming because "social work is no exception to the tendency of established institutions to dig in and become increasingly less keen for advancing to new lines of trenches. The vigorous attacks from the left have been disconcerting, but they have undoubtedly had a wholesome effect upon the right."

Fitch, Dutcher, Lurie, and the others spoke as individuals; it was less likely that professional bodies as such would take cognizance of unionism in social work. There were exceptions. In 1934 the Committee on Employment Practices and Relationships of the National Conference of Jewish Social Service recommended approval by the conference of the right of social agency employees to organize, without necessarily endorsing trade union tactics in social work, and urged recognition by agency boards of the right of employee associations to speak on behalf of their members on issues affecting their economic security. This was part of a larger package, accepted by the conference at its business session, covering desirable standards on salaries, sick and vacation leave, and such fringe benefits, not common then in social work, as retirement benefits, and health and accident insurance.

About the same time, the Division of Employment Practices of the AASW also endorsed the principle of collective bargaining in social work.

The association as such had no occasion, however, to take a position on the subject and none was sought by the protective organizations in the field. Some of the chapters became involved, on the other hand, when specific abuses were brought to their attention. In response to the dismissal in 1933 of six investigators at the Cook County Bureau of Public Welfare, an incident referred to earlier, the Chicago chapter issued a strongly worded protest on the use by the state's Relief Commission of the phony issue of Communism in ordering the discharges; their dismissal was attributed in the chapter's report to union organizing activities. The report expressed sympathy with many of the principles embodied in the code for social workers, drafted by the Social Workers Discussion Club and accepted as its program by the Social Service Workers Union to which the dismissed employees belonged; and concluded by affirming support of the civil rights of state and county employees, among which it included the right to join a union.

The issues on which social work opinion was most divided concerned tactics. The pros and cons of demonstrations, stoppages, strikes, and other practices common in labor disputes in industry were fiercely argued, particularly within AASW chapters appealed to by the unions in labor disputes in public relief agencies. Because the disputes involved primarily tactics, the chapters felt more comfortable, on the whole, not taking sides and offering instead a role as mediator.

In 1935 Helen Grulich and Gertrude Nillson were summarily discharged by the New Jersey ERA for union-organizing activity. Although not members, they appealed to the New Jersey chapter of the AASW for help in reinstatement. A chapter committee interviewed the two women and the officials of the ERA. No recommendation was made on reinstatement, but the committee took the occasion to issue a broad statement on the principles at stake. Its report recommended that ERA establish employment and discharge procedures in conformity with standard practices in social work. The discharge procedure proposed proscribed any dismissal except for incompetence, with reasons to be stated in writing, and an opportunity for a hearing before an impartial board and for appeal from the board's decision. Grulich and Nillson were not rehired, but the chapter's recommendations led to some reforms in the agency's procedures.

More difficult issues were presented by the Dawson case. Sidonia Dawson was an investigator on the staff of the New York Emergency Home Relief Bureau. In October 1934 she was fired for conduct incompatible with her duties as an employee of the agency. The Dawson case illustrates graphically the hostility marking both recipient-administration and union-administration relationships in New York in the early years of the EHRB. According to the union, Dawson was separated because she fought discriminatory practices against blacks (she herself was white) and the use of police to clear relief offices of recipients with grievances. The series of events which triggered the firing began with the appearance at the local office in which Dawson was employed of a delegation representing an organization of relief recipients. The delegation rushed past the guards at the door and attempted to force its way into the room occupied by the local office administration. The police were called in and the delegation was ejected, but not before a number of its members were beaten up. The next morning a flyer appeared on every desk captioned "Is the Police Department Running This Precinct?" It was unsigned but assumed by staff to have been prepared by the union's local grievance committee, of which Dawson was chairman. According to the agency, while a union delegation was meeting with the local office administration to discuss the incident, Dawson was in the street outside haranguing a hundred or more employees she had induced to leave their desks, calling for an end to "police brutality."

The union demanded her reinstatement and, among other moves to exert pressure on the bureau, called on the local chapter of the AASW for support. The chapter committee designated to consider the request interviewed all the parties concerned. Its report, which appeared in the December 1934 issue of the *Compass* under the catchy title "Disruptive Tactics and Summary Discharges," found much to criticize in both administration and union practices. It called supervision by the administration poor and the physical equipment of the office inadequate; it affirmed the right of recipient delegations to be heard, criticized the use of police to eject them, and faulted the administration for not developing a better working relationship with its employees.

The report made sympathetic references to the desire of investigators to see relief standards raised, but critized both union and client delegations for using intimidation and violence to achieve their aims. It condemned specifically what was referred to as the union's "Political and Social Philosophy," its "revolutionary tactics," and its use of "disruption to hasten the revolutionary order." The AASW, said the report, believed in social justice but did not think it could be attained by the use of "violence." The report made no recommendations on the disposition of the Dawson case. It offered the services of the chapter to set up grievance machinery to mediate conflicts between clients and administration and between administration and union before they deteriorated into violent confrontations. There is no record that either union or administration took up the chapter's offer. In time they learned to live together.

Chapter 10

The Rank-and-File Movement:
Social Work Today

The purpose of *Social Work Today*, as given in the first issue, March 1934, was "to meet the need for a frank, critical analysis of basic social problems and their relation to social work not obtainable through established professional channels. Its province will be all of social welfare. It will promote an interest in the fundamental reorganization society must undergo to provide security for all, and will support labor's struggle for a greater measure of control as the basic condition for that reorganization."[1]

Starting Out

This ambitious undertaking was not matched by either staff or resources, which were quite modest. Staff consisted entirely of volunteers with full-time jobs who devoted evenings, weekends, and holidays to soliciting articles, editing copy, promoting circulation, and scrounging for money to pay printing and mailing bills. The primary source of income was subscriptions, never enough to meet costs, as the frequent appeals for contributions in its pages and the money-raising parties and forums attested. Advertising income was minimal. Circulation was never large. From an initial printing of 1,000, it rose to 4,800 by 1936, when the annual budget was about $5,000. Single copies sold for 15 cents; an annual subscription for the nine issues which came out during the year was $1.00. The price was kept low to attract readers; it reflected also the salary level of social work employees in the thirties.

Volume 1, Number 1 appeared under the imprint of the Social Workers Discussion Club of New York, which remained the publisher until 1936. (The club's name was changed in February 1935 to the Association of Workers in Social Agencies of New York.) Between May 1936 and June 1937 the periodical was published under the aegis of the National Coordinating Committee of Social Service Employee Groups, the new name of the National Coordinating Committee of Rank and File Groups in Social Work. These changes were formal rather than real and reflected only modifications in the organizational structure of the Rank-and-File Movement in response to changing conditions in the field. Editorial direction and policy remained consistent throughout these years, guided by the rather small New York group responsible for the theory, strategy, and tactics of the movement. The present writer was listed as the sole editor from March to July 1934, and as a member of the board of editors from October 1934 to June 1935, the others being Flora Davidson, Clara Miller, and Elizabeth Sherman. Between October 1935 and May 1936 the board of editors comprised George Wolfe, Edith Weller and Luba Wender.

Since these persons were not known outside the radicalized wing in social work, the editors thought it advisable to invite as contributing editors sympathizers with well-recognized names in the field, such as Gordon Hamilton and Eduard Lindeman of the New York School of Social Work; Harry Lurie, Mary van Kleeck; Ira de A. Reid, industrial secretary of the New York Urban League; June Purcell Guild of the Richmond Professional Institute's School of Social Work; Winifred Chappell, Methodist Federation for Social Service; Bertha Reynolds, associate director, Smith College School of Social Work; and Frankwood E. Williams, psychiatrist and medical director of the National Committee for Mental Hygiene from 1920 to 1931, who had taught at the New School for Social Research and at the New York and Smith Schools of Social Work. They were not consulted on editorial policy; it was mutually understood that the presence of their names on the masthead simply meant they believed dissidents in social work had a right to a voice of their own. As the magazine's circulation and its reputation grew, the need for such a crutch was no longer felt. The list of contributing editors was dropped with the January 1935 issue.

The articles *Social Work Today* carried in its initial years dealt only in small part and then only tangentially with the grand design implicit in the aims set out in the first issue. But the point of view reflected was well left of center. Treatment was critical, satirical, or sympathetic, depending on the subject.

Social Work Today, wrote a disgruntled reader in 1935, was not a social work journal, since it scarcely treated social work philosophy and published nothing on social work techniques. It was another left-wing periodical, and unnecessary at that, because one could get its point of view on the subjects treated by reading the many publications put out by the Socialist and Communist parties. "To be a member of the rank and file must one be a radical?" he asked. Not at all, the editors replied, in the April 1935 issue, in which the complaining letter had appeared, but they went on to imply that the rank-and-filer couldn't help winding up as a radical when he looked into the close relationship between social work and the social setting in which it was practiced. The commendable objectives of social work, such as the profession's pronouncements on the nature of a desirable direct relief and public jobs program, were thwarted by the class nature of America's society. *Social Work Today* saw as part of its job the obligation to call attention to the consequences of this class nature by running articles on the inadequacy of relief standards and personnel practices, and the desirability of protective organization among social agency employees. "If by doing these things we are radical then we plead guilty. We can be called worse things."

One of the few articles inspired by the statement of purpose in Volume 1, Number 1 was "Social Work and Liberalism," which appeared in the May 1934 issue. The article reflected the present writer's idea in 1934 of a Marxist analysis of the function of social work under capitalism: social work was part of liberalism's effort to ameliorate the grosser abuses. The article talked, among other things, of the bankruptcy of liberalism, attacked the leadership of social work as bankrupt also, and called on younger social workers to take their stand with class-conscious workers fighting for a better social order. (Schemes for Marxist histories of education, the law, medicine, the natural sciences, the social sciences, engineering, architecture, the arts, were popular then among radicalized professionals attracted by what seemed to them the liberating and exhilarating vision of History as the Class Struggle, Dialectical Materialism, and other Grand Insights.)

Taking Exception

For the most part the articles in Social Work Today were less ambitious in scope, however heterogeneous in subject—the social work scene, the government's social welfare program, the New Deal, the state of affairs in the United States in general, the state of affairs in Europe and in the world at large. Since there was little here to approve, the treatment generally was disparaging. Among the objects of the journal's critical eye in its early years were the social work Establishment, the administration's unemployment program, U.S. foreign policy, and international developments.

The social workers who applauded Harry Hopkins were chastised. Hopkins and other social workers in the administration were viewed as faithless to the profession's noblest ideals, as spineless trimmers, coopted and bribed intellectually by appointments to high office. Social work leaders who defended the New Deal, like William Hodson, were termed naive. The AASW was arraigned for timidity in criticizing inadequacies in the federal relief and work programs; for its silence, with a few notable exceptions in some chapters, on the use of police to clear recipient protesters from relief offices. Reports on the National Conference of Social Work and on AASW conferences read like jottings by a spy in the enemy's camp. They were often written under pseudonyms; were censorious in tone when not indulging in ridicule or irony—except for the favorable references to the occasional Rank-and-File Movement leader present as speaker or discussant and to such friends of the movement as Mary van Kleeck and Harry Lurie.

The FERA was condemned for the low assistance levels and the degrading eligibility conditions it permitted in local public relief programs; abandonment of the program in 1935 was termed disastrous because the states and localities were wholly unprepared to take on the financial burdens entailed. The CCC program was the subject of an article, "Shovels and Guns," describing it as an effort to prepare its beneficiaries for the next war. CWA was attacked for its low wage levels and its abrupt termination, WPA for its limitations on weekly earnings and the use of a means test to screen applicants. The administration program for social insurance, as embodied in the Wagner-Lewis bill, was dismissed as wholly inadequate because it provided for forty-eight state unemployment insurance systems rather than one national system; it excluded firms with fewer than eight workers, and did not cover workers in government, in nonprofit organizations, and in domestic service. The old age benefit title of the bill made no provision in its financing for a government contribution. Adoption was urged of the Lundeen bill, whose complete—and brief—text was printed in the February 1935 issue.

The magazine scored the economic recovery program of the New Deal, expressed in the NIRA and the triple A, as benefiting big business and big agriculture only. Section 7a of the NIRA, ostensibly a guaranty of labor's right to collective bargaining, said the editors, was used by industry to establish company unions; it provided no relief against racial discrimination in hiring and firing. After two years of the New Deal, said *Social Work Today* in July 1935, there were still 14 million unemployed (as noted earlier, there were no official figures; data developed later indicated the number of unemployed in '35 averaged 11 million monthly); relief rolls were as high as they were in '33 (they were actually higher, in persons aided, dollars spent); corporate profits were up and real wages were down.

The administration's budget was found wanting in more respects than the inadequacy of its funding of relief and emergency job programs. An editorial in the March 1936 issue saw in the larger funds proposed for the War and Navy Departments the prelude to a "war of economic aggression, most likely in the Far East, against Japan." Behind this threat, the journal said, were the same banking and industrial interests that drew the United States into the World War. An alarming view of war-threatening activities was not limited to those presumably undertaken by the American government. An article by Margaret Schlauch, "On the Brink, War and Fascism Today," December 1935, called attention to the growth of Fascism in Europe and the preparations for war by Germany and Italy.

An Upsetting Experience

The 1914–18 war, particularly the position of social work on American participation, and the threat of a second world war, were of concern to the editors. The part that social work played in what was still called the Great War was the subject of perhaps the most controversial article *Social Work Today* ran in its first year, "Social Workers Present Arms," by Flora Davidson, which appeared in October 1934. Modeled on *Preachers Present Arms,* a small book by radical clergymen on the role of churchmen when America entered the war in 1917, it accused the leadership of social work of "whole-hearted support" of American participation in a "military struggle so destructive of human values." While acknowledging the pacifist stand taken by Jane Addams, Lillian Wald, and Roger Baldwin, the author quoted a number of prominent social workers who said in 1917–18 that the most important item on the nation's agenda was to win the war; criticized the settlement houses for allegedly cooperating with army recruitment efforts; and underscored the close working relationships of the Red Cross, the YM and YWCA with the military at home and abroad.

Copies of the article were sent to the social workers quoted or referred to with a request that they define their position in the event of another war.

Not many days later a rather small, pale, agitated, but tightly self-controlled man came to the tiny office of *Social Work Today,* identified himself to me (I was alone at the moment, the other editors were out) as Paul Kellogg, a name I recognized as that of the editor of the *Survey,* although I had never met him before, and put in my hands several typed pages. Kellogg had been quoted in the Davidson article and this was his reply. Apparently he was not wholly satisfied with it, because he almost immediately asked for an opportunity for a last going-over and in my presence toned down the sharpness of some of his comments.

Kellogg's reply was a spirited defense of the social workers, among whom Kellogg included himself, who were aware of imperialist rivalries in Europe, feared the existence of secret agreements which came to fruit in the Versailles treaty, and when the United States entered the war, fought against the development of a militaristic spirit on this side of the Atlantic. Some social workers, like Roger Baldwin, who went to jail for his pacifism, helped organize the American Civil Liberties Union to defend the victims of jingoism. Davidson's article ignored the insurgents who voiced opposition to the war at the 1917 National Conference of Social Work, 500 of whom signed a round robin letter asking the administration for its peace terms. The letter condemned territorial changes and punitive indemnities contemplated by the belligerents who expected to emerge as victors at the war's end; and it called for a democratic league of nations to prevent future wars. Kellogg himself, a signer of the round robin, was denounced by the leader of the pro-war wing of the Socialist Party, William English Walling, and by AFofL president Samuel Gompers, as guilty of insidious pro-German pacifist propaganda.

How to stop World War II? Kellog asked in conclusion. By fighting the munition makers and the "big navy" crowd. By strengthening peace organizations. By solving our economic and racial grievances in other ways than war.

It was a moving response. I experienced guilt, remorse, emotions felt also by some of my fellow editors. Had we been unfair to Kellogg and to the others, named and unnamed in his letter, who shared his views on the war? Had Davidson, in her research for the article, looked at all the evidence or only that part of it which put social work in an unfavorable light? Perhaps behind "Social Workers Present Arms" there was not only the muckraker's zeal to expose evil, but also the youthful rebel's need *pour épater le bourgeois,* to scandalize the respectable, and the devil take the consequences, including the hurt inflicted on innocent people. Had we gone too far?

The November issue carried Kellogg's piece and a response by Karl de Schweinitz, another social worker quoted in the article, and a rejoinder by Davidson. Roger Baldwin's comment, which came late, was printed in February 1935. Baldwin said a minority of social workers, of whom he was one, fought U.S. participation in the war, worked for better treatment of conscientious objectors, and were active in the American Union against Militarism, whose members included such prominent social workers and persons on the edge of social work as Jane Addams, Lillian Wald, Owen R. Lovejoy, Florence Kelley, John Lovejoy Elliott, Norman Thomas, Baldwin himself—and Paul U. Kellogg.

OK Causes

Not all the articles *Social Work Today* published in its early years were reprobatory in tone. The organizations, activities, and causes winning its endorsement reflected, however, a similar leftist outlook on the issues of the day—in social work, in public policy, and international developments.

One of the primary interests of the editors was the progress of unionism in social work. Articles on the subject noted discriminatory practices by agencies against union activists, the militancy of unions in response, the gains won by unions, the spread of the union idea across the country. Beginning in October 1934 a directory of Rank-and-File organizations was printed in each issue, listing name, address, name of principal officer, purpose, coverage. They were for the most part, and increasingly with the years, protective organizations, i.e., unions. The expansion in the size of the directory was a measure of the growth of the union idea and a spur to further effort.

In the same vein—sounding a note positive, commendatory, optimistic—were articles on social work unions or near unions in other countries, and on unions, new and old, in other professions in the United States.

The labor movement, per se, was treated in very general terms. Most labor unions in the country belonged to the AFofL, whose leadership was considered in left circles as reactionary in its politics, timid in its approach to collective bargaining, too feeble to seize the opportunities for organizing the unorganized potentially present in section 7a of the NIRA. Consequently it was the labor movement idea or ideal rather than the labor movement reality that won *Social Work Today* support. Calls to social workers to recognize their identity of interests with other workers and to join with them in promoting labor's cause—expressed for example in van Kleeck's 1934 national conference paper, "The Common Goals of Labor and Social Work," and in her 1935 conference paper, "Sources of Power for the Social Work Program" published in the October 1934 and December 1935 issues respectively—assumed a labor movement that did not exist in 1934 and 1935, emerging in embryo form only late in 1935 with the formation within the AFofL of the dissident Committee for Industrial Organization (CIO).

Closely related to the belief in the importance of a vital labor movement was the hope that a radically-oriented Labor party along the European model could be developed in the United States. This thesis was best expressed in "Sources of Power for the Social Work Program." Here van Kleeck noted that the 1912 report of the Committee on Standards of Living and Labor resulted in no reforms worth speaking of; that in 1924, as related in chapter 2, a follow-up committee presented a report, "Sources of Power for Industrial Freedom," which attributed the failure to the absence of a "political class party of the producers." In 1935, van Kleeck said, this meant a third party, a Labor party in which social workers concerned with living standards could play an important role in formulating standards and goals.

Other causes towards which *Social Work Today* took a sympathetic attitude were the efforts of organizations of the unemployed and of relief recipients to win recognition from relief administrators when protesting inadequacies in the relief program and demanding the correction of injustices or abuses in specific cases. The activities of the unemployed councils in blocking evictions were publicized and their national conventions favorably reported.

Critical articles and comments on U.S. foreign policy and on the triumphs of Fascism and the dangers of war in Europe were matched on the other side by friendly references to the American League Against War and Fascism and to the U.S.S.R.

Perspective on the political outlook reflected in *Social Work Today* may be gained by noting that its first few years coincided in time with the growth of a strong left trend among American writers, the beginnings of what was referred to as a "proletarian literature,"and the publication of a spate of books, generally favorable, on the Soviet Union, the revolutionary movement in China, and anti-fascist activities in Europe. Some of these books were commented on in *Social Work Today*, whose book review section gave first place to publications in the field of social work, though not to the neglect of books of more general interest.

How unabashedly at times the journal revealed its political stance was illustrated by the May 1935 issue, which devoted a full page to the reproduction of four cartoons from *Hunger and Revolt*, a collection of drawings by Jacob Burck, the political cartoonist of the *Daily Worker*, the book's publisher. The four cartoons reproduced were "Section 7a at Work," depicting a mounted policeman, whip in hand, driving before him a horde of pick-and-shovel workers; "Too Much Wheat," showing in the foreground the skeletonized figure of a farmer on his back, surrounded by a field of wheat stretching to the farmhouse on the horizon; "The Cloak," a skeleton, cane in hand, wearing a fur-collared coat and a top hat and smoking a cigar; and "Fall In," marchers carrying signs which said "We Refuse to Starve," "No Evictions," and "Down With Breadlines." The drawings were described as possessing a "magnificence and a strength that reflects as much the power of the revolutionary movement they serve as the first-rate talent they embody." The editors referred to Burck as the best political cartoonist in America, and to the *Daily Worker* as the best labor daily.

The characterization of the *Daily Worker* by the editors of *Social Work Today* as the best labor daily is not to be construed as an effort at deception, since the paper identified itself on the first page as the organ of the Communist Party of the United States. The nonreference to the connection of the paper and the party was part of the posture of the editors that the subject was unimportant, that the words Communist and Communism should be avoided because some people had hangups about them, and that of greater importance were the underlying themes the drawings dramatized—the evils of hunger, unemployment, exploitation, police violence, capitalism; and the necessity of struggle against them.

Chapter 11

The Rank-and-File Movement: The Wider Involvement

The Rank-and-File Movement encouraged cooperation among social agency employee groups on issues of common concern, and between such groups and non-social work organizations interested in the same goals. The present chapter describes some of these activities.[1]

Organizations of the Unemployed

The New York Social Workers Discussion Club, as noted, contributed money for the national hunger march in Washington in 1932, and sent delegates to the National Convention Against Unemployment held in the nation's capital in January 1934, at which representatives of an estimated 1,200 unemployed councils, according to the account in *Social Work Today*, organized the Unemployed Councils of America.

Perhaps the most ambitious effort undertaken by the Unemployed Councils of America was the Congress for Unemployment and Social Insurance held in Washington January 5–7, 1935. It drew 3,000 delegates and observers from council locals, trade unions, professional bodies, women's organizations, church groups, and fraternal organizations. Eleven Rank-and-File groups in social work sent delegates or observers. The call to the conference was signed, among others, by Heywood Broun, president of the American Newspaper Guild; Mary E. Beardsley, American Red Cross; Paul Brissenden, Columbia University; and other persons prominent in education, religion, social work, and labor circles. Well-attended regional meetings in a dozen or more cities in December 1934 served to publicize the congress and attract attendance. It met at a critical moment. It was on January 4 that Roosevelt had told Congress the federal government "must and shall quit this business of relief."

Congress chairman was Harry Elmer Brown, president of the National Typographical Union, and the speakers at general sessions included T. Arnold Hill, director of the Department of Industrial Relations, National Urban League; Broadus Mitchell, professor of economics, Johns Hopkins

University; Mary van Kleeck; Congressman Ernest Lundeen, sponsor of the Lundeen bill, to mobilize support for which was the primary aim of the congress; and Earl Browder, general secretary of the Communist party.

The big old Washington Auditorium, which occupied the triangle formed by New York Avenue, E Street and 19th and 20th Streets, and has since been torn down, was rented for the occasion and became a beehive of activity during the three days of the congress. There were general sessions; caucuses of the delegates from unions, from unemployed councils, from professional organizations; special committee meetings; the selection of delegations to visit (with appropriate "demands") the White House, the office of the vice-president, the FERA, the PWA, the secretary of Labor, and the AFofL.

From some rough notes the present writer made at the time as a member of the delegation that met with the FERA: It is a large delegation, maybe twenty-five or thirty, headed by Israel Amter of the National Unemployed Councils. Amter an old hand at confrontations with public officials; tough, hard-boiled, direct; conveys strong sense of command in any situation in which he finds self. Hdq. of FERA is on New York Ave., only a block and a half from auditorium. At door guard says will admit only small committee. But pressure of delegation behind Amter too much. We flood into small lobby, filling it. We want to see Hopkins, says Amter. Hopkins is sick, says the guard; get out of here. No one moves. Guard phones for a policeman. An FERA official appears from nowhere; says Aubrey Williams, assistant administrator, will see a small committee. Amter is invited into the reception room off the lobby. We all push in; occupy chairs, stand against the wall. Williams enters, a tall, thin, dark-haired man. Sits on the edge of a desk, says "Go ahead and talk, I'm listening." His folksy manner is disarming, for some of us, but Amter is not susceptible to its charms. He ticks off counts in bill of indictment against government's program. Relief payments are inadequate. Wages on work-relief are too low. Negroes get short end of stick in size of relief allowance, number and kinds of jobs on work projects.

Williams says nothing, takes notes, smiles now and then at a vivid turn of phrase. Amter calls on members of the delegation to speak their piece. Personal experiences looking for a job, getting relief, working on a project. They come from Olathe, Kansas; Abbeville, Louisiana; Flint, Michigan; New Bedford, Massachusetts; Klamath Falls, Oregon. A woman from Jacksonville, Florida thrusts at Williams a voucher for a week's wages on work-relief: $1.24. "We want an answer," says Amter at end.

"We'll look into all complaints," says Williams. "We have programs, but we don't always get what we want out of them. Some local administrators are mean and hard. We're trying to weed them out. We're not sure we have all the answers, but the administration is doing its best to protect the unemployed against the forces trying to destroy them—powerful private interests, local officials in league with them, reactionary senators and congressmen." He asks patience and trust. FDR will go down in history as the man who made the first great move to help the unemployed in the Depression. Derisive shouts. Amter demands a timetable, figures on how many dollars will be spent, how many families aided, how many people employed on the new work program. Williams pushes him off, says he is in no position to make promises, wants to finish the discussion, get back to his office. The meeting ends lamely as the exchange between the two becomes repetitive, dwindles, and Williams leaves.

This is how my notes read. But Amter's report to the congress, the write-up in the *Daily Worker*, limned another portrait; heightened a contrast between outraged protesters and cowed officials; converted William's acknowledgment of problems and deficiencies to confessions of failure, his plea for patience and trust into a cloudcuckooland of vague promises of a better future. Thus was reality transformed in the pressure cooker of the politics of the day.

The congress wound up with a strongly-worded assault on the administration's relief and job programs and its social insurance proposals as expressed in the Wagner-Lewis bill. A ringing endorsement was given the Lundeen bill.

The meeting with Aubrey Williams was one vivid experience I recall from the congress. The other was an incident which took place the morning of the second day; it is illustrative of the persistence of racial segregation in the Washington of the New Deal and of Mary van Kleeck's forthrightness on the subject. I was attending the congress as a member of the delegation from the Inter-Professional Association for Social Insurance. IPA delegates had taken rooms in a small hotel near the auditorium and had agreed to have breakfast the following day at the Allies Inn, which occupied a small brick building at the corner of 17th Street and New York Avenue. It went back to World War I and maybe earlier, and its entrance was marked by the crossed flags of the principal allies other than Russia in that war—the United States, Britain, France, and Italy. (The Italian flag was still flying in 1942, when we were officially at war with Italy.) The Allies Inn provided no lodging, at least not in 1935, and confined its activities to the operation of a cafeteria which served excellent southern -style dishes. Patrons took their trays outdoors in mild weather and ate at tables set on flagstoned terraces shaded by dogwood, crape myrtle, holly in variety, and underplanted in season with impatiens, begonia, pinks, and petunias. An elegant place.

That January morning we took our trays and began moving down the line, making our selections. Some of us had almost reached the cashier when a commotion broke out behind us. A black congress delegate was standing at the beginning of the counter, his tray empty except for napkin and silver. Opposite him a flustered server opened and closed her mouth. I couldn't make out her words but they evidently expressed strong disapproval of his presence. A moment later the manager appeared from the kitchen and in a voice loud enough for us all to hear said, "We don't serve nigras." The black stared at her, his fingers still gripping the tray. "You don't?" said van Kleeck, who was about midway in the line. "I'm sorry to hear you say that." There was a half-disdainful half-pitying edge in her words. "We're not eating here." For the IPA members on the line and our black fellow-delegate, it was a command. We left our trays on the counter, moved past the astonished cashier without a word, and trooped out. "The YWCA," said one knowledgeable member of the group when we reached the sidewalk. The YW, then as now at 17th and K, was one of the few nonsegregated eating places in the District. We walked the four blocks to K Street and had our breakfast there.

Protesting Relief and Job Program Cuts

Not all visits to Washington in '35 and '36 by delegations representing the National Coordinating Committee of Rank and File Groups in Social Work were for the purpose of attending conferences, conventions or congresses. The NCC organized a number of protests against reductions in the administration's relief and job programs and against appropriation cuts which were viewed as evidence of callousness to the needs of the unemployed and of relief recipients and which affected affiliates in the form of staff reductions. An ad hoc committee would be organized in New York, board a Friday late-afternoon Washington train at Penn Station and arrive in the District that evening. It checked in at a low-price hotel, such as the cavernous Cairo, where members would get together, when time allowed for the necessary arrangements, with representatives from other cities. The next morning (federal offices were then open half-days Saturdays) the committee would go to FERA or WPA headquarters, meet with a middle-echelon official, engage in a half-acrimonious, half-humorous discussion with him, leave in his hands a statement prepared in advance, listing its "demands," and take the afternoon train back to New York. But not before a stop at the National Press Building to leave copies of press releases at the offices of the AP, the UP, the *New York Times*, the New York *Herald Tribune*, and two or three other dailies we deemed of importance. The releases were usually ignored, but one Monday morning New York's social workers, union and nonunion members alike, were astonished to open the *Trib* and find the NCC's story on page 1, and given a full column. It must have been a Sunday singularly devoid of news, a day for which fillers are reserved.

Sometimes the New York group stayed over to Sunday because Saturday afternoon was spent conferring with NCC representatives from other cities on some upcoming development. On one such occasion we decided to explore Washington before we took the train back. It was a cloudless August day. The nation's capital, prostrate under the airless tropic heat of a Washington summer, was a dead city, its stores and offices closed, its residents immured in their shuttered houses, or fled, God knows where to. We walked south down an empty 14th Street, past the Liberty Loan Building and the Bureau of Engraving and Printing, and striking east emerged on the other side of the elevated railroad tracks to find ourselves in what might have been a small southern town. Tree-shaded streets, their pavements as wrinkled as the face of an old man; their curbs canted, fallen, like teeth in a ruined mouth. Frame houses in faded white, green, and brown, set well back from a sidewalk which in places disappeared altogether and became a dusty path through the crabgrass. In front of some houses, or in the driveway, one saw an ancient abandoned car, hoodless, its tires stripped, its fenders porous with rust, its doors hanging on one hinge, the cloth top in shreds. Visible beyond the car in the driveway, sometimes, was a weathered shanty, high in weeds—a privy, said one of the more knowing persons in our group. A cicada would suddenly break the summer Sunday stillness with a loud swelling rattle, like seed shaken in a dried gourd, then stop abruptly, as though seized by an unseen hand. Occasionally one caught a glimpse of a black face in a window. We were in the old Southwest, a black slum in the shadow, as the papers said then and later, of the Capitol. Another side of Washington, unforgettable.

Fighting Racism

The Allies Inn incident, the glimpse we caught that Sunday morning of the black slum, were reminders of the persistence under the New Deal of one of the major evils of twentieth century America, the second-class status of blacks, or Negroes as they were called in the thirties. Part of the radicalization social workers underwent in the Rank-and-File Movement was to be sensitized to this issue, in large part because it was stressed as an issue by the Communist party and its sympathizers, and the radicalism in social work, in other professional fields, and among writers, the arts, the theater, took many of its cues from the Communists. One did not have to swallow the Communist party program as a whole, including the slogan of self-determination for the black belt, to recognize that the Communists spoke up on the subject when liberals were silent; that the AFofL hierarchy condoned the existence of lily-white unions in its midst; and that it was a Communist lawyers' group, the International Labor Defense, which was the first to come to the rescue of the nine Scottsboro boys in 1931, after they had been sentenced to death in a farcically brief trial for allegedly raping two white women of dubious virtue, who had been their fellow-travelers on a freight train near that Alabama town.

It was common knowledge that Washington was a segregated city, and that a number of New Deal programs accepted and perpetuated discriminatory policies based on race. Most hotels and restaurants in the city were off-limits to blacks, even the often dingy little lunchrooms in department stores, which employed only white sales personnel. One theater accepted the presence of blacks on the stage, but not in the audience. Illustrative of the irrationality of such social conventions, this policy was applied in reverse by the DAR when its auditorium, Constitution Hall, was used for concerts. The celebrated incident to which it led later in the decade, giving the Daughters unwanted publicity, was the DAR's cancellation of a concert in 1939 by Marian Anderson, and her performance before a much larger audience on the steps of the Lincoln Memorial. The new site had the blessing of the National Park Service of the Department of the Interior, whose secretary, Harold Ickes, was a former president of the Chicago chapter of the NAACP.

Racial covenants confined the black population pretty much to selected areas of the District, largely the slums. Washington's schools were segregated, as were the public playgrounds and public swimming pools run by the city's recreation department. New Deal defenders attributed such practices in public facilities to the District committees of House and Senate, which influenced the appointment by the President of the city's governing body, the Commissioners of the District of Columbia (there was no self-government), appropriated the city's budget, and determined municipal policy and practices. These committees were invariably chaired by Southerners. But this explanation could not account for the denial of service in government building cafeterias to black federal employees, with the outstanding exceptions of the Interior Department under Ickes and the Labor Department under Frances Perkins. (Labor employees who took offense at the presence of blacks went across the street to the segregated cafeteria in Commerce.) When federal employees organized Group Health Association, a prepaid medical care plan, it was limited to whites.

Any fair assessment of the impact of the New Deal on the condition of blacks in the country must take into account, to be sure, the indirect effects of policies which had a larger influence on the condition of some groups than others, for reasons related to the socio-economic structure of the population rather than race per se. Because they were over-represented among the poor, America's blacks benefited perhaps more than whites did from the New Deal's relief and work programs, and from the increase in federal employment and in private industry. More blacks had jobs. Their average income gained. CCC gave jobs to 200,000 black youths; except in the South, the camps were integrated. FERA regulations forbade discrimination based on race in the distribution of federal relief funds; although subtly evaded in the South, where local relief officials found them a bitter pill to swallow and said they "spoiled the niggers," they had the effect of ameliorating such practices in other parts of the country.

On the other hand, blacks in the federal service held lower-level jobs for the most part. They were messengers, porters, maintenance personnel. Few were secretaries, typists, clerks; even fewer had jobs of a professional, supervisory, or administrative nature. The explanation usually offered was lack of experience, training, or education. This was true, but few or blacks were accepted for the in-service training programs either. That snobbish branch of the military establishment, the Navy, FDR's pride and joy, accepted blacks for enlistment as messmen only.

The National Industrial Recovery Administration approved industrial codes providing for black-white differentials in wage rates in the South, and the manual of the Federal Housing Administration (FHA) permitted racially-restricted covenants in the residential housing it insured. Under the AAA program, Negro tenant farmers and sharecroppers were among the first to be pushed off the land when crop acreage was reduced. Black applicants for participation in the model subsistence homestead program sponsored by Eleanor Roosevelt at Arthurdale, West Virginia, learned from the manager it was for "native white stock" only. This was not of course what Mrs. Roosevelt had in mind, as she quickly made clear. Her views on race were far in advance of her time and her class; she resigned from the DAR in 1939 over the Marian Anderson incident.

With the exception of Ickes and Perkins, perhaps, no one in high office in the government considered racial discrimination of major significance when compared with the greater objectives of business recovery, the end of mass unemployment, higher farm prices, banking reform, social security, and the other stated objectives of the New Deal. Roosevelt refused to push an antilynching bill, of prime importance in the thirties to the NAACP, and when appealed to by Walter White, its executive secretary, offered as explanation that the chairmanships of all major committees in House and Senate were held by Southerners and he needed their support for his legislative program. The same rationale accounted presumably for his seeming indifference to segregation practices in the government of the District and in federal agencies, and to other aspects of discrimination cited here. He was no racist, but, unlike his wife, he didn't feel deeply on the subject, any more than he felt or thought deeply on any subject. He had the sure instincts of the successful politician; he liked to be liked, and by the right people. He could afford to offend the blacks who ran the NAACP, but not the Southern senators. (These qualities were later to determine his unconcern with the fate of Europe's Jews in the Holocaust.)

It was this aspect of the administration which, among others, soured the Rank-and-File Movement on the New Deal in the period 1933–35. The unions whose organization the NCC encouraged in public relief agencies took a strong stand on the employment of blacks on the staff and their promotion to supervisory and administrative jobs. Outstanding in this regard was New York's Association of Workers in Public Relief Agencies (AWPRA), which had a black vice-president and enjoyed a substantial membership in the Home Relief Bureau's offices in Harlem.

At the 1935 National Conference of Social Work, held in Montreal, three black members of the AWPRA group were denied accommodations at the six hotels they tried the day of their arrival. An NCC committee went to see Howard Knight, the general secretary of the conference, who got rooms for the three and agreed to take up the issue of discrimination with the conference executive committee. Publicity was given the incident by Mary van Kleeck, who inserted some condemnatory remarks on the subject in one of the papers she gave. (NCC officers made sure she learned about it.) When the executive conference committee met, it issued a general statement deploring discrimination based on race in hotel and restaurant facilities. The NCC considered the statement insufficient and proposed that the national conference adopt a policy of not meeting in any city whose hotel and restaurant convention bureau could not pledge complete access by all attendees to every housing, eating, and drinking establishment subject to convention bureau rules.

The conference executive committee, some of whose members agreed with the NCC position, agonized over the issue for months, in part because adoption of the position meant that the conference could not meet in the South. The conference followed a general policy of covering over the years all regions of the country and of Canada in the selection of conference cities. Eventually the executive committee came out foursquare for meeting only in cities which could make a pledge of absolute nondiscrimination. Because such a guarantee could not be obtained from the convention bureau in Washington, selected earlier as the site of the '36 meeting, the conference was shifted that year to Atlantic City. *Social Work Today* hailed the decision as a victory for the progressive forces in social work.

Overlooked in the dispute between the NCC and the executive committee of the National Conference—overlooked, that is, by all NCC officers—was the better-than-average record of social work in race discrimination, recognition of which on the part of NCC might have avoided some of the abrasive aspects of NCC-executive committee contacts on the issue. Social work was probably in advance of the other professions in this regard. The AASW was open to all persons in social work who met its membership requirements, which made no mention of race. By contrast, the American Bar Association admitted on blacks; both the American Medical Association and the National Education Association condoned lily-white state and local affiliates. Negro physicians had to organize the National Medical Association to find a national voice; and Negro teachers, the National Teachers Association. (Some black lawyers joined the National Lawyers Guild when it was established in the thirties by white liberal and radical lawyers and made open to all attorneys.) There was no separate black social workers organization, in part becaase where were few black social workers in the thirties (they were limited for the most part to employees of the National Urban League, and members of the teaching staffs of the two black schools of social work, Atlanta and Howard, established in 1920 and 1936 respectively) but in greater part because they were welcome in the AASW.

III The Second New Deal, 1935–37

Chapter 12

The New Deal in its Populist Phase

The second New Deal is the term historians use to describe the new direction in the policies pursued by the administration after the destruction at the hands of the Supreme Court of the two pivotal economic measures of the first New Deal, the National Industrial Recovery Act (NIRA) and the Agricultural Adjustment Act (AAA). The actions of the highest court of the land coincided and fitted in with a reordering of Roosevelt's political strategy, growing out of his resentment of the continued hostility of the die-hard big business conservatives he thought he was helping in the first New Deal. He was also moved by fear of the political threat posed by Senator Huey Long's demagogic appeal to the poor and the dispossessed of the nation ("Share the Wealth," "Every Man a King"), a fear compounded by the coolness of organized labor towards him because of the growth of company unions under section 7a of the NIRA. The net effect was a turn to the left in the alignment of his political base, and in the economic programs proposed for legislation or pursued by executive direction.[1]

The new politics that emerged with the second New Deal were almost unnoticed or ignored by social work as represented by the professional associations. They exercised a major influence, however, on the radicalized wing of social work, particularly the Rank-and-File Movement.

To win the White House again in 1936 and to consolidate his hold on House and Senate, Roosevelt forged a new Democratic party, a coalition of white supremacists in the South; of corrupt city machines in the North; of a revived and expanding, if divided, labor movement, politically conscious of its power and making effective use of it through Labor's Nonpartisan League; of liberal reformers from coast to coast with backgrounds in Teddy Roosevelt's Progressive party of 1912, in Robert LaFollette's party of the same name of 1924, and in the Socialist party; of liberals whose frosty attitude toward FDR was thawed by the demise of the first New Deal, and Roosevelt's denunciation of the nine old men on the Supreme Court, the last stronghold of the old order in Washington; and of agrarian reformers battling under the banners of the Nonpartisan

League of the upper Middle West and the Farmer-Labor party of Minnesota, inheritors of the populist tradition of the nineteenth century.

The Socialist party split as Roosevelt succeeded in wooing into his coalition Sidney Hillman, David Dubinsky, and Emil Rieve, presidents respectively of the Amalgamated Clothing Workers of America, the International Ladies Garment Workers Union, and the Hosiery Workers Union, all former Socialist party members, whose defection deprived the party of major elements in its financial and voting base. The Communist party, adopting the Popular Front line promulgated by the Communist International in 1935 (the Communist U.S.S.R. and the Western democracies have a common stake in the defeat of fascism—more of this later), assumed an ambiguous position on the '36 election, putting up a candidate of its own but stressing in its campaign the primary importance of defeating the Republican party, an endorsement, in effect, of Roosevelt.

Union backing for Roosevelt was assured by such symbolic acts as the talk secretary of Labor Frances Perkins made to steelworkers at the Homestead, Pennsylvania, post office after being driven out of a hall and a park by steel company police and forced to find safety on federal property. The rural electrification and rural settlement programs won the adherence of the small farmer, the tenant farmer, and the sharecropper. Help in pushing New Deal legislation through Congress by Republican party progressives in House and Senate and participation in the management of the new programs by other Republican party progressives assured the fealty of the Republicans' followers. By pinning the donkey's tail of a WASP image on the Republican party, FDR attracted to himself strategic blocs of voters of other ethnic origins, including blacks in the North; and by appropriate appointments he captured the political loyalties of Catholics and Jews.

As for the Republican party, which took such a licking in '32, it had never been in such bad odor. It retained its hold on the more rural conservative voters of New England and the Middle West, but for the American public as a whole it had acquired a new image. It was, in Roosevelt's phrase, the party of the economic royalists, the rich and the once-rich, a minority party, a shadow of its former opulent, starched-shirt, stiff-collar self of the twenties.

The 1936 election was a triumph for the coalition Roosevelt had put together. He drew 28 million votes to the 17 million of Republican candidate Landon, sweeping all the states except Maine and Vermont. In third place was a maverick Republican from North Dakota, William Lemke, who attracted less than a million votes under the banner of the Union party. This was a hastily put together coalition of radical rightists like the radio priest Father Coughlin and Gerald L. K. Smith; of populists distrustful of Roosevelt; and of such one-issue crusaders as Dr. Townsend, who proposed to cure the Depression by paying persons over sixty $200 a month, provided they spent it all in thirty days. The Socialist party vote fell below 200,000; that of the Communist party dropped to 80,000. Republican governors were reduced to a bare seven. Democratic majorities in House and Senate had never been bigger.[2]

The second New Deal was a return, in a sense, to the economic goals outlined by Roosevelt in his '32 campaign speech before the Commonwealth Club of San Francisco, but given low priority in the first New Deal. In his address he had described the basic task of government as "distributing wealth and products more equitably, of adopting economic organizations to the service of the people." "Unless prosperity is uniform," he had said, "unless purchasing power is distributed throughout every group in the nation," the safety of the existing order was imperiled. The importance of these goals was introduced by a summary reference to the alarming growth of monopoly and the economic power of large corporations, and the narrowing-down of economic opportunities for the small businessman, the farmer, and the wage and salary earner.[3]

The Supreme Court ruling in the NIRA case restored the antitrust laws and regulations, in particular the prohibition against price-fixing in industry and commerce. Roosevelt had denounced the nine old men but, agile to adjust to the new political reality, he now hailed price competition as a stimulus to further recovery. Bigness and monopoly were once again seen in Washington as evil. "Private power," said FDR to Congress, was reaching a point at which it was becoming "stronger than the democratic state itself . . . a concentration of private power without equal in history is growing . . . The power of the few to manage the economic life of the nation must be diffused among the many or be transferred to the public and its democratically responsible government."[4] Legislation was introduced to break up business combinations and to promote more price rivalry among firms competing for the consumer's dollar. TVA, conceived as an experiment in regional planning, was expected to compete with private industry in the production of power and fertilizer.

To publicize monopoly in business the Temporary National Economic Committee (TNEC) was appointed. Its investigations, stretching over several years, made a major contribution to the store of information on the subject, and are significant, in retrospect, of the gap between promise and performance of much of the second New Deal, since the monopolization they documented was little affected in its growth by the administration's program. The TNEC was in this respect like the rhetoric of the second New Deal, sufficiently populist in tone to win the approval of liberals who had been critical of the first New Deal's marriage to big business and big agriculture, and to receive the unreserved endorsement of a resurgent, vigorously growing, administration-supported labor movement, but equivocal in delivery. Labor, however, got a little more than populist rhetoric. The Wagner Labor Relations Act (1935) established collective bargaining rights on a firmer footing than the discredited section 7a of the NIRA. It was quickly taken advantage of by the AFofL's newly established Committee for Industrial Organization (CIO) to launch energetic drives in the largely unorganized auto, steel, and textile industries, drives that had the sympathetic support of the National Labor Relations Board set up under the act.

In agriculture, there was no more Triple A, but its principal objective, to raise farm prices, had been achieved. To make sure farm income would not drop, benefit payments were paid for soil conservation rather than for taking land out of production, which had the desirable effect of encouraging the planting of soil-conserving rather than soil-depleting crops, mostly in surplus anyway (e.g. corn, cotton). The little farmer was still in trouble. He was to be helped, however, via the Resettlement Administration and the Farm Security Administration, its successor, which bought up exhausted land, returned it to forest and pasture, and resettled its farm owners; and via the Farm Tenancy Act, a low-interest loan program to enable farm tenants and sharecroppers to buy their own farms.

Of all the four periods viewed here as significant for the changing nature of the decade, the second New Deal, covering roughly the middle years of '35–'37, witnessed the most solid support for the administration among liberals, groups with a left-of-center political orientation, and the labor movement. Its moral tone was set by Roosevelt's Second Inaugural, with its reference to the third of a nation ill-housed, ill-clothed, ill-fed, attesting to official recognition of the faults in American society and to administration commitment to take remedial action. Contributing to the heady atmosphere of the period and the feeling of moving forward were the gains in Gross National Product, in gross wage and salary income, and in gross farm income.

Gross National Product, in current prices, went up from $58 billion in '32 to $83 billion in '36, and to $90 billion in '37. (The figures cited here were developed later; their general magnitudes were apparent at the time, however.) Employment rose from a low of 38 million in '32 to 44 million in '36, and to 46 million in '37. There were still 8 million unemployed in '37, the best Depression year yet, a sobering fact, but the 8 million were 4 million fewer than in '33. Gross wage and salary income increased 25 percent between '35 and '37, and gross farm income 13 percent.[5] People had more to eat, felt they had more to live for.

Chapter 13

The Lost Battle for a Federal General Relief Program

The response of social work to the second New Deal was mixed. Radicalized social workers, disarmed by its populism, muted their criticism of government policy. The Rank-and-File Movement, its focus more and more on union organization, viewed sympathetically the administration's near alliance with the labor movement, became its supporter on most issues. For the profession as a whole, however, as represented in such organizations as the AASW and to a lesser extent in the American Public Welfare Association, the touchstone was federal policy on responsibility for general relief. The dominant attitude toward the administration remained critical, as it had been in the latter period of the first New Deal, and for the same reason, namely Roosevelt's belief that federal public aid responsibilities should be confined to work-relief and the special categories under the Social Security Act; and his insistence that general relief should be and would be left to the states and localities.

A Dissenting Profession

Social workers not in the federal service found it difficult to reconcile themselves to the withdrawal of the government from direct relief. They fought unsuccessfully all through the middle years of the thirties for the return of federal sharing in the cost of general relief, or general assistance, as it came to be called after the passage into law of the Social Security Act in August 1935 and the establishment under the act of federally aided programs for the three categories: Old Age Assistance, Aid to Dependent Children, and Aid to the Blind. They challenged the administration's estimates of the effect of the termination of FERA, the number of relief cases that would be picked up by WPA and the three categories, and the residual number that would become the responsibility of the states and localities. In his message to Congress, March 18, 1936, requesting $1.5 billion for WPA, the President put at 5.3 million the number of families and unattached individuals in need of public assistance that month, of whom 3.8 million were benefiting from WPA, CCC, and National Youth Administration (NYA) job programs under federal auspices, leaving 1.5 million, containing mostly unemployable persons, to be cared for by state and local governments. This relatively small group, said the President encouragingly, could be expected to decline rapidly as selected parts were picked up by the Social Security Act's categories.

The AASW, speaking through the pages of the *Compass* in April, quoted with approval Roosevelt's assertion that persons suffering from the effects of the Depression "must continue to be the concern of the federal government"; such a commitment "wins full support from social workers." It noted, however, a wide gap between the optimistic calculations underlying the message to Congress and its own estimates. Families on relief totalled 6 million rather than 5.3 million; those with members employed on federal work programs numbered 3.2 million rather than 3.8 million. On this more realistic basis, as the AASW saw it, states and localities would have to care for 2.8 million not 1.5 million cases—almost twice as many as the President assumed. "It is a matter of grave doubt whether state and local governments can provide adequately at the present time for so large a number as 1.5 million," let alone 2.8 million, the statement continued. It predicted that "relief in many jurisdictions will not be given," expressed the fear that "great deprivation and suffering" would ensue.[1]

Chapter reports from widely scattered parts of the country, summarized in succeeding issues of the *Compass*, seemed to confirm the fears expressed by the national office of the AASW. They spoke of reduced budgets, of restrictive eligibility conditions, of needy families cut off from the relief rolls.

Indicative of the pinch felt by state and local governments as FERA phased out its program early in 1936, was the opposition to the administration's policy voiced by the American Public Welfare Association, which generally avoided taking sides on major issues, shunned in particular any criticism of the administration, and left to the AASW the expression of dissident views concerning depression programs sponsored by the White House. APWA's board of directors in April 1936 affirmed its belief that the federal government had a continuing responsibility to meet the relief requirements of all needy persons, not only those falling into the categories. "This Association is . . . strongly of the opinion that the WPA program must be supplemented and underpinned by a federal grant-in-aid program for direct relief."[2]

Two concerns animated the APWA; not only the inability of the states and localities to carry unaided the residual relief program and the suffering that would ensue as a result, but fear also of a deterioration in personnel standards whose introduction under FERA regulations in 1933 had been hailed as the first step toward broad acceptance of a merit system in public welfare. (Existing merit systems covered only a tiny fraction of the tens of thousands employed in the country's public welfare departments and independently administered emergency relief agencies.)

A study of the effects of the withdrawal of federal grants for direct relief, made by Catherine Dunn of the APWA staff, concluded in language uncharacteristically severe for the Association, that it had paved the way for a "starvation scale of relief," and "the entrance of poor personnel, and of politics in its most destructive form. The result is the destruction of all that we want to preserve in people and the sapping of the very life blood of society."[3]

A third voice in the chorus of social work disapproval was the National Committee on the Care of Transients and Homeless, which issued a statement in January 1936 deploring the termination of the federal transient program the previous fall and recommending its reinstatement. A study made by the committee documented some of the consequences which flowed from the program's demise—the insufficiency of local resources to meet the needs of this special group, the restrictions hostile state and local legislators imposed on public assistance to persons lacking legal residence, the impact on families with children.[4]

Dunn's APWA study was based on telegraphic reports from local officials. Hurried, impressionistic, they reflected the immediate situation, and served to buttress the belief of most social workers that the administration had abandoned millions of needy persons to an uncertain fate when it limited its principal responsibility to jobs for employables. But that such first impressions were in the main on the mark was confirmed with the publication later of detailed studies by the WPA research division, tracing the erosion of living standards among families on general relief with the ending of FERA.

The irony of the executioner making public the sufferings of his victims was not lost on some social workers. The more cynical said it was cheaper to study the effects of the end of the FERA than to restore the program. Policy-makers in the administration, to judge from the course of events, ignored the studies. Perhaps they never saw them because they were too busy to read reports. Besides, the WPA research division poured out reports by the scores and by the hundreds on all kinds of subjects. Most were for specialists in narrow areas; justified because, among other reasons, they employed people who would otherwise be jobless, made a contribution to scholarship, and met with the approval of most experts in the subject areas covered. It is quite possible that the WPA studies on how families coped when public assistance was reduced or stopped altogether had no impact, owing to their categorization as reports for scholars only, or to their publication long after the federal policy at issue had become fixed. In any event, when they appeared, the situations they described and analyzed had become primarily of historical interest.

In the critical year 1936, however, the AASW, not waiting for the documentation the WPA research division would eventually supply, kept up a steady drumfire of criticism of the Roosevelt-Hopkins policy, quoting in the *Compass* such typical June 1936 newspaper headlines about the situation in New Jersey as:

"New Jersey Experiments with Starvation."

"Relief Costs Cut in Half by Home Rule in N.J."

"N.J. Set-up Found Deplorable . . . . Commissioner Ellis Holds Needy Are Treated Like Elizabethan Paupers."[5]

In one community, not identified, town officials, their relief funds exhausted, authorized families on the rolls to beg their food from merchants and residents.[6]

"Hunger is once more abroad in the land, as it was in those three winters of bitter memory from 1930 to 1933," wrote Edith Abbott, dean of the University of Chicago's School of Social Service Administration, in the *Nation* of March 18, 1936. She expressed fear of a drift back to the "old days of pauper relief" because the end of federal grants for families qualifying neither for WPA jobs nor for categorical aid put them at the "tender mercies of petty local officials." Transients, she said, would be told to "move on," and to "get out of town." The three categories deserved approval, but the flow of federal funds to them was slow in starting, and "in the meantime heart-breaking tragedies are reported" for families dependent on general relief. "The end of the FERA," she concluded, "has been one of the tragedies of the administration program. Our most promising experiment in public welfare has been destroyed in the house of its friends."

For mingled with disapproval of administration policy was a sense of betrayal at the hands of the man in the White House, who had earlier been hailed as the embodiment of compassion for the poor and the hungry, and of the social workers who carried out his policy, from Harry Hopkins down.

Meeting in Washington in February 1936, a delegate conference of the AASW reaffirmed, in principle, stands taken the previous year (and in 1933 and 1934) on national relief and work policies. Its updated four-point program called for: 1. Federal grants to the states for general assistance, to be administered by a permanent agency, such as the Social

Security Board, with the federal share to be fixed at 25 percent (it was 50 percent for Old Age Assistance and Aid to the Blind and 33 1/3 percent for Aid to Dependent Children), or, alternatively, to vary with the fiscal capacity of the state. 2. Assistance standards under the program high enough to maintain "life, health and decency," and to include medical care. 3. A federal work program for employables, eligibility for which was to be based solely on unemployment, not unemployment plus need, as in WPA; paying prevailing hourly rates or the union hourly scale where appropriate; providing working conditions to conform to state and union standards for health and sanitation; offering workmen's compensation protection; and recognizing the right of employees to organize and to bargain collectively. 4. An enlarged and strengthened public employment service, to be responsible for referring the unemployed to jobs not only in private employment but in the federal work program as well.

Referred to the chapters for study was Congressman Marcantonio's relief and work projects bill, whose endorsement had been requested by the Inter-Professional Association for Social Insurance, and which authorized $2 billion for a new FERA program, $2 billion for WPA, and $2 billion for state-administered work projects. In some of its provisions, particularly those affecting the WPA and the state work-project programs, the Marcantonio bill bore a striking resemblance to the standards endorsed in the delegate assembly four-point program. Marcantonio had the public image of a radical, and the bill's supporters were largely radical, among them the Unemployed Councils of America; which was perhaps why the AASW was reluctant to endorse it. But never had the AASW and the Communist-led organization of the unemployed seemed to see so nearly eye to eye on an issue of interest to both.[7]

As a follow-up of the delegate conference, the Division of Government and Social Work prepared for presentation to the Democratic and Republican party committees engaged in drafting platforms for the crucial 1936 presidential election, an outline for a federal assistance program which summarized conference conclusions, adding for good measure support of a federal low-cost housing program, ratification of the Child Labor Amendment (still alive, but barely), and extension of the Social Security Act to Puerto Rico.[8]

When the National Conference of Social Work met that June, there was a flattering letter of greetings from FDR himself, commending social workers for their part in the New Deal's rescue effort. But except for social workers in the administration, the speakers who commented on federal programs were generally critical. The critics included even such pillars of the social work establishment as Joanna Colcord of the Russell Sage Foundation, who made unflattering references to the patchy character of the programs and the large areas of need left uncovered, and Solomon

Lowenstein, executive director of the New York Federation of Jewish Philanthropies, whose paper, "What Price National Security," called attention to the deficiencies in the Social Security Act rather than the good things in it, as one would have expected from a person holding his job. He criticized the low benefit levels in both the unemployment insurance and old age insurance programs, the occupations and industries excluded from old age insurance coverage, and the absence of personnel standards in the administration of the categorical assistance titles.[9]

The program adopted at the AASW 1937 delegate conference reiterated the association's position on the need for federal participation in general assistance and on the principles to govern the federal work program. Added were recommendations for amending the Social Security Act to raise the federal share of Aid to Dependent Children from 33 1/3 percent to the 50 percent in the other two categories, to extend the coverage of the old age and unemployment insurance titles of the act, and to add a new insurance title covering the risks of illness and disability. The establishment of a federal department of social welfare was proposed, a recommendation earlier made by the President's Committee on Administrative Management and forwarded with his approval to Congress January 12, 1937. It would put in one agency the government's social security, health, education, welfare, prison, probation, and parole programs; its principal appeal to social workers was the cachet of acceptance and permanence it seemed to give the newer programs.[10]

The program was drafted by the association's National Division on Government and Social Work. In presenting it to the delegates, the division's chairman, William Hodson, had unusually sharp words to say about the administration. The absence of federal funding for general assistance had reduced standards in that program to "indecently low levels." States and localities lacked the funds, the will, or both, to do a decent job. There was public acceptance of a permanent assistance program in the three categories in the Social Security Act, he said, but not of a permanent program for general assistance; this was commonly thought of as temporary, made necessary only because of mass unemployment, and to be dispensed with when the economy recovered. Furthermore, for reasons having to do with the checkered history of poor relief, general assistance had a bad public image; it was deemed corrupting in its influence. Social workers did not, of course, share these views, but to make general assistance acceptable to the public, said Hodson, the categories in the Social Security Act should be abolished and one public assistance title substituted, making federal aid available to meet need arising from any source, not only that associated with old age, blindness, or the absence or disability of the father of dependent children.

Hodson looked unkindly too at the WPA program. He castigated it as hastily put together, inadequately funded, limited in coverage with respect to numbers employed and skills put to use, and unnecessarily tied to a need requirement. He concluded by calling for a reassessment of national policy by a federal commission to study unemployment and relief. A resolution to create such a commission was introduced in the Senate by Murray of Montana and Hatch of New Mexico. It passed June 14, 1937, but died in the House when Congress adjourned late in August.[11]

Edith Abbott, in her presidential address at the National Conference of Social Work, voiced still another view, equally critical of the administration. Abbott, uncommitted to any program not of her own making and indifferent to organization and organizational positions in social work, described public assistance in the United States as a thing of shreds and patches under some gaudy outer garments. She assailed the administration for abandoning general assistance. The flinty dean of the Chicago School, the junior member of the formidable Abbott-Breckenridge team which had dominated the school since its founding in 1907, stood foursquare for state intervention on behalf of the underprivileged and the exploited (the terms reflect their Progressive Era background, whose values influenced the two all through the twenties and thirties), for protective legislation for women and children, and for an enlarged, modernized public welfare program to meet need. In the twenties Abbott had regarded with a cold eye the absorption in social casework of social workers she called the "Easterners." She now disagreed with Hodson and the others about the desirability of one public assistance title in the Social Security Act. Long an advocate of the categories (Progressive Era, again, in origins), she preferred an additional general assistance title as such, if that was the only way to restore federal responsibility. To abandon the categories was to invite a return to the discredited poor law approach to public assistance.

Pointing out that wars, past and future, were taking a larger share of the federal budget than social welfare, Abbott appealed for reordering of national priorities. More of the country's resources should be going to the people at the lower end of the income scale. She advocated abolition of the means test in Old Age Assistance and of the employer-employee contributory system for financing old age benefits in the Social Security Act. Government-financed old age pensions should be based on age only and should be sufficient in benefit level to meet a person's minimum requirements. She proposed pensions to women responsible for the support of dependent children. She said it was time for the government to guarantee a minimum income for all families in the United States as recommended for Britain by the Webbs as long ago as 1909, in their famous minority report as members of the Royal Commission on the Poor Laws.[12]

The Politics of Relief

Social workers in the administration hit back at its critics by calling attention to the assault on the government's program from the right, which threatened, they claimed, its very existence, minimal as it seemed to most social workers. The reference was not only to the Republican party and its representatives in Congress, but to the nation's press, largely Republican in political outlook, and to business organizations from the U.S. Chamber of Commerce down; they had succeeded in convincing large sections of the public that WPA was a "boondoggle" (originally a word describing a craft product made in one of the WPA programs, converted by Madison Avenue's magicians into a synonym for trivial, useless, wasteful activity), and that people on relief, or the "dole," as they preferred to call it, were too lazy to look for work.

Speaking at an NCC session at the 1936 National Conference of Social Work, Aubrey Williams acknowledged WPA's deficiencies with respect to coverage and wage levels, but expressed fear that liberalization of these aspects would bring the program down. Despite the limitations seen by social workers, it was all the public would "countenance," and in a democracy the wishes of the majority had to be respected. He warned that agitation for a federal role in general assistance would undercut WPA. The choice, he said, was between the two; Congress would not give the President both.

Harry Lurie, one of the discussants at the same session, dismissed Williams's reference to the public and to majority wishes as another way of saying the administration was motivated in its course by political expediency.[13]

The major party platforms in the 1936 presidential campaign seemed to bear out Williams's political assessment. To social workers who cared to examine them, they were a cold shower. They showed no evidence of having been influenced by the recommendations made by the AASW's Division of Government and Social Work; what examination did reveal was the discouraging fact that, however high-minded social workers were in their concern for the poor, they constituted a small group and as a political constituency threatened no one. No surprise, since they had no lobby in Washington, not even an office.

The Republican party platform echoed the National Economy League's report on federal relief programs. It affirmed state and local responsibility for public assistance of all varieties, categorical and general, but among the categories specified only Old Age Assistance; called the Social Security Act a fraud, proposed its repeal except for the two insurance programs, but advocated conversion of the old age insurance provisions from a federal to a federal-state program, paralleling in the minor nature of the federal role the federal-state unemployment insurance program. All these references to social welfare and social insurance were within the context of a call for the "restoration" of "free enterprise," and a denunciation of waste and extravagance in government spending. The platform ignored WPA; one could assume its abandonment was favored, as had been recommended by the National Economy League.

The Democratic party platform was a self-congratulatory paean to the party which had lifted America out of the depths of the Depression. It cited among its accomplishments the passage of the Social Security Act, and the inauguration of the WPA and other work programs for the unemployed. It contained no hint that these measures required improvement.[14]

The administration kept to its course on work and relief policies, trimming to meet opposition on the right from congressional enemies, but hardly affected by social-work criticism. WPA employed 2.7 million persons at the end of '35, reducing the number to 2.2 million by the close of '36 and to 1.6 million in December 1937 as economic conditions improved. In each of these years between one and one and a half million individuals were employed on CCC projects or benefiting from National Youth Administration or other federal work programs. Earnings in the programs amounted to $1 billion in '35, $2.5 billion in '36, and almost $2 billion in that relatively good business year 1937.[15] Confronted by a flood of new applications for general assistance, social workers disputed Hopkins's contention that the reductions in WPA in 1937 were justified by the gain in employment opportunities in industry. They quoted a survey by the U.S. Conference of Mayors which indicated that applications for relief following WPA layoffs were as high as 75 percent of the number laid off.[16] Hopkins, who by now regarded himself less as a social worker than as a presidential advisor, a White House confidant, a mover and a shaker, a political realist, an expert in the strategies that govern White House–Capitol Hill relationships, was not impressed.

Hopkins claimed Roosevelt was right in his decision to pull the federal government out of general assistance, in his estimate of the combined effects of WPA employment and categorical assistance on the size of the population in need, in his belief in the ability of state and local governments to carry the residual load. Social workers might complain, but the figures coming into his office told another story. He could cite economic indicators, such as gains in GNP and employment, to justify curtailment in WPA, for one thing. Growth in GNP meant a better tax base for state and local governments, for another. They were able to raise $500 million for general assistance in fiscal year '35–'36, and $400 million in '36–'37; to increase such expenditures to $450 million in '37–'38, the latter half of which saw the end of the '37 boomlet and a sharp increase in unemployment and in need. Over the same three years, the outlays of states and localities on the three categories of public assistance in the Social Security Act had gone up from $123 million to $261 million. A major inducement was the rise in federal matching grants from $19 million to $201 million.[17] In 1937 recipients under the categories totaled 2.4 million, as high as half the 4.8 million on general assistance.[18]

Most social workers, on the other hand, believed the transition over these years had been accompanied by considerable suffering, documented in the cases they got to know in their day-to-day work in relief offices. And the numbers on general assistance were far more than either Roosevelt or Hopkins wanted to talk about, to judge by their silence on the subject.

Disagreement between administration and social work on the nature and size of the problem of need and on policy was at its peak, perhaps, as 1937 ended and a turn for the worse overtook the once-again ailing economy.

Chapter 14

Social Work's Left Wing
Sets a New Course

A Qualified No to the Administration's Social Welfare Policy

The Rank-and-File Movement in Social Work was not unaffected by these developments. It shared the critical views of the AASW on Washington's desertion of the general assistance program and on the shortcomings of both the WPA and social security programs; it went beyond the association in its proposals for greater federal involvement in all three areas. At the same time, it moderated its hostility to the administration and saw in a populist New Deal aspects meriting unqualified approval. A movement increasingly centered on union-organizing campaigns in social agencies could not ignore the unavowed alliance between organized labor and the administration. In the political polarization marking the second New Deal, it was for FDR and the "people" in '36 and '37, and against his enemies on the right—big business, the Liberty League, the union-busters, the antispending crowd, and the extremist fringe elements such as the Coughlinites and the Jew-baiting Silver Shirts of William Dudley Pelley.

Employed for the most part in public aid programs, activists in the movement had first-hand familiarity with program shortcomings. *Social Work Today* ran a series of articles in 1936 on the chaos in state and local relief agencies with the withdrawal of FERA funds and on the effects: for relief recipients, deprivation; for employees, loss of job. In the March issue it summarized the strong statement ("shocking," "pitiful," "horrible") issued by the AASW in February. Harry Lurie's "Quitting the Relief Business" in the May issue took the government to task for its seeming callousness toward the poor, exhibited not only in dumping general assistance, but in meeting every upturn in economic indicators with a reduction in WPA rolls, in hours of work per week permitted an individual, and in policy toward relief supplementation of inadequate wages.

The problem became particularly acute in '37, when rising employment and payrolls prompted the administration to order wholesale slashes in WPA rolls and to reduce the number of jobs on the program to the lowest point since it began. At its second conference, held in Cleveland in

February 1936, the National Coordinating Committee of Rank-and-File Groups endorsed Representative Marcantonio's federal relief and work projects standards bill, and offered cooperation to the AASW in its campaign for the resumption of federal responsibility for general assistance.[1] The NCC Conference voted support also for the Frazier-Lundeen bill. Introduced in the Senate in January 1936 by Lynn Frazier, a progressive Republican from North Dakota, and in the House by Lundeen, the bill was the product of an intensive effort by a committee of the Inter-Professional Association for Social Insurance, composed primarily of members of the National Lawyers Guild, to flesh out the skeleton of the old Lundeen bill by specifying in detail the risks to income covered—unemployment, disability, old age, maternity, death or desertion of the family earner—the benefit programs to be established for each risk, benefit amounts, eligibility conditions, and administration. Unlike the Social Security Act, under which only the Old Age Benefits program was wholly federal in character, the Frazier-Lundeen measure provided for 100 percent federal administration for all its programs. The bill, said an approving editorial in the February 1936 issue of *Social Work Today,* would not only meet all the deficiencies social workers called attention to in the insurance titles of the Social Security Act, but would also obviate the need for both general assistance and the three public assistance categories in the act. The reason was the approach taken by the bill. With coverage universal, interruption of income from any cause made one eligible for the appropriate benefit. With no showing of need required for benefit, public assistance became unnecessary.

The Frazier-Lundeen bill was characterized by its opponents, in and out of social work, as unrealistic if not utopian. It retained, in general, the financing and administrative features of the Lundeen bill—funding out of general revenues, with heavy reliance on higher personal and corporate income taxes; and operation of the entire system by a commission appointed by the President from panels of names to be submitted by "national workers' organizations." Benefits were to be equal to average earnings, but in no case less than $10 a week and $3 a week for each dependent, with a maximum of $20 a week plus $5 for each dependent.

Unrealistic, utopian, the Frazier-Lundeen bill was nevertheless a symbol of all that was desirable in social insurance in a just social order. It had the firm support of all the newly organized left-leaning groups of professionals in the country—not only the NCC, but also the Book and Magazine Guild of America (publishing); the Federation of Architects, Engineers and Technicians; the National Lawyers Guild. Proponents of the bill had less success winning endorsement from trade unions, or among such professional groups as the American Federation of Teachers and the American Association of University Professors.

Endorsement of the Marcantonio and Frazier-Lundeen bills comprised only two items in the national social welfare program adopted by the NCC at its 1936 conference. Reflecting a broad interpretation of that term, delegates approved support also of the Child Labor and Workers' Rights Amendments to the Constitution; the antilynching bill; and the American Youth Act, which would enlarge the NYA program, limited to needy families, to provide jobs, education, recreation, and health services for all American youngsters. Enactment of a five-day week and a six-hour day with no loss in weekly earnings was urged, as well as an enlarged program of government aid to small farmers, tenant farmers and sharecroppers. Opposition was affirmed to the operation of CCC camps by the War Department. Resolutions were adopted expressing sympathy with the aims of the organizations of the unemployed (Unemployed Councils of America, Workers Alliance of America, and the National Unemployed League), and supporting the establishment of a National Farmer-Labor party. The IPA was endorsed; member groups were urged to affiliate. Congratulations were extended the National Negro Congress, created by civil rights activists dissatisfied with the cautious approach of the National Association for the Advancement of Colored People (NAACP). NCC affiliates were requested to cooperate with local chapters of the American League Against War and Fascism.[2]

Political Strategy in the 1936 Election

Advocacy of a national Farmer-Labor party was an idea popular for years in left circles influenced by the Communist party and among radicalized noncommunist liberals. The idea reflected sentiment in these groups going back to the beginnings of the Depression, expressive of disapproval of both major parties for their support of a profit-motivated economy; and a belief that a third party, dedicated to the establishment of an economic and political order meeting the needs of wage earners and small farmers, would attract the support of major segments of the population. The idea had its ups and downs all through the Hoover years and the early years of Roosevelt's first presidency, but was never realized because of the inability of its proponents, who ranged over the political spectrum from the middle left to the extreme left, to agree on a program. Roosevelt's triumph in '32 put a temporary damper on hopes for a third party, but opposition among liberals and radicals to the first New Deal for its seeming commitment to a planned economy favoring big business and big agriculture served to revive the proposal. The Democratic party was the principal target of criticism of third-party proponents since none of the groups to whom a

Farmer-Labor party could appeal would have to be wooed away from the wholly discredited Republican party.

By the fall of '36, however, support for a Farmer-Labor party had evaporated, not only in the radicalized wing in social work but everywhere else. The primary factor was the populist stance taken by Roosevelt following the Supreme Court decisions on NIRA and Triple A, and the political polarization which took place as the presidential election approached. By November, the primary issue had become the people vs. big business, the poor vs. the rich, the exploited vs. the exploiters, a development only in part based on underlying political and economic realities, and largely the result of the political strategy devised by FDR and his advisers in the new Democratic party, as noted in chapter 12.

The declining fortunes of the Farmer-Labor party idea in the radicalized wing in social work between February and December 1936 may be traced in the pages of *Social Work Today*.

Early in the year the editors invited comments from a number of prominent social workers, social work union leaders, and educators, on such questions as, What kind of political program should social workers support? Which program would best yield a comprehensive integrated system of public assistance, work projects, and social security? Should social workers as a group support a particular political party or candidate? Answers from eight respondents were published in the June issue.

T. Arnold Hill of the National Urban League professed pessimism about political action by social workers, disavowed support for any political party, and advocated limitation of political activity by social workers to collaboration with liberals for the support of, or opposition to, particular bills before Congress. A somewhat similar position was taken by Arch Mandel, a voluntary agency executive, who favored working with all parties to influence their relief, work program, and social security planks. Grace Coyle of the Western Reserve School of Social Work said social workers should act in politics as individuals; she had always voted for third-party candidates; but more fundamental changes (for the worse?) would have to take place in the economy, she believed, before a political organization could emerge capable of having any major impact and meriting, therefore, support of social workers as a group.

Paul Douglas, University of Chicago economist, called the Republican party the servant of big business; said the Democrats were controlled by the planters and mill-owners in the South and by the big-city machines in the North; advocated support of a third party representing workers and farmers. Joseph Levy, Chicago social work union leader, came out for a national Farmer-Labor party, recapitulating the NCC position and rationale. Forrester Washington, director of the Atlanta School of Social Work, favored a third party, a united front of liberals and radicals dedicated to the organization of a planned society devoted to humanitarian ideals. Henry Pratt Fairchild, New York University sociologist, said he would support only a party committed to a complete recasting of the social order with the avowed goal of production for use, not profit. Benjamin Glassberg, director of the Milwaukee public welfare department, proposed social worker support of a party of agricultural, industrial, and professional workers committed to support of the Frazier-Lundeen bill and similar measures and to the struggle against Fascism.

However they differed in detail, the eight respondents agreed, with two exceptions, in repudiating the two major parties and in their advocacy of a third party identified in one way or another with a socialized political and economic order.

The editors addressed an inquiry also to six political parties, asking where they stood on relief, work, and social security programs, and why social workers should support their candidates. Their replies, printed in the November issue, contained few surprises. Of particular interest to *Social Work Today's* readers was the endorsement given the Frazier-Lundeen bill by the Socialist and Communist parties and their support of a WPA program at union wages for all unemployed persons.

Where *Social Work Today* stood on the election appeared in an editorial in the October issue. It revealed a divided mind resulting from an unhappy compromise between professed principles—disapproval of the two major parties, approval of a third party dedicated to a just social order—and the political choices facing voters in 1936. The editors endorsed a national Farmer-Labor party, but for 1940 not 1936. The overriding issue in 1936, they asserted, was the defeat of Landon, the Republican candidate, who stood for everything social workers were against. No candidate was endorsed.

How to Keep the Second New Deal on Course

But a seeming indifference as to how social workers voted, other than against Landon, was denied by an affirmation that the utmost importance attached to a vote for FDR. Why? Because, said the editors, FDR vacillated; was subject to pressures from both right and left. For radicals to give him their vote—how he would know it was not made clear—would be to push him left. Far more unequivocal in its reasoning was that part of the editorial which urged support of House and Senate candidates pledged to vote for the Frazier-Lundeen and Marcantonio bills.

The same issue voiced approval, probably for the first time in the journal's history, of a position taken by the administration. An editorial applauded the decision of a WPA official in Tennessee, confirmed by

Washington, not to cut back the program, as requested by cotton growers looking for cheap labor to pick cotton as the harvest approached.

Whatever conflicts may have troubled the editors in their advice to readers on how to vote were resolved by the time the election was over. The results, said *Social Work Today* as the year closed, proved that the American electorate rejected reaction. The people, by reelecting Roosevelt, had endorsed an administration interested in experimenting with devices—borrowing, higher taxes, legislative curbs on business and financial abuses, labor legislation, relief, job, and social security programs—that would stabilize capitalism and help ease the burden a shrunken economy imposed on the poor. The election results were unmistakable evidence of the desire of the majority for progressive policies in government, for increased governmental controls over business, and for economic security for wage earners. In language new to *Social Work Today*, the government was now referred to as a "popular" government, subject to pressure from labor organizations and other "progressive" forces.

At the same time, as though to reassure its readers that it was still a dissident voice, the journal warned that the immediate outlook for the relief and social security programs was not promising. The federal government was adamant in its refusal to get back into general assistance, payment levels in the categorical assistance programs under the Social Security Act were inadequate, and first benefits under the act's old age insurance title would not be available until 1940. (The editors goofed; such benefits in the 1935 act were not payable before January 1, 1942.) But the big problem, the December 1936 editorial went on to say, was the continuing need for WPA because of the persistence of large-scale unemployment. To round out its summary of issues in the foreground requiring attention, support was urged of the CIO's organizing campaigns, and of labor union demands for wage increases to meet rising prices.

Links with the earlier *Social Work Today* were provided also by reproductions in the June issue of cartoons by William Gropper, staff cartoonist of *Der Freiheit*, the Yiddish Communist daily; and the appearance in the December issue of two pages of drawings from Hugo Gellert's book *Aesop Said So*, a Communist commentary on the Depression, America and the first New Deal.

The theory of pressure from the left to keep the second New Deal on course found expression in the leading article in the February 1937 issue. The new managing editor, and *Social Work Today's* first full-time paid editor, Frank Bancroft, quoted from Roosevelt's Second Inaugural address—"I see one third of a nation" etc.—and asked, What will he do about it? Bancroft proposed an enlarged WPA program, a 20 percent increase in wage rates, and recognition of collective bargaining rights for project workers. The article set out these additional goals for the second

Roosevelt administration: an improved National Labor Relations Act (the statute on the books did not cover governmental employees and workers in nonprofit agencies, to cite one of its limitations); reform of the Supreme Court (a reform called by its enemies FDR's court-packing plan); passage of the American Youth Act; liberalization of the Social Security Act along the lines of the Frazier-Lundeen bill; enactment of a federal antilynching bill.

The programs advocated were for the most part not supported by the White House. But the disparity in views on legislative program did not induce in *Social Work Today* the hostility to the administration it would have done in the years '34 and '35. Editorials and articles in '37 and '38 called attention to shortcomings between promise and performance, but the tone was friendly, or at its most critical, chiding rather than admonitory.

Applause for Uncovering the Nation's Sores

A favorable view of the government was also encouraged by administration support of studies whose results in some cases were to uncover the nation's festering sores.

Under the imaginative direction of Howard B. Myers, the Research Division of the WPA issued hundreds of bulletins and monographs, relatively few of which dealt with the WPA program as such. Created in large part to give employment to jobless economists and other social scientists, it initiated the first large-scale inventory of the social and economic characteristics of the country. The resultant publications were not puffs designed to create a favorable image of a nation on the mend under the beneficent influence of a benign, all-seeing, all-knowing leadership in Washington. The division thought it important, however damaging to the administration, to look not only into the consequences of the withdrawal of the federal government from direct relief, but also at local relief practices in different parts of the country (generally deplorable); state public welfare legislation (generally antiquated) and the changes (mostly for the good) prompted by the Social Security Act; the living conditions of migratory cotton pickers in Arizona (bad); labor mobility in Michigan; farming hazards in drought-stricken areas; child nutrition; the in-service training of teachers; the plantation South in the thirties; urban youth in the labor market; etc. The Research Division of WPA conducted surveys of local historical records, made real property inventories, studied low income housing projects. One of its most ambitious research efforts was the National Research Project on Reemployment Opportunities and Recent Changes in Industrial Techniques, located in Philadelphia and headed by a brilliant young economist named David Weintraub. Under his direction several hundred economists turned out scores of monographs on the effects on manpower needs of a changing technology in agriculture, commerce, and in industries ranging in size from cigar manufacturing to steel. It provided employment to scholars who would otherwise have been used as payroll clerks on more conventional WPA programs. More importantly, it documented in detail what economists had suspected was happening under the stress of the Depression—the vast gains in productivity per worker in most sections of the economy, a development with far-reaching consequences for the millions still unemployed in the country.

In cooperation with WPA's Division of Statistics, it participated in and furnished the field staff for two major path-breaking studies—the 1935–36 Consumer Income Study and the 1935–36 National Health Survey.The income study, published by the National Resources Committee under the title *Consumer Incomes in the United States*, was based on a canvass of 300,000 representative families and produced the first national data on income by size of family, occupation of family earner, race, and other characteristics. It revealed shocking inequalities in the money families had to live on. The health survey, also derived from interviews with a representative sample of the population, afforded the first look at the prevalence of disabling illness and chronic disability in the country as a whole, and at the receipt of medical care. The carefully collected and analyzed data verified the common observation of the inverse relation between income and health and the close correlation of size of income and receipt of medical care. They also documented the greater incidence of illness, disability, and inadequate medical care among black families as compared to white.

The two WPA divisions were responsible also for initiating the monthly population sample surveys, which were taken over later by the Census Bureau and formed the basis for the Bureau's studies of changes in the demographic, social, and economic characteristics of the population, continuous since the middle forties. They also initiated the monthly survey of the labor force of the Bureau of Labor Statistics, and the continuing assessment of the nation's health in the postwar years by the National Center of Health Statistics.

The WPA research programs were part of a large-scale upgrading of the government's research and statistical activities in the thirties, not only in the field of economics, but in areas which threw new light on the conditions under which people lived and on their standard of living, documenting the need for new and improved governmental programs to help Roosevelt's third of a nation at the bottom of the heap, and providing ammunition for organized labor's campaign for a larger share of the income generated by the economy.

On another level in popular appeal, but moved by the same passion to record the truth about life as lived by the people at the bottom, was the photographic record on rural poverty compiled by the historical section of the Resettlement Administration, renamed the Farm Security Administration in 1937. Under the direction of Roy Stryker, formerly of Columbia's economics department, the section commissioned such well-known or since-famous photographers as Walker Evans, Ben Shahn, Dorothea Lange, Carl Mydens, Arthur Rothstein and a host of less well-known camera artists to capture on film the look of the Depression visible in the bare cabins and churches of southern sharecroppers, the dust-covered roads and fields of the drought-stricken plains of the Middle West, and the ravaged faces of migrants on the move to California in their broken-down rattletrap cars and pickups, pictures that told an unforgettable story when released to magazines and published in book form. Many have since become celebrated in the history of American photography. In all, close to 300,000 photographs were assembled, one of the greatest collections of pictures in American history.[3]

All this was a plus for the government in the eyes of the Rank-and-File Movement.

Social Work Unions Enter Organized Labor

In 1935 a number of unions in social work applied for and received AFofL charters. The decision to affiliate with an organization earlier dismissed as timid, inept, and led by political conservatives, if not reactionaries in league with employers to keep labor down, reflected a conjunction of several influences: the growing number and strength of social work unions; the self-confidence bred by gains won in job security, hours and wages; the new approval, in the political left dominated by the Communist party's Popular Front policy, of affiliation by unions with the main body of organized labor; administration support of collective bargaining in labor-management relations; and its indirect encouragement of union organizing efforts.

In the ensuing developments, which stretched over a period of several years, the National Coordinating Committee of Rank and File Groups in Social Work, renamed the National Coordinating Committee of Social Service Employee Groups at its second conference in February 1936, disappeared from the social work scene. Its philosophy lived on, however, in union-sponsored activities at the National Conference of Social Work and in the pages of *Social Work Today*.

Such an outcome was not foreseen by the NCC leadership, which envisaged eventual AFofL affiliation of the unions in social work, but as a national organization, somewhat akin to the relationship of teachers with the AFofL through the American Federation of Teachers. When NCC officers met in June 1935 they approved the report of the Committee on National Coordination, rejecting piecemeal local affiliation with the AFofL on the ground that the craft union philosophy of the federation would destroy the social service unions as such, dispersing their members among existing unions on the basis of occupation. Until a national union of social service employees was established, a task put into the hands of a committee on constitution, AFofL affiliation was to be discouraged.[4]

Events later that year overtook and made obsolete the position adopted in June. Faced by layoffs and other problems, workers in public agencies in a number of cities sought protection by turning to the AFofL rather than the NCC, which had neither staff nor money to throw into any local union struggle. In September, employees of the Baltimore Transient Bureau obtained a charter as a lodge of the American Federation of Government Employees (AFGE), an AFofL national union. Similar moves were under consideration by the Practitioners' Council of the Cincinnati Department of Public Welfare and by the Association of Workers in Public Relief Agencies (AWPRA) in New York. What AW-PRA would do was decisive, since its membership constituted 40 percent of the organized strength of the groups affiliated with the NCC.

By the end of 1935 AFGE lodges were in existence not only in Baltimore but in public relief agencies in Washington, Milwaukee, and Minneapolis as well. The committee on constitution of the NCC reluctantly decided to adapt to the trend and recommended local affiliation with the AFofL. Its draft report expressed the hope that joint application by the social service locals for national charter as an independent organization could be made as soon as the locals felt strong enough to take the step.

The recommendations of the committee on constitution were approved by the thirty delegates from the thirteen NCC affiliates represented at the February 1936 Cleveland meeting, its second national convention. (Observers from sixteen other organizations were present; the twenty-nine groups had 12,000 members in the fifteen cities from which they came.) A continuing need for the NCC was recognized, however, to keep groups within and outside the AFofL in touch with one another for discussion and joint action on issues of common interest.

By June 1936, AFGE charters had been issued public relief workers in New York, Philadelphia, Pittsburgh, Cleveland, and Chicago; and second lodges had been established in Baltimore and Washington. When the AFGE lodges in state and local government employment were granted a national charter of their own by the executive council of the AFofL, the social service unions in the AFGE were included in the newly named

American Federation of State, County, and Municipal Employees (AFSCME).

The largest union of private agency employees, the New York Association of Federation Workers, applied for and was granted a "federal" charter as an independent local union. It changed its name to the Social Service Employees Union (SSEU) and with 400 dues-paying members was able to afford a full-time paid secretary. Within a year the number of SSEU federally chartered locals had grown to five; the number of public welfare agency locals in the AFSCME, to twenty-one. Combined membership numbered in the thousands, largely in the public agency locals. Gains claimed by the new unions included salary increases, reinstatement of workers discharged for union activities, improved vacation and sick leave policies, the five-day week, reductions in average caseload, workmen's compensation coverage.[5]

More difficult to attain was job tenure for public welfare workers, expressed in the demand for civil service status. On this issue AFSCME locals had the indirect support of the Social Security Board, charged with the operation of the three public assistance titles under the Social Security Act. The titles called for "efficient administration," among other requirements for the approval of state public assistance plans. The Bureau of Public Assistance interpreted "efficient administration" to include the basics of good social work personnel practices, i.e., appointment on the basis of qualifications; job tenure; no discharge without cause; written policies governing salaries, promotion, sick and vacation leave, etc. Lacking the authority of law, the bureau sought these goals via persuasion, with varying results. It was not until the adoption of the 1939 amendments to the act that the establishment of a "merit system" was required for state plan approval, construed by the bureau as necessitating not only appointment on a "merit" basis (i.e., minimum educational and experience requirements, competitive examinations, etc.) but also the other personnel practices just mentioned. Between 1936 and 1939 many state and local public welfare departments, particularly in the poorer states, offered strong resistance to pressures by the bureau to ensure "efficient administration." They rationalized their footdragging as reluctance to surrender local autonomy; but the underlying reasons were the old reasons, money and politics. It cost more money to do what the bureau wanted and it deprived the local agency of the freedom to appoint to the job persons with the right political connections.

The efforts of the bureau were confined, of course, to agencies or agency divisions administering the public assistance titles of the act; they had little or no impact on personnel practices in agencies or agency divisions operating general assistance, institutions, hospitals and other programs not under the act. Compounding the difficulties of both bureau and unions in the public welfare field was the crazy-quilt pattern of state and local administration. State welfare department functions and the division of responsibility between state and local governments for financing and administration almost defied classification. There were integrated departments of public welfare in some cities and counties; separate agencies for the categories and for general assistance in others; and varying combinations of these programs in still others. In some states, one or more of the categorical assistance programs were wholly state-operated. The public welfare department in some states was responsible for the operation of long-term institutions for the chronically ill or disabled; in others it was not. Corrections and public welfare were in one department in a number of states; in still others, public welfare was combined with public health or with mental hygiene.

The diminishing role of the NCC in union-organizing efforts stood out clearly in its third conference, held in conjunction with the 1936 National Conference of Social Work in June. No proposals were advanced for activities in the year ahead, other than plans for the presentation of papers at the 1937 national conference. The NCC met for the last time at the '37 national conference. It voted to dissolve, recommended the incorporation of *Social Work Today* as an independent publication and the establishment of a joint committee of trade unions in social work to plan for sessions at meetings of the National Conference of Social Work.[6]

The demise of the NCC was anticipated, but not the organizational realignments which followed. The transitional character of the NCC had been recognized from the first, but it was expected to be succeeded, as noted, by a national membership association. The rush to the AFofL by NCC affiliates made such a dream obsolete. "Dream" is the right word to use, because the idea of a national membership organization of social service employees, cherished particularly by the NCC leaders from private agencies primarily responsible for its organization and program, overlooked both the organizational structure of the AFofL and the many differences between public agency workers and private agency workers in the groups attached to the NCC. The AFofL, and the CIO when it became independent in 1938, contained national unions claiming jurisdiction, based either on occupation or place of employment, over every segment of the social welfare field. Had an application been made for a charter for one national union in the field, they would have fought it tooth and nail, and successfully.

The second factor in the dissolution of the NCC was a reluctant recognition that direct-service personnel in public and private agencies had dissimilar views about their professional identity, arising out of differences in training and background. Union members in both types of agencies shared a common belief in industrial as against craft unionism and in the inclusion in the same union of both direct-service personnel and clerical, maintenance, and other employees. The dissimilarity in views concerned understanding of their roles on the job. Direct-service personnel in the private agency unions were for the most part professional social workers; large numbers were graduates of schools of social work and members of the AASW, and they felt responsible for defining and articulating a philosophy regarding their professional obligations as social workers. Direct-service personnel in the public agency unions came from a variety of educational and occupational backgrounds. What they knew about social work skills they generally learned on the job, or in brief training programs the unions often had to extract from a reluctant administration. They saw themselves as government workers, primarily, rather than as social workers. It would be years before the agencies in which they worked would institute training-leave programs enabling them to enroll in schools of social work and earn professional degrees. In the thirties they felt closer, perhaps, in the problems they faced as employees to such fellow public service personnel as teachers, policemen and firemen, than to social workers in private agencies.

The NCC sun may have set on the union scene; it shone bright however at both the 1936 and 1937 National Conference of Social Work. In 1936 it sponsored sessions on "The Problem of the Negro in Social Work;" "Political Action for a Social Welfare Program;" "The Individual and Social Change—A Mental Hygiene Approach;" "Security for the Social Worker;" and "Fascism and Social Work" Speakers, in addition to social work union leaders, included Francis Gorman, vice-president of the United Textile Workers; Edwin Burgum of the American Federation of Teachers; John Davis, executive secretary of the National Negro Congress; Philip Klein, New York School of Social Work; and Bertha Reynolds, associate director of the Smith College School of Social Work. A booth distributed literature and information on unions in social work. Mimeographed daily bulletins were distributed to conference attendees containing notices of NCC meetings to be held, and quoting speakers at meetings held under NCC or other auspices. The tone was now condemning, now urgent, now hortatory, but always breathless. "This year's conference takes place at a time when social work programs and social workers are under attack and when the fundamental goals of social work are seriously threatened," said Bulletin Number 1.[7]

The 1936 conference was held in Atlantic City, having been shifted from Washington, as noted in chapter 11, because the convention bureau in that city could not give the conference executive committee an ironbound agreement on nondiscrimination. When black attendees were denied service at bars in two hotels included in the Atlantic City agreement, the NCC brought the issue to the attention of conference general secretary

Howard Knight, in accordance with an arrangement worked out following a similar incident at the 1935 meeting in Montreal. Knight checked and found that bar service had been denied. He maintained, however, that the agreement with the Atlantic City convention bureau covered housing and restaurant service only and not hotel bars. The NCC committee countered that, while the letter of the agreement had been honored, the discrimination at the two bars violated its spirit. Knight disagreed. The committee held to its stand and issued a bulletin on the subject.

As a follow-up, a committee of the NCC met with Knight in October to review policy on the question and its application at the 1937 conference, scheduled for Indianapolis. The convention bureau in that city affirmed a nondiscrimination policy, but inspection of the written agreement by the NCC committee indicated that the nondiscrimination, as in Atlantic City, referred to housing and food service only and said nothing about service at bars. Knight commented that drinking at bars was not essential to attendance at the National Conference of Social Work, but agreed to put the issue before the conference executive committee. The latter reaffirmed its earlier decision limiting the ban on discrimination to hotel rooms and restaurants. When the NCC expressed its dissatisfaction, Knight said that an appeal could be made to Edith Abbott, 1937 conference president. A letter to Abbott brought a rather typical acerbic, ascetic Abbott response. The business of the conference, she wrote, required that attendees be assured the availability of food and housing, not recreation. The NCC then issued a statement, addressed to the social work community at large, deploring the impasse, asserting the issue was not recreation but civil rights and appealing to social workers of conscience for support.[8]

As it turned out, no instances of discrimination at hotel bars occurred at the 1937 conference; if they did, they were not brought to the NCC's attention. There were two new issues, both big, of concern: the civil war in Spain, and the AFofL–CIO controversy. The NCC cooperated with the Social Workers Committee of the Medical Bureau to Aid Spanish Democracy in sponsoring a meeting on Spain at which Ferdinand de los Rios, the Spanish Ambassador to the United States spoke, as well as the journalist, Anna Louise Strong, and Wayne McMillen of the University of Chicago School of Social Service Administration. The NCC meeting on the AFofL–CIO conflict featured as speakers Robert Travis of the CIO's United Auto Workers, and Lewis Merrill of the AFofL's Bookkeepers, Stenographers, and Assistants' Union.

A session on trade union organization for social workers had as speakers Jerome Davis of Yale, president of the American Federation of Teachers, and Lester Granger, secretary of the Workers Bureau of the National Urban League. At another NCC meeting, Mary van Kleeck gave a paper on "Trends in Standards of Living." Goodwin Watson of Teachers

College, Columbia University, Erika Mann, and Anna Louise Strong spoke at still another session on "Individual Growth and the Social Order—Opportunities for the Individual Under Democracy, Fascism, and Communism." The NCC ran a meeting also on "Basic Social Work Concepts in the Administration of Public Relief"; conducted roundtable discussions on organizational tactics in public and private agencies, and on education and training for social work; cooperated with the Social Workers Branch of the American League for Peace and Democracy in sponsoring a meeting on internal problems; and held a luncheon meeting for students of schools of social work. Four bulletins were issued and, as in 1936, a booth dispensed information and literature. It was a busy week, the last of its kind under NCC auspices at the National Conference of Social Work. Future activities at the conference would be entrusted, as already noted, to the Joint Committee of Trade Unions in Social Work.[9]

The National Conference of Social Work was held only once a year. To meet the need for more frequent meetings at which current issues could be discussed and interesting speakers heard, *Social Work Today* launched a series of Social Work Today Forums, which resembled in some ways the meetings formerly conducted by Social Workers Discussion Clubs, now no longer in existence. Typical of such forums was the one held in New York in January 1937, with the formidable title of "The Impact of Social Structures on the Individual and the Family." The two speakers were Dr. Nathaniel Ross, assistant clinical professor of psychiatry at New York University ("In Our Society"); and Dr. Otto Klineberg, instructor in anthropology and psychology, Columbia University ("In Other Societies").

The Left Wing and the Profession

The middle years of the decade witnessed a growing acceptance by the profession of the Rank-and-File Movement, as it continued to be called, and of its legitimate place in the field. In part it reflected familiarity, and here and there even friendliness, with a phenomenon that seemed to be more than temporary, particularly as the social work unions increased in number and size and acquired a certain respectability as AFofL affiliates. More important, perhaps, was the decline in the intransigence and abrasive rhetoric of the movement, its identification with the aspirations of the second New Deal and its approval, if qualified, of Roosevelt and the administration.

The *Survey* ran accounts of the two major NCC conferences (Pittsburgh,1935; Cleveland, 1936), and from time to time reported on or published comments on social work union philosophy and tactics. (Frankwood Williams, "Understanding the Rank and File," May and June 1935; John S. Gambs, "Should I Join a Social Work Union?" January 1936; Maurice Taylor, "Tactics of Social Work Unions," August 1936.) *Better Times*, the optimistically named organ of New York's Welfare Council, opened its pages to articles by practitioners on the rationale of trade unionism in social work, organizational developments, and specific union grievances.

Writing in the *Family* in December 1935, Porter Lee, director of the New York School of Social Work, found the "unintelligent intrusive methods of radical propaganda" of Movement spokesmen as much an embarrassment to social workers' efforts "to promote justice and human well-being" as "the equally unintelligent restrictions of conservative donors and boards of directors." But early in 1936 he invited the author, as chairman of the NCC, to speak at a student seminar on the subject. In June the school published a forty-nine-page bulletin, *The Rank and File Movement in Social Work 1931–36*, prepared from notes assembled for the seminar. In his generous foreword, Lee wrote: "There is a natural sympathy between a student body and the rank and file due to the kinship of their vocational status. Hence the student interest. For the field of social work as a whole, the movement has in a sense even deeper significance for it appears at an intersection of social forces that may determine a realignment of social work, and a possible redefinition of the objectives of social work and of its relation to the economics, political and social currents of the day."

The Social Work Year Book, published by the Russell Sage Foundation beginning with 1929 and, despite its title, coming out only every two years during the thirties (after skipping '31), published articles on trade unionism in social work in its 1937 and 1939 issues.

The Special Committee on Relief of the National Conference of Social Work invited the present writer in his capacity as chairman of the NCC to participate with Aubrey Williams, assistant administrator, WPA, Walter West, executive secretary, AASW, and Josephine Brown of the Russell Sage Foundation, in a panel discussion at the 1936 conference on "The Present Status of Public Relief in the United States." A similar development was taking place at state conferences of social work, whose roster of speakers began to include social work union officers, a phenomenon more pronounced, however, toward the end of the decade than in the middle period covered by the present chapter.

One subject which troubled some social work spokesmen and continued to do so to the end of the decade and beyond, was trade union tactics. Most bothered were those, perhaps a minority, for whom unions had no place at all in social work. Rejection of unionism—lock,stock and barrel—

dominated the article Maurice Taylor, executive secretary, Pittsburgh Federation of Jewish Philanthropies, wrote for the August 1936 issue of the *Survey*. Taylor had had occasion to follow the views of the New York Association of Federation Workers (AFW) as expounded by its leaders at the annual meetings of the National Conference of Jewish Social Service, and what seemed to have left the deepest impression on him when he wrote the *Survey* article was the class struggle philosophy implicit in the attitude of the AFW leadership in its early years. Taylor found it repulsive.

In his article Taylor invoked all the familiar arguments against unions in social work, such as the presumed inconsistency between service to the poor and needy and the emphasis by the union on the economic interest of its members, but added a few more. He attributed the growth of the AFW and other protective organizations to the psychological coercion exercised by them on social workers who feared isolation if they did not belong. He theorized that membership in the union led to bad morale in the staff as a result of the conflict social workers felt between union tactics and their professional obligations. He found no community of interests between social workers and clerical and other nonprofessional employees; attributed their common membership in the AFW and other protective organizations to slavish adherence to the practices in industrial unions. He condemned, out of hand, strikes, picketing, demonstrations, protest telegrams, and other forms of "mass pressure." They were inappropriate in social work and counterproductive, since they served to offend lay boards and to arouse hostility in the public. Unionism in social work invited these evils because it represented an effort to adapt to a nonprofit, helping profession tactics appropriate only in industry and commerce. The relation of social worker and client was not at all comparable, he said, to that of industrial worker and consumer. He conceded one point only. The coming of unions to social work had resulted in greater awareness by board members of neglected problems in personnel practices in social agencies. But he thought that greater progress could be made in their solution via arbitration and "responsible" discussion than by collective bargaining with unions. Implicit in the entire article was the assumption that unions limited their tactics to those he cited and found objectionable, that they rejected arbitration of disputes, and refused to enter into "responsible" discussion with executives and boards.

More typical, however, of the profession's views on the subject was the report prepared by the Procedure Committee of the Detroit chapter of the AASW, which had been appealed to by the union in the public relief agency to secure the reinstatement of two employees who had been discharged, the union claimed, for organizing activities.Like the Newark AASW committee in the Grulich-Nillson case referred to in Chapter 9, the committee interviewed the parties in the dispute, but made no recommendations concerning the discharged employees. It suggested study by the chapter of the collective bargaining rights of social agency employees, the protection of the professional rights and civil liberties of employees afforded by existing practices, and the need for machinery to resolve via discussion the settlement of issues in dispute between administration and staff. Implicit in the recommendations, reported in the *Compass* of June 1936, was approval of the rights listed for study.

"Should Social Workers Use Labor Tactics?" asked the editors of *Social Work Today* in 1935, inviting responses from a number of persons prominent in the profession and in union organization. The responses of Paul Kellogg, Harry Lurie, Mary van Kleeck, Ewan Clague of the Social Security Board, Bertha Reynolds of the Smith College School of Social Work, Howard Cullman, president of the Beekman Street Hospital in New York, Jennie Berman, chairman of the New York Association of Federation Workers, and Frank Bancroft, active in the public welfare union in Cincinnati, appeared in the January and February 1936 issues. All answered the question in the affirmative, but qualified their approval with respect to the tactics appropriate under given circumstances. Clague and Reynolds specifically ruled out picketing, demonstrations and stoppages, however brief. Such tactics, said Clague, harmed agency clients and alienated the public, whose support was needed to raise personnel standards in both public and private agencies. Berman said she would hesitate to endorse a strike because clients would suffer, but Bancroft accepted resort to a stoppage if all other tactics failed. Reynolds, as would the Detroit AASW chapter committee, urged arbitration of disputes.

The shift from the early to the middle years of the decade in the profession's attitude towards the Rank-and-File Movement is best illustrated perhaps by the contrast between the paper Grace Marcus read at the 1935 National Conference of Social Work, and the paper Virginia Robinson gave at a forum held under NCC auspices in Philadelphia in March 1937, printed in the *Compass* for May that year. Both women were eloquent exponents, in a decade inhospitable on the whole to their views, of the basic importance of social casework in the therapeutic management of individuals with personal problems.

In 1935, as will be recalled from chapter 6, Marcus, in a *cri du coeur* from the depths of her outraged soul, attacked social workers who indulged in "economic dogmas that caricature Marxian theory," who called social casework "a sop to the underprivileged," and were blind to the "unique and indisputable contribution" it made to "social insight, improvement and change."

In 1937, Virginia Robinson of the Philadelphia School of Social Work, prestigious author of *A Changing Psychology in Social Case Work* (1930), the authoritative exposition all through the thirties of the role of social casework, also had harsh words for such social workers. *"Social Work Today"*, she said in her paper, "Is Unionism Compatible with Social Work?", which covered more ground than was indicated by the title, "started off with an attack on everything in social work. It reviled its philosophy as conservative and reactionary; it accused it of capitalistic domination. Social action alone was worthwhile and social work as a technical, professional field received scant consideration in its columns. As you know if you follow this magazine its interest had shifted in the past year and there is now some real concern with technical problems." She went on to say that *Social Work Today* and the social workers who shared its views had matured since its founding.

"We've lost naive faith in panaceas in which enthusiastic idealists saw the solution four or five years ago. No longer can those who find our democratic process too slow and awkward point with unshaken confidence to another country as having found the perfect solution. There is more acceptance of this country with all its bungling as the place where we have to work out our social and economic salvation if we can, more willingness to struggle with our democratic forms as having the possibility of including and protecting more human values than do the extremes of Fascism or Communism . . . " Therefore, "social workers and rank-and-filers are nearer today in social philosophy than they were five years ago."

She expressed the hope that unions would recognize the absolute need for social workers to have "professional training, professional development, and professional responsibility," but was critical of the unions' stand on whose responsibility it was to pay for training, and the kind of training required in social work. It was not enough to ask, as did the NCC, for "a comprehensive training program at agency expense on agency time." This did not yield true professional preparation. "Professional education is always on the individual's time, at individual expense, at the cost of struggle and sacrifice to the individual."

What the NCC was asking for in training programs in the years '35–'37 would be achieved a decade or more later. Perhaps in the light of the limited funds at the disposal of public welfare agencies in the thirties it was unrealistic to make such a demand, but no more so than was Virginia Robinson in expecting relief workers to fund their professional education from the savings possible under the low salaries prevalent when she spoke. Not too many, it may be hazarded, were prepared to undergo the "struggle and sacrifice" she viewed as an "ineluctable element in the training of the social worker."

If anything, Robinson dismissed too quickly the hunger among public welfare workers for professional guidance and growth, expressed not only in the demand for training programs on the job and agency funding of attendance at schools of social work, but also in the growing interest in professional literature. One response, by the editors of *Social Work Today*, was the inauguration in 1936 of a regular column called "The Casework Notebook," featuring a different professional subject in each issue. *Social Work Today* forums discussed professional problems as well as topics of more general interest. Implicit in these developments was a recognition of the permanance of the public assistance programs inaugurated on an emergency basis in the Depression; of the transformation effected by the categorical assistance titles of the Social Security Act in the character of the state old age pension and mothers' aid programs; and of the importance to the people served by these programs of improvement in the professional level of the services provided.

IV The Last Years, 1937–40

Chapter 15

Social Work: Acquiescence in the Administration Program

Three Eventful Years, in Summary

The last years of the decade were marked by a temporary recession, followed by recovery and the reestablishment of the growth pattern of the third period (1935–37). An increasing interest in developments abroad emerged as Americans became concerned about the retreat of democracy in Europe before Fascist aggression, and the administration saw in Nazi Germany's absorption of Austria and Czechoslovakia and Japanese dismemberment of China potential threats to our national security. The period culminated in the outbreak of World War II and a hasty enlargement of the country's military defenses.

Social workers reacted vigorously to the turn of events on both the domestic and international fronts. The 1938 recession, with its attendant suffering, prompted a call for an immediate enlargement of the WPA program and a drumfire of criticism of the administration for its slowness in responding to the need for more project jobs and for its unwillingness to shore up state and local general assistance programs, all but drowned in the flood of new applications for aid. As WPA rolls expanded and more jobs became available in industry, disapproval of the administration receded. The campaign for federal grants for general assistance was abandoned, as was the push for a liberalized and enlarged social insurance program. The final years of the decade, 1939 and 1940, saw social work, except for such dissidents as Mary van Kleeck, Harry Lurie, Bertha Reynolds, the magazine *Social Work Today*, and the social work unions, reconciled to the administration's view of its responsibilities in social welfare and social insurance. These were, in brief, jobs for the needy unemployed via WPA, the size of the program to be determined by the state of the economy; federal grants for public assistance limited to the three categories in the Social Security Act; and a federal social insurance program confined to old age, survivors, and unemployment insurance, restricted in coverage and meager in benefit levels.

The eruption of the Spanish civil war aroused anxiety among many social workers, as among liberals in general, for the survival of democracy in that country and led to the organization of the Social Workers Committee to Aid Spanish Democracy. The flight of social worker refugees from Nazi Germany similarly prompted social workers in this country to organize Hospites, a rescue and placement program. Europe's slide to war was followed with apprehension; the war's outbreak in 1939 split social work down the middle. Many social workers shared *Social Work Today*'s views on the importance of American neutrality; other social workers, particularly after the fall of France, aligned themselves with the Allies in their struggle against the two Fascist dictatorships in Europe, and urged American aid to Britain.

The 1938 Recession and the Profession's Response

The 1938 recession came swiftly and unexpectedly but, to the relief of the administration, didn't last too long. Gross National Product fell from $90 billion in '37 to $85 billion in '38, but regained its loss in '39. Unemployment rose by two and a half million, prompting the government to double WPA rolls, which were cut back in '39 when the number of jobless fell by a million. Nearly all business indicators were up in '39, and by the end of that year were pointing to another surge in the economy.[1]

To put it this way is to gloss over the privation suffered by millions of families during 1938. Employment on WPA may have doubled between December 1937 and December 1938, but in the interim people who had lost jobs in private industry exhausted their savings and crowded into the offices of public welfare agencies unprepared for them. As early as January 1938, when the recession had been under way for several months and its probable duration was unknown, Grace Abbott, former head of the Children's Bureau, Paul Kellogg, and other prominent social workers, issued a statement calling for an increase of 100 percent in the WPA program to provide 3 million jobs for the newly idle and the long-time out-of-work. Their appeal, publicized in the press, drew immediate endorsement from the AFofL and the Workers Alliance, the organization of the unemployed.[2] The administration responded by pressing Congress for an enlarged WPA appropriation, against conservative opposition in both parties. The battle lines were familiar. Industry and big agriculture saw in more WPA jobs a threat to the reduction in wage levels deemed an essential part of the classic cure for recession. They did not, however, command in House and Senate the support Hoover had had in his years in the White House, and in the end, with some compromises, Roosevelt and

Hopkins got the money they wanted to add a million and a half jobs to WPA, enough to take care of perhaps six out of ten of the newly unemployed.

In the meanwhile, the families without resources had to make out and they made out poorly. The AASW, on the basis of information from local agencies, released a report in March on the sharp increase in applications for public aid and the failure of state and local agencies to respond adequately to the new situation. The report illuminated an area of American life obscured until then by newspaper and radio stories of recovery and by the good feeling induced in most listeners by FDR's sanguine fireside chats over the radio. To stretch funds, said the AASW, public assistance agencies were reducing grants, cutting some cases off altogether, denying applications. Average monthly aid ran as low as $12 in Nebraska, $8 in Alabama, $6 in Arkansas and Georgia. Wholesale evictions were reported in cities where the relief allowance made no provision for rent. Aliens, nonresidents, families with an employable member, were denied relief altogether. As in '31–'33, some agencies stopped payments for longer or shorter periods as funds ran out. In parts of the South, always the worst-off region in good times and bad, federal surplus commodities were being issued in the absence of relief in cash. Some agencies reported children were not going to school for lack of clothing; others that malnutrition was common.[3]

In the same month that the AASW's report was released, its Division of Government and Social Work held a two-day meeting in Washington, attended by representatives of twenty-five national health and welfare agencies, to consider recommendations appropriate to the crisis. The ten-point program which emerged, presented to the White House and to the Social Security Board, proposed among other things the replacement of WPA by a federal employment authority to inaugurate a federal work program large enough to provide jobs for all the unemployed; the establishment of federal training and retraining programs for the occupationally displaced and for young persons entering the labor market for the first time; restoration of federal grants for general assistance; establishment of a social welfare department to consolidate all social welfare programs under federal auspices.

In the area of social insurance, the division recommended unemployment insurance benefit levels high enough to render supplementary relief unnecessary; strengthening of U.S. Employment Service; the establishment of a sickness insurance program to compensate wage loss in temporary illness; broadening of federal health services for the prevention and treatment of illness. Study of the nation's needs in health, welfare, employment, and social security by a presidentially-appointed commission was recommended; and the development by such a commission of guidelines for a permanent program.[4]

The federal government had washed its hands of responsibility for general assistance years earlier; it was not to be persuaded now by social workers, city mayors, or county supervisors to step in again as it had in FERA days. When Roosevelt in April sent Congress his request for money to meet the recession's relief needs, he limited himself to $2 billion for WPA and other federal work programs and an authorization to lend up to $1 billion to states and localities for their own emergency employment projects. The $3 billion was almost exactly the amount the newly independent CIO was asking Congress to vote.

The congressional authorization and appropriation wheels ground slowly. After the money was voted, projects—federal, state, and local— took time to plan, to be put into operation, to fill the job slots assigned them. As late as October, the AASW called the relief situation "chaotic" and the standards in effect in some local agencies "shockingly low."[5]

But as the WPA rolls swelled, the pressures on public assistance agencies slackened and the concern of the AASW moderated. Gains in employment in '39 and '40, reflected in declines in both the general assistance and WPA rolls, further cooled AASW interest in the subject. From a high of 3.2 million in December 1938, persons employed on WPA were reduced to 2.1 million in December 1939 and to 1.8 million in December 1940. Over the same two years the average monthly number of general assistance cases fell from 5.2 million to 3.6 million.[6]

Whether due to the decline in need, as measured by the size of the public aid programs, or discouragement resulting from the administration's seeming indifference to its recommendations, a change may be observed over the years '38–'40, both in the stand taken by the AASW on public policy in the areas of unemployment and public assistance, and in the importance of the subject in the association program as a whole. In 1940 the Division of Government and Social Work still called for a federal work program large enough to provide employment to all unemployed persons regardless of need; for a noncategorical public assistance program for all persons in need, under conditions conserving family integrity and dignity; and for a program of "public social services" for all persons whose resources fell below a level sufficient to maintain them in "health and decency." But the recommendations sounded more like muted echoes of the programs advanced in prior years than the results of a fresh look at a rapidly changing picture. The proposal for a federal department of social welfare was dropped, and in the recommendations concerning administrative reforms—a merit system requirement for state plan approval in the public assistance categories under the Social Security Act, for example— there could be detected an acceptance of the existing federal social welfare program and of the modest recommendations of the Social Security Board for their improvement.[7]

Reawakened Interests

Accompanying this acquiescence, if qualified, in the administration program, was a reawakened interest in the association's traditional concerns with the subjects of training and education, i.e., with the enhancement of the professional status of the social worker. It seemed important once again to measure the gap between the public image of the physician and lawyer on the one hand, and of the social worker on the other. The bitter taste of the ugly social worker in Elmer Rice's Pulitzer Prize play, *Street Scene* (1929), still lingered on the tongue of the social work Establishment. Although the social worker in the thirties was generally praised by journalists for doing a heroic job under trying circumstances, the influx of untrained and partly trained persons into the new or expanded public welfare agencies had diluted beyond recognition the gains in professional requirements for employment won in the twenties. With the financial and administrative pressure on agencies now somewhat reduced, the time seemed right to recoup the loss.

The change in emphasis could be observed as early as 1938, when Linton Swift in his presidential address to the delegate conference noted that "for several years after the beginning of the depression one might justifiably have thought social action was our major concern, at least in practice. Now, however, we are beginning to reexamine our basic reasons for existence as an Association and the ways in which, jointly or individually, we can most effectively define and achieve professional purposes." As though to buttress his position, the issue of the *Compass* (July-August 1938) carrying his address also printed papers on Professional Strengths and Their Attainment, and The Relationship of the Trained Social Worker to Social Work Education.

The Current Relief Situation had gotten page 1 in the *Compass* in February 1938; the report in the October issue of the "shockingly low standards" in relief agencies appeared on page 26. From late October 1938 through 1940 the principle AASW interest, to judge by *Compass* articles, concerned such subjects as Training and Education for Social Work, Social Work Standards, AASW Membership Standards, Personnel Standards, Staff Development, Social Work Skills, Principles in Worker Evaluation Process, etc.

The cooptation of the profession by the administration was particularly pronounced in the American Public Welfare Association (APWA), an organization rarely taking a stand in opposition to the government. In 1935 the APWA had called for a federal department of public welfare and had passed a resolution critical of the low wage level in WPA; in 1936 it urged the inclusion of a general assistance title in the Social Security Act, in defiance of the administration's position on the subject. That proved to be the last dissent registered by the association. With the selection of APWA's director, Frank Bane, as executive director of the Social Security Board, and the establishment in the forty-eight states of programs to take advantage of the three categorical aid titles under the act, the APWA, whose members were, after all, directly involved in the process as administrators and supervisors at state and local levels, focused almost exclusive attention on the problems involved in implementation. It organized round tables and panel discussions on state plan requirements, on personnel standards, on merit systems, on federal-state relationships, in-service training, public interpretation, medical-care administration, supervision, etc. Such meetings had the participation of officials from the Social Security Board and the Public Health Service. The dinner meeting in Washington, December 1938, featured speeches by WPA Administrator Harry Hopkins, Chairman of the Social Security Board Arthur Altmeyer, Surgeon-General Thomas Parran, former Assistant Secretary of the Treasury Josephine Roche. A meeting with the President was arranged. They were partners in a common enterprise. Their get-togethers were very chummy, very heart-warming.[8]

By the end of the decade the social work Establishment, as represented by the AASW and the APWA, had abandoned its demand for a general assistance title under the Social Security Act or, alternatively, a comprehensive public assistance title open to all needy persons, irrespective of age, disability, marital, or parental status. It had become reconciled to the administration's social welfare program, and gave wholehearted support to its major features, namely, a temporary federal work program, its dimensions roughly cut to fit the number of needy unemployed in the population, and a federal-state-local program of assistance to three specialized groups of needy unemployables: the aged, the blind, and children with a dead, disabled, or absent father. These boundaries to federal responsibility for the needy, to whom the permanently and totally disabled were added in 1950, were to remain fixed for the next four decades.[9]

The Influence of the 1939 Amendments to the Social Security Act

In part, the identification of social work leadership with the administration program was the result of the incorporation in the Social Security Act, under the 1939 amendments, of reforms tending to promote staff professionalization in the public assistance and related titles advocated by both AASW and APWA. Based largely on recommendations of the Advisory Committee on Social Security, jointly appointed by the board and the Senate Special Committee on Social Security, and made public in

December 1938, the amendments, approved by the President August 1939, required the states to establish a merit system in the selection of personnel in the administration of the three public assistance titles, and in the maternal, child health, child welfare, and public health titles. This meant primary reliance on written examinations, which tested knowledge of the law and of the nature of public assistance and child welfare services, and tended to favor the appointment of applicants familiar with social work principles and practices. The new procedure was interpreted to give preference to persons with experience in social work and, most important, to persons whose training was evidenced by the number of courses taken in approved schools of social work and by possession of a degree from such a school.

Other amendments to the three public assistance titles could have been written by social workers, since they embodied procedures long standard in private social work: in the determination of need, for example, the states would have to take into consideration income or resources available to the applicant or recipient, and the records maintained on applicants and recipients were to remain confidential.

The other amendments affecting the five titles, while not crucial from a social work point of view, were likewise favorably received: the increase in the federal share of the Aid to Dependent Children payment from one third to one half, making the program uniform in this respect with the Old Age Assistance and Aid to the Blind programs; and increases in the annual authorizations for the maternal, child health, child welfare, and public health service programs.

Of greater significance, perhaps, because they affected more people, were the changes in the 1939 amendments wrought in the Old Age Benefits (OAB) program. The most important was the establishment of a "survivors" program, which paid benefits to the dependent survivors of deceased workers insured under the program, primarily widows and children under eighteen. It was viewed in '39 as a potential replacement, in time, of the public assistance given under the Aid to Dependent Children title of the act, just as in '35, when the act was passed, Old Age Assistance was considered a transitional program, the need for which would diminish and eventually become unnecessary as the OAB program matured.

Benefits to retired workers were increased for beneficiaries with dependent wives sixty-five years and over or with dependent children under age eighteen. Other changes in the OAB program under the '39 amendments were perhaps of greater interest to organized labor than to organized social work. The date for first payments was advanced from January 1942 to January 1940. Eligibility conditions were liberalized, the benefit formula was changed, and a lump-sum benefit at death (the socalled funeral benefit) was added. These changes incorporated some, but by no means all, the reforms recommended by the AFofL and the CIO. They ignored proposals for more complete coverage of the population at work, higher benefit levels, a federal contribution to the funding of benefits, and the establishment of a health insurance program.

The unemployment insurance title remained largely unchanged. A merit system for the appointment of personnel was made mandatory, as in the public assistance and other federal-state programs under the act, effective January 1, 1940.[10]

Social Welfare Policy: Five Groups and their Views

Some comment is indicated on the major determinants affecting the attitudes of social workers toward the administration's social welfare programs in the last half and particularly the last quarter of the decade. Their attitudes varied, depending largely on how close the individual was to policy determination and to policy execution. Five groups may be distinguished.

1. Top federal officials, who helped make policy through their recommendations to the White House and to congressional committees, wrote the rules and regulations under which policy was made explicit, and enforced the program by monitoring through field staff the compliance of state and local agencies. Such persons—WPA's Harry Hopkins and Aubrey Williams, Katherine Lenroot of the Children's Bureau, Frank Bane of the Social Security Board—were the strongest defenders of the administration program. For them the task of justifying appropriation requests and new legislation before hostile, conservative, and economy-minded congressmen and senators, the bruising they took in the process, was the reality. They took pride in seeing themselves as on the firing line. They were strongly loyal to Roosevelt. When they faced social workers at the National Conference of Social Work, they defended their programs ardently and called attention to the great gains made since the Dark Ages under Hoover.

2. Middle-level operators, the intermediate echelons of the federal establishment and state and local administrators, wrapped up in the problems of administering the new programs. They tended to push aside large policy issues: these had been or would be decided by the people higher up—the President, Congress, the governor, the state legislature—and were in any event not their responsibility. Their responsibility was to get the job done as best they could with what they had in the way of money and program guides in the form of rules and regulations. Their primary interest was in administrative techniques: how to run the program on a day-to-day basis, how to recruit and train staff, how to interpret programs

to the public, how to deal with people who looked to them for orders, guidance, counsel.

3. Lower-echelon people on the job in public welfare agencies as supervisors and case-workers. They were aware of limitations in the programs and knew that large areas of need were not covered, but, as a rule, were too busy doing the job assigned them to have time to look at the larger picture they believed lay out there if they lifted their eyes. We can have, we should have, better programs, they said, in terms of people coverage, assistance levels, eligibility standards, caseload size, merit-system protection, etc. But these things were beyond their control, unfortunately. A minority among them entertained radically different views, not so much on program goals as on whether social workers could do something to achieve them, and how. This minority constituted such mass base as the Rank-and-File Movement had.

4. Academics administering or teaching in schools of social work. A mixed lot, quite varied in the issues which concerned them. These issues ranged from the need for social action and social legislation of a broad and sweeping character, which led them to take a critical attitude towards the administration program, to the prime importance of a better understanding of the springs of human behavior, seen by them as hidden in sources beyond the reach of even changes in the social or economic order. The academics included technicians skilled in program operations, in upgrading performance, and in promoting professionalization, who were delighted to be called in by administrators in group 2 above as consultants on specific problems.

5. Most critical of the administration's social welfare programs, perhaps, were some of the social workers employed by private agencies or by national professional organizations (group or individual in membership), perhaps because they were furthest removed from operations—from the firing line. They saw, or claimed to see, most clearly the gap between operating programs and program needs, and felt free to talk about it. As noted with respect to the social workers in group 3, the critics could not be said to constitute more than a minority of private agency workers. Most private agency staffers stood in the broad middle: mildly critical, indifferent, or mildly approving. Executives among them included men and women of ability and ambition, who held power in high regard, envied the people in groups 1 and 2, hoped to be tapped for appointment, and identified in advance with the programs they would help administer if appointed.

Chapter 16

Social Work:
The Unconverted Dissidents

Lurie and van Kleeck Again

Perhaps the most articulate voices in the last of the five groups identified in the preceding chapter were Harry Lurie and Mary van Kleeck, who were earlier mentioned as raising within the AASW, in the middle years of the decade, fundamental questions concerning the nature of the economy and the appropriate response of social work to the problems raised by the Depression. They remained, through the end of the decade, unsparing critics of the administration's course in social welfare and social insurance.

In 1936, for example, Lurie gave a series of lectures under the auspices of the Los Angeles Council of Social Agencies, one of which was devoted to the subject of the responsibility of the social worker for social action. He looked askance at the AASW for what he described as its failure to call attention to the inadequacies of the Social Security Act; for its indifference to, or neglect of, proposals for needed reforms in medical care, and for better housing for low-income families; and for ignoring altogether the subject of labor standards and labor's organizational struggles. He favored the alignment of social work with the progressive forces in labor and politics on those issues in which social work could provide support based on professional knowledge.

In a letter in 1938 to David Lasser, president of the Workers Alliance of America, the organization of the unemployed, who had requested comment on and support of the alliance's work and relief program, Lurie endorsed a public assistance program adequate in scope and in level of payment to meet need, irrespective of state of residence, age, marital and parental status, and other considerations he deemed irrelevant. He urged a work program at prevailing wages open to all the unemployed, designed to protect their skills and their right to organize, and emphasizing socially useful projects; also repeal of contributory taxes in the Social Security Act and the financing of benefits out of general funds.

In 1939 he wrote Lasser again, stating that most social workers were in sympathy with the Workers Alliance in its fight against reductions in the

WPA rolls necessitated by the Senate's cut in the appropriation requested by the administration. It was a distressing experience for social workers, he said, to make the selection of persons to be laid off, for whom the outlook for employment in private industry was uncertain and whose future on the inadequate general assistance program was precarious at best.[1]

Writing in *Social Work Today* in 1938, Lurie argued that a larger GNP was necessary to finance adequate public welfare and social insurance programs. He expressed the belief that further growth in GNP was contingent on economic planning, and the hope that such planning would involve the democratic participation of all segments of the population.[2]

Mary van Kleeck's comments on the administration's social welfare and social insurance programs were less frequent than they had been in the middle years of the decade, perhaps because of her involvement in activities related to international political developments growing out of the Spanish Civil War and the spread of Fascism in Europe. When she did turn her attention to WPA and the Social Security Act, her remarks reflected no softening in her disapproval of the deficiencies she saw in both programs.

The extent to which the views of Lurie and van Kleeck were shared by national figures in social work, other than a few fellow dissidents like Bertha Reynolds, is difficult to determine. The leadership of the APWA became, as noted, supporters of the administration program, and one may assume acceptance and approval of such support by all but a handful of the membership. While the AASW as an organization also went along with the administration in Washington, however qualified in some details, the extent of concurrence among association members is not known. The practitioners councils, through which opposition could have been expressed, had disappeared. Some part of the membership undoubtedly identified with AASW officers on the issue; some may be assumed to have been in disagreement; still others, perhaps the majority may have been indifferent.

There is little question, however, that the disaffection expressed by Lurie and van Kleeck had the approval of most of the unions in social work, particularly in the larger cities, and of the editors of *Social Work Today*.

Social Work Unions

Members of public welfare departments felt the impact of the 1938 recession in increased caseloads and in recipient protest against reductions in general assistance grants. Their unions spoke out for federal aid in the general assistance program, for additional staff, for a restoration in levels of assistance where reduced. A number of the unions endorsed the work and relief program of the Workers Alliance. The shift from AF of L to CIO affiliation in 1938, noted below, brought most of the public welfare department unions within the fold of a labor center strongly committed to a larger WPA program and a more comprehensive Social Security Act.

Social work union dissent with the administration's social welfare policy was more concerned, however, with its impact on staff than on clients. For the vigorous growth in the number and size of unions, particularly in the public welfare field, was accompanied by a subtle change in their character. Public policy issues, such as the size of WPA program and the scope of the Social Security Act, were still of interest to them, to be sure, but did not have the high priority they had had earlier in the decade, when ideology loomed larger in the thinking of the leadership than union strategy and union administration. The change reflected the transformation in political alignments in the middle years of the decade, particularly union identification with the populist aspects of the second New Deal, and the consequences of growth and affiliation with organized labor.

How to win more members, articulate their grievances, and score gains, seemed more important now than finding a rationale for unions in the irreconcilable differences between labor and management and raising the class consciousness of workers in social agencies. The decline in the importance of ideology meant a lower priority for issues of concern primarily to public assistance recipients and to the unemployed on WPA. The unions took the "progressive" stand on social issues, of course, but the latter did not have the urgency of trade union issues. Resolutions of support for Workers Alliance and American Youth Congress programs, for the bills in which they were embodied, for the appointment of delegates to conferences these organizations called, were passed with little debate, almost pro forma.

The relatively rapid growth of unions in social agencies in the last years of the decade may be attributed to their increasing acceptance among employed personnel, professional and nonprofessional, and to the organizational and financial assistance furnished by the labor movement, particularly the CIO (the Committee for Industrial Organization). Suspension in August 1936 of the ten unions in the CIO by the AFofL executive council on a charge of dual unionism, spurred the committee, whose affiliates had a million members and the financial strength to support the effort, to accelerate its organizational drives, and to take the unprecedented step of chartering new national unions attached to the CIO rather than to the AFofL. In 1938 the CIO cut its last formal links with the

AFofL and set up as a rival union center under the name of the Congress of Industrial Organizations.

Among the beneficiaries of these developments were the State, County and Municipal Workers of America (SCMWA), chartered by the CIO in 1937 to organize all nonfederal government workers; and the United Office and Professional Workers of America (UOPWA), to which a charter was issued the same year with jurisdiction over all white-collar workers not claimed by other CIO unions (such as the Newspaper Guild; the Federation of Architects, Engineers and Technicians; the Book and Magazine Guild). Among the first to affiliate with the two new unions were most of the public welfare locals in the AFofL's American Federation of State, County and Municipal Employees (AFSCME) and all of the AFofL federally chartered Social Service Employees Union locals in private agencies. The SCMWA was headed by Abram Flaxer, president of the large and militant AFSCME local in New York's Department of Public Welfare; the UOPWA, by Lewis Merrill, president of an AFofL office-workers union. They gave able experienced leadership to the new unions.

In its first year SCMWA signed up 35,000 members, of whom 8,500 were in 28 public welfare locals. Some of the growth, but by no means all, was attributable to the flight from the AFofL, which fought a losing battle to retain the loyalty of locals attracted to the CIO. Among those remaining in the AFSCME were approximately 1,000 in public welfare locals.

The UOPWA grew even more rapidly, claiming 45,000 members by mid-'38, the result largely of an intensive drive in the insurance industry. The social work contingent comprised seven SSEU locals and two SSEU divisions in UOPWA locals with a catchall membership. SSEU members numbered 2,000, of whom 1,500 were in the New York local. Indicating the importance the national union attached to the SSEU Division, it funded two positions, that of national director, to which Leo Allen of the New York local was appointed, and a Midwest representative, a job filled by Joseph Levy of Chicago. The New York local had its own full-time organizer, William Piehl.

The pace of growth slackened after the initial surge, but in 1939 there were thirty-six SCMWA public welfare locals in almost as many cities, four AFSCME public welfare locals, and eight SSEU locals. In 1940 membership in SSEU locals and divisions totaled 3,000.[3]

The major programs of the public welfare locals in the SCMWA remained largely those which had engaged them as independent unions earlier in the decade: a shorter workweek, wage and salary increases, smaller caseloads, longer vacations, better sick leave policies, workmen's compensation, etc. Of prime importance was job tenure, seen as achievable via civil service status, a goal whose attainment was accelerated by the requirement for a merit system in the 1939 amendments to the Social Security Act. The merit system applied, of course, only to agencies and divisions administering the three public assistance titles under the act, but could not help affecting public welfare departments as a whole because of the trend toward the integration of all public aid programs in one agency. The demand for job tenure was expressed via letter-writing campaigns to public welfare officials, members of city councils, county boards of supervisors and the state legislature; testimony at hearings conducted by state legislative committees; mass picketing of public welfare offices; and, in places, sit-ins.

Salary increases were won for lower-paid employees and in some cities mandatory salary increases were gained for all employees, based on years of employment. The right to a hearing prior to dismissal was recognized in a number of agencies. Gains were made in vacation and sick leave policy. Periodic written evaluations and opportunities for promotion were incorporated in personnel practices.

In the private field, the major issues were standardization of employment practices, job security, and coverage under the insurance titles of the Social Security Act and under state labor relations acts. The latter coverage was seen as a help in winning union recognition, collective bargaining rights, and the establishment of standardized procedures for settling grievances. In New York the SSEU, Local 19 of the UOPWA, endorsed the campaign appeal of the Greater New York Fund for the first time, but expressed criticism of coercive practives in some firms in obtaining employee contributions and regretted the lack of labor representation on the board of the fund.

In June 1938 the New York SSEU won the first contract between a private social agency and a social work union. The contract was with the national office of the National Council of Jewish Women, which recognized the union as the exclusive bargaining agent for its employees, twenty-five professional and clerical workers. The contract provided for a five-day week, time and a half for overtime, paid sick leave. That fall another contract was signed with the Russell Sage Foundation, and a third with a children's home. Two more contracts were won in 1939, and in 1940 a major gain was recorded when the National Refugee Service signed a contract with Local 19 covering its 500 employees. The climax of these developments came in 1941, with the negotiation of a written contract with the Jewish Social Service Association, the largest Jewish family agency in the country.[4]

The acceptance of trade unions for social workers was promoted by favorable articles in *Social Work Today* by faculty members of schools of social work: "Trade Unionism for Social Workers," by Wayne McMillen, University of Chicago School of Social Service Administration; and

"Security in Social Work," by John Fitch, New York School of Social Work. At the 1939 meeting of the Pennsylvania Conference of Social Work, Marion T. Hathway, executive secretary of the American Association of Schools of Social Work, read a supportive paper on the topic, "Trade Union Organization for Professional Workers." The articles and the Hathway paper were reprinted by the SSEU division of the UOPWA and used as promotional material in recruiting new members.[5]

Some members of the New York School faculty joined the SSEU. In 1938, Clara Rabinowitz of New York's SSEU was invited by the Smith College School of Social Work to speak to a meeting of students interested in the place of social work unions in the field.[6]

In a new departure for that organization, the Division on Recruitment and Personnel Management of the American Public Welfare Association issued a statement in 1938 to the effect that unions for civil service employees were here to stay, would grow in influence, had been helpful in obtaining desirable personnel practices, and should be encouraged.[7] As if to confirm the respectability of civil service unions in the public eye, Governor Earle of Pennsylvania appointed Robert Weinstein, field representative of the SCMWA, a member of the Philadelphia County Board of Assistance in 1939.[8]

The Journal Social Work Today

The reduction in the WPA rolls made by Hopkins in response to the improvement in economic conditions in 1937 prompted the publication in the October issue of *Social Work Today* of two articles: "Where Are the Jobs, Mr. Hopkins?" by Maxwell Stewart, which called attention to the difficulties laid-off WPA workers encountered in finding employment; and "Why We Marched," by Herbert Benjamin, secretary of the Workers Alliance, who described the protest the layoffs provoked.

Social Work Today was quick to pick up and reprint the calls for increases in the WPA program when the recession struck in the winter of '37–'38—including the Abbott-Kellogg appeal in January for 3 million WPA jobs; the March report by the AASW on the suffering caused by the recession and the inadequacies in the relief programs to which recession victims turned; and the recommendations made by the AASW Division on Government and Social Work that same month.

Roosevelt's request to Congress in April for $2 billion for WPA and other work programs was criticized editorially as insufficient to meet the needs of the 14 million unemployed (an AFofL estimate; there were no official figures). A favorable reception was given, on the other hand, to the program urged by the Workers Alliance at its March Conference on Work and Security, whose planks included a $3.5 billion public works program; an increase in WPA wage rates; the resumption of federal grants to the states for general assistance; liberalization of the Social Security Act; a strong, well-financed youth program; a $500 million public housing program; $500 million for flood control; and other measures.

Articles and editorials in the years 1938–40 directed attention to the deplorable consequences of the liquidation of the federal program for transients; the inadequacies of the social insurance programs under the Social Security Act with respect to coverage and benefit levels; the shortcomings of WPA; the deficiencies in the general assistance program; the absence of any program for people who fell between the cracks that divided a shrinking WPA, a pinchpenny general assistance program, and the rigidly defined categorical assistance programs under the Social Security Act.[9]

Since these views were advanced in a magazine no longer formally affiliated with the trade union movement in social work, some reference may be in order at this point to the editorial direction and financing of *Social Work Today* in the closing years of the decade.

The dissolution of the NCC in June 1937 ended union sponsorship of the magazine, but by no means its character as a vehicle for news about social work union developments, for articles and editorial comment on the relationships between social work unions and professional organizations, and on the place of social work unions in organized labor. Of more general interest were articles which ranged in scope from public assistance standards to the threat the spread of Fascism in Europe posed for democratic values.

Its ties with NCC cut, *Social Work Today* was independently incorporated in the fall of 1937. A full-time, paid managing editor was engaged, raising the number of salaried employees to three, the other two being Blanche Mahler, the business manager, and a secretary. The managing editor selected was Frank Bancroft, a graduate of Princeton and of the Virginia Episcopal Theological Seminary, who had served as a missionary in India, and whose Depression years' working experience included a stint with the local office of the U.S. Employment Service in Cincinnati and one with the public welfare department of that city as a caseworker. In the latter job he had become active in the agency union and had displayed a marked talent for public relations and for writing and editing.

To put the magazine's financing, always precarious, on a more secure footing, a drive was launched to increase circulation and obtain more advertising. Theater benefits were conducted and other fundraising affairs organized. Readers were asked to contribute to the magazine's support by becoming *Social Work Today* Cooperators, whose sponsors in the October 1938 issue, in which they were listed for the first time, included Mary van

Kleeck as chairman, and such well-known names in the field as Harry Lurie; Bertha Reynolds, until 1937 associate director, Smith College School of Social work; Ellen Potter, director of the medical department of the New Jersey Department of Institutions and Agencies; Mary Simkhovich of the Greenwich Settlement House, New York; T. Arnold Hill, National Urban League. Schools of social work were represented among the sponsors by Forrester B. Washington, Atlanta; Grace Coyle, Western Reserve; Wayne McMillen, Chicago; Phillip Klein, New York; Marion T Hathway, Pittsburgh. Some sponsors were prominent lay persons in social work: Helen Buttenwieser, New York; Sidney Hollander, Baltimore; Stanley Isaacs, New York. Abram Flaxer and Lewis Merrill, presidents respectively of the State, County and Municipal Workers of America (CIO), and of the United Office and Professional Workers of America (CIO), the two principal national unions enrolling social-work employees, were sponsors. Other names added later included Kenneth Pray, director, Philadelphia School of Social Work; Inabel Lindsay of the social work school at Howard University; and Grace Marcus.

The contributions and theater benefit parties helped keep the magazine afloat, but subscriptions never exceeded 6,000 (although the press run for the special issue on "The New Immigration," December 1939, was 16,000), and when *Social Work Today* finally went under in 1942 it was because, among other reasons, it was not popular enough to be self-supporting on the basis of subscriptions, sales, and advertising, nor could it find a continuing source of subsidies.

To guide Bancroft, an editorial board of sixteen was designated in 1937, representing a broad range of social-work fields, from local public welfare departments to the YWCA and the National Urban League. The magazine's purpose was described now as the "defense and extension of those social values to which the profession is rightly committed." These were not defined, but the reference to "progressive American social work" suggested that the reader could expect editorial comment oriented to the left rather than to the right of center. That the philosophy and rhetoric of 1934, its first year of publication, had been left behind, was clear. There was no more talk of the "fundamental reorganization society must undergo to provide security for all." As the selection of articles in '37–'39, editorial comment, and the writers requested to contribute indicated, the magazine identified with the populist aspects of the second New Deal. In this respect it shared the view in some liberal-radical circles that Roosevelt's presidency in his second term was subject to pressures from both left and right, as noted in chapter 14, and could be pushed to the left, or the "progressive" or "democratic" side, as the current terminology went, if the push was strong enough. Bancroft and his conferees on the editorial board hoped to add their mite to that push. This entailed a selective approach to administration programs; approval of some, disapproval of others.

Some examples. *Social Work Today* supported Roosevelt's unsuccessful effort to enlarge the Supreme Court, but was sharply critical of the administration's timid, poorly financed slum clearance and housing program. The White House-supported Fair Labor Standards Act, finally passed in 1938, and setting a minimum hourly wage in interstate commerce and industry (40 cents an hour) for the first time, was heartily approved. On the other hand, the administration's foot-dragging on antilynching legislation was castigated. *Social Work Today* hailed Roosevelt's Quarantine the Aggressor speech of October 1937; assailed him for his neutrality in the Spanish civil war. Cutbacks in WPA in 1937 were deplored, as was Washington's slowness to respond to the 1938 recession. The limitations of the Social Security Act were repeatedly examined, in both its social insurance and public assistance aspects.

Yet in May 1938 the editors asked its readers to write their congressmen to support unqualifiedly "Roosevelt's Program for Recovery." The reductive approach, the either-or attitude was most pronounced at election time, and 1938 was a congressional election year. "The people and Roosevelt vs. special privilege and popular betrayal," was the big issue in 1938, wrote the editors, noting FDR's support by the CIO, AFofL, the Railroad Brotherhoods, Labor's Nonpartisan League and the Workers Alliance; and the opposition of big business. However "imperfectly, unevenly and inadequately," the New Deal administration and its congressional supporters had carried forward a program of recovery and reform since 1936 against the opposition of all the "antisocial forces" in society. A double-page spread in the June 1939 issue, entitled "New Deal Landmarks—Recapitulation of Six Years of Social Achievement," listed the major legislative gains of the two New Deals, including programs subjected in the journal's earlier years to savage attacks. The list was introduced by a quotation from FDR affirming the administration's search "to save for our common country opportunity and security for citizens in a free society." A full-page editorial proclaimed "The New Deal is Our Deal."

Such affirmations of support for Roosevelt and his New Deal lay comfortably, if paradoxically, side by side with editorials urging readers to join such mass organizations as the American League for Peace and Democracy, called a Communist front by the House Committee on Un-American Activities, and to participate in such mass activities as the annual May Day parades, which were under open Communist Party sponsorship and control, organizations and activities hardly calculated to stir the enthusiasm of the President or his advisors. *Social Work Today* proudly reported that in the '37 May Day parade in New York, 2,000 members of the AFSCME union in the Home Relief Bureau took part, and close to 600 members of the Social Service Employees Union. The '38 and '39 parades drew an even larger response from the two unions. The editors commented that the 1939 parades "in every free country of the world" represented a "demonstration of unity and power behind the greatest of all aspirations and determinations—a just social order."[10]

The years 1937–40 were perhaps the magazine's best years in terms of readership, influence, range of articles, and the interest they aroused. An effort was made to broaden subject coverage to include more professional content: developments in social casework, which reemerged toward the end of the decade from the doldrums into which it had been jostled by the stormy weather of the early and middle years of the Depression, as well as what were called nuts-and-bolts discussions of training, personnel standards, supervision, and administration. The vehicle chosen was a column appearing in every issue, called "The Case Work Notebook," varying in length, in the detail with which the subject was treated, and in contributing authors. A leading role in its development was played by Bertha Reynolds, whose three articles in 1938, "Rethinking Social Case Work" (reprinted as a pamphlet by the magazine), summarized a major effort to integrate the fundamental findings of psychology and psychiatry on individual behavior, with the insights into the interaction of the individual and society afforded by the social sciences, in particular as interpreted by writers on the left influenced by what has been loosely denominated Marxism. "The new scientific orientation of social casework," she wrote in the second article, was "pushing relentlessly toward a democracy of approach to human beings." And in her concluding third article, her eyes on the darkening clouds over Europe, she linked the "fate of social casework" to the "fate of democracy."[11]

Reynolds was not alone in her effort to widen the horizens of traditional social work thinking. In an article bravely titled, "Toward a Science of Society," Harald Lund said social work faced a unique opportunity to contribute to a "catholic" human science of individual growth in a dynamic society. Books mentioned favorably as contributing to such a science included the Lynds' *Middletown in Transition* (1937), Karen Horney's *The Neurotic Personality of Our Time* (1937), Dollard's *Caste and Class in a Southern Town* (1937), Mary van Kleeck's *Creative America* (1936), and Margaret Mead's *Sex and Temperament in Three Primitive Societies* (1935).[12]

Public policy issues brought to the attention of the readers included not only the social welfare and social insurance programs of the administration, but the housing needs of the country, racial discrimination, and the state of civil liberties in general. The growth of the labor movement was reported. An increasing number of articles and editorials were devoted to the meaning for social workers of the war in Spain and the growth of Fascism in Europe. The special issue on the new immigration (December 1939), dealing with efforts to rescue refugees from Germany, Austria, and Czechoslovakia, resettlement services for them in the United States, and the contributions to American science, art, literature, of world notables among the refugees, received widespread favorable comment. Stories based on some of the articles appeared in the *New York Times*, the New York *Herald-Tribune*, and the New York *Post*.

New names appearing among authors included members of faculties of schools of social work and prominent administration figures, such as secretary of Labor Frances Perkins; Katherine Lenroot, chief of the Children's Bureau; and Thomas Parran, surgeon-general of the U.S. Public Health Service. John L. Lewis, president of the CIO, contributed an article, as did Roger Baldwin, executive director of the American Civil Liberties Union, and A. Philip Randolph, president of the Brotherhood of Sleeping Car Porters and of the National Negro Congress.

Chapter 17

Social Work and Politics Abroad: Becoming Involved

The last years of the decade were characterized by a growing concern with international developments in official circles in Washington, among members of the public at large, and among social workers. As domestic troubles receded in importance with the fading of the 1938 recession, the troubles of other countries commanded greater interest. It was an interest in marked contrast, however, with the typical attitude toward events abroad at the beginning of the decade.

Isolationism in Retreat

Isolationism, today a pejorative, was the proud boast of the America of the twenties. In its revulsion against World War I, the country rejected Woodrow Wilson and his League of Nations and saw in George Washington's warning against entangling alliances an appropriate guide for the twentieth century in framing its attitude toward Europe and its centuries-old rivalries and quarrels. "Hands off China and Latin America" summed up American foreign policy.

But since the Depression was a worldwide phenomenon and the health of the American economy was dependent in part on the size of its exports, the country found itself involved willy-nilly in international economic and political developments. Exports dropped by over half from '29 to '33.[1] Increasing competition for dwindling foreign markets and unfavorable trade balances led to the abandonment of the gold standard by Britain and a dozen other countries in '31, and by France, the last major holdout, in '36. The United States, to defend itself against the edge given its foreign trade rivals, went off the gold standard in '33. These successive blows to what had once been a stable international economic order, and the failure of international conferences to resolve the problems involved, emphasized both the gravity of the illness which had overtaken the world economy and America's stake in a cure.

For the general public, however, economics took second place to politics, their close interrelationships notwithstanding. Although primarily interested in their own troubles, many Americans saw in the course of events in Europe a repudiation of the democratic ideals for which America stood. However remote Europe seemed, and for all the lingering doubts about involvement, their sympathies were engaged and their fears aroused.

In Germany, the Hitler regime, which came to power in '33, the same year Roosevelt was inaugurated president, abolished the democracy of the postwar Weimar republic, proscribed all parties except the Nazi party, filled concentration camps with dissidents from the regime, real and presumed, and undertook the systematic exclusion of Jews from all spheres of the nation's life, economic, political, and cultural. Sworn to restore Germany as a great power, Hitler disavowed all reparation payments imposed by the Versailles Treaty ending the Great War, withdrew Germany from the League of Nations, reoccupied the Saar and the Rhineland, and, in defiance again of the 1919 treaty, undertook the country's rearmament and the reestablishment of universal military service. To cap Germany's restoration as a great power, he wrested from Britain a naval pact which gave the Reich a larger fleet than France.

Emboldened by Hitler's successes and the seeming inability of France, Britain, and the other European democracies to stop him, Mussolini, Fascist dictator of Italy since 1922, whose foreign policy until then had been all bluster and no action, invaded Ethiopia in '35 and annexed it in '36, defying a helpless League of Nations.

And in that same year, 1936, war broke out in Spain when a group of rightist generals, headed by Francisco Franco, revolted against the newly elected left-of-center government, invading Spain from Africa with an army composed largely of Moroccan troops, stiffened by barely disguised German and Italian contingents. Government attempts to purchase arms for defense were rejected by the appeasement-dominated European democracies in the name of nonintervention in a purely domestic quarrel, a policy in which the United States joined. Limited to supplies furnished by the Soviet Union, meager in comparison with those provided the rebel side by Italy and Germany, loyalist forces, although augmented by an International Brigade of anti-Fascists from many countries, including the United States, were slowly pushed back, and completely expelled from Spain by '39, when the last refugees, military and civilian, flooded across the border to be interned by a suspicious and pusillanimous French government.

Democracy in Europe from 1932 on seemed to be almost everywhere in retreat. Germany had joined Italy in going Fascist; Fascism won out in Spain; and there were strong Fascist movements in Austria, Hungary, Rumania, and even in France itself. In Britain, the world's oldest democracy, Oswald Mosley quit the Labor party to organize the British Union of

Fascists. The democracies were paralyzed by fear of offending the new aggressive regimes in Berlin and Rome; by fear of domestic appeasement forces whose sympathies were with the new Fascist governments on the move, or who were convinced they could not be stopped; by fear of Communist Russia, whose government denounced German and Italian aggression and called for an alliance between the Soviet Union and European democracies to check Fascism, an alliance that seemed to the men in power in the democracies a worse threat than appeasement; and by a pacifist public opinion, particularly in Britain, reflected, to cite two illustrations, in the Oxford pledge not to fight for king or country and in the paradox of a Labor party calling on the government to take a stand against Fascism while voting against rearmament. In France the anonymously authored slogan "Who wants to die for Danzig?" reflected the general unwillingness of most Frenchmen to get involved in other peoples' quarrels.

Numerous Americans viewed with growing dismay the seemingly relentless march of Fascism in Europe. French and British nonintervention in Spain was followed by passive acceptance of the German *Anschluss* with Austria in March 1938. At Munich six months later, the two governments acceded to Hitler's demand for the incorporation of the German-speaking Czech Sudetenland into the Reich. A Fascist-dominated Slovakia declared its independence from Czechoslovakia in 1939, and when Prague appealed to Hitler, the latter's response was to make of the truncated country a German protectorate.

Events now began to move at an accelerated pace. Hitler wrested Memel from Lithuania in March 1939 and demanded cession of the free city of Danzig. In April Italy occupied Albania, and in May Hitler and Mussolini transformed the Berlin-Rome Axis into a ten-year military alliance pledged to reorganize Europe to achieve unspecified but alarming objectives.

Adding to American concern over the success attending aggression were developments on the other side of the globe. In 1931 Japan had taken over Manchuria; when condemned by the League of Nations in 1933, it walked out, as Germany did the same year. Between 1937 and 1939 the Japanese army penetrated China proper, occupying Peking, Shanghai, and other major cities and establishing a puppet regime in Nanking. Every sign pointed to an early alliance between an expanding Japan and the Axis powers in Europe.[2]

The Spanish Civil War and Social Work

Of all these developments, the one which stirred American liberals and radicals most was the Spanish civil war. Not since the Sacco-Vanzetti case of the twenties had so many well-known writers, editors, journalists, clergymen, college and university presidents and professors, as well as large segments of the labor movement, been so seized by an issue. The Franco rebellion's aims, the brutal massacres of which it was guilty, and the open intervention of Germany and Italy, particularly the destruction of Guernica by the Nazi Condor Legion, immortalized in Picasso's painting of the crime, struck such Americans as an assault not only on the democratic values embodied in the American and French Revolutions, but on the whole idea of civilized behavior by governments toward civilians and in international relations. To help the Spanish government was not only the decent thing to do, but a welcome opportunity to strike a blow against the new barbarism represented by Fascism.

An open letter to President Roosevelt and to the Foreign Affairs Committees of Senate and House in February 1938, sponsored by the American Friends of Spanish Democracy, urged amendment of the Neutrality Act to permit the purchase of arms by the Spanish government. It was signed by Henry Stimson, former secretary of State; William E. Dodd, ex-ambassador to Germany; Roger Baldwin, American Civil Liberties Union; writers Upton Sinclair and Dorothy Canfield Fisher; the presidents of the Brotherhood of Railroad Trainmen, the United Textile Workers, and the American Federation of Hosiery Workers; and, from the academic world, Paul Douglas of the University of Chicago, Crane Brinton and Arthur F. Schlesinger of Harvard, Horace M. Kallen, Wesley C. Mitchell, Alvin Johnson; and a host of others, including in the social work field, Paul Kellogg, editor of the *Survey*.[3]

The appeal fell on deaf ears.

Success, however, attended efforts to raise funds by the Medical Bureau of the American Friends of Spanish Democracy. The Bureau was organized in the fall of 1936 in response to an urgent plea by the Spanish Red Cross for sera, vaccines, antitoxins, surgical instruments and other medical supplies. Tons of medical supplies and equipment were shipped, and two base hospitals were established with over 1,000 beds, staffed by American doctors and nurses.

The officers of the Medical Bureau, loosely federated through the North American Committee to Aid Spanish Democracy with organizations engaged in refugee resettlement, food shipments, and other forms of aid, read like a roll call of the leading American liberals of the day. The chairman was Bishop Robert L. Paddock of the Episcopal church; the vice-chairman was John Dewey, perhaps the country's foremost philosopher and educator. Members of the national committee or the executive committee included writers John Dos Passos, Stephen Vincent Benet, Archibald MacLeish, Lewis Mumford, and Harry Elmer Barnes; Heywood Broun, Bruce Bliven, Maxwell Stewart, Alfred Bingham, George

Soule, Max Lerner, and Oswald Garrison Villard, among editors, colum-
nists, journalists; such university presidents as William Allen Nielson,
Frank P. Graham; and among the clergy, Bishop Francis J. McConnell,
Stephen S. Wise, John Haynes Holmes, Guy Emergy Shipler, Reinhold
Niebuhr.[4]

Some 3,000 Americans slipped out of the country to join the Abraham
Lincoln Brigade, the American contingent of the International Brigade,
thrown into the struggle to halt Franco at the gates of Madrid. Among the
first to fall was Julius Rosenthal, social worker, member of the New York
Association of Workers in Public Relief Agencies; "killed while fighting
Fascism that Democracy might live—April 1937," *Social Work Today*
noted in a tribute in its June 1937 issue. How many other social workers
fought in the brigade is not known, since participation was illegal under
American law and generally concealed. Jennie Berman, president of the
New York Association of Federation Workers (AFW) before it became
the SSEU, lost her husband, one of a number of teachers among the
volunteers.

As early as October 1936, three months after the rebellion erupted, the
AFW named a committee to raise money for Labor's Red Cross Fund for
Spain, established by members of the teachers union, the musicians union,
the needle trades and other unions.[5] When the AASW delegate conference
met in February 1937, an informal meeting of some of the delegates under
the chairmanship of Peter Kasius, director of the Community Council and
United Charities, St. Louis, discussed the issues at stake in the war, and
decided to organize a social workers' committee of the Medical Bureau.
Harald Lund, assistant director, Family Welfare Association of America,
agreed to serve as chairman; Kasius was designated vice-chairman; and
Saul Carson, secretary.[6]

This was the modest beginning of what became, before the year was
over, the Social Workers Committee to Aid Spanish Democracy. Lund
remained chairman. The two vice-chairmen were Wayne McMillen of
Chicago's School of Social Service Administration, and Helen M. Harris,
head of the New York office of the National Youth Administration.
Gordon Hamilton of the New York School of Social Work was the
treasurer, and Jennie Berman of the New York SSEU the executive
secretary. The fifteen-member executive committee included Dr. John A.
Kingsbury, secretary of the Milbank Fund from 1921 to 1935; Harry
Greenstein, Maryland State Relief Administrator, 1933–36; Mildred Fairchild, director, Graduate Department of Social Economy, Bryn Mawr
College; Mary van Kleeck; Walter Pettit and Antoinette Cannon of the
New York School; Morris Lewis, former director of the federal program
for transients under FERA; and a number of officers of social work
unions. In 1938 Blanche Mahler left *Social Work Today* to become the

committee's full-time salaried executive secretary. The national committee, headed by Lillian Wald of the Henry Street Settlement as honorary
chairman and containing seventy-three names ranging alphabetically from
Edith Abbott to Walter West, was a blue ribbon list of American social
workers.[7]

In the summer of '37 a committee of five members, headed by Jennie
Berman, went to Spain for a first-hand view. They interviewed government
officials and representatives of international relief organizations and made
a detailed study of the work done in evacuation centers, refugee camps,
children's colonies, milk stations, hospitals, clinics. Their findings were
reported at a large meeting in New York in October, and publicized in
written form in a pamphlet prepared by Wayne McMillen.[8] On their
recommendation, the national committee voted in 1938 to assume support
of a facility established near Valencia housing fifty homeless children, now
named the Ethel C. Taylor Home, in honor of a dedicated committee
member who had died in 1937.[9]

Contacts with the Taylor Home and related American-supported efforts
at aid were maintained through Constance Kyle, who had been a member
of the group which visited Spain in '37 and made several return trips in '37
and '38. Eventually she found herself supervising the distribution not only
of the aid sent the Taylor Home by the Social Workers Committee, but of
all foreign aid to Spanish children under the International Commission
for Aid to Children, whose headquarters were in Paris.

Between 1937 and 1939 the committee, with the aid of chapters in half a
dozen cities, raised $33,000 among social workers for the support of the
Taylor Home and related activities. It supplied Spanish agencies with
American literature on child care. It circulated among social workers a
petition for lifting the embargo against shipment of arms to the Spanish
government. It issued bulletins on changing relief needs in Spain, based
largely on Constance Kyle's field reports.[10]

With the collapse of the resistance to Franco early in 1939, a major
reorganization took place in American and international aid groups. In
this country the Medical Bureau, the North American Committee to Aid
Spanish Democracy, and the American Friends of Spanish Democracy
merged in April 1939 to form the Spanish Refugee Relief Campaign, with
Harold Ickes, Interior Department secretary, as honorary chairman and a
new distinguished list of sponsors. The campaign raised a million dollars
plus half a million in kind for the relief of the refugees in France. The
Social Workers Committee renamed itself the Social Workers Committee
of the Spanish Refugee Relief Campaign; Helen M. Harris replaced
Harald Lund as chairman; the principal officers otherwise remained the
same. Committee funds were now allocated to the International Coordi-

nating Committee in Paris for the support and medical care of the 60,000 children included in the 400,000 refugees who fled to France.

The Spanish civil war and its aftermath spawned other organizations. Americans who had fought in Spain came home and formed the Veterans of the Abraham Lincoln Brigade. People who felt committed to the Spanish Republican cause joined and contributed funds to the Friends of the Abraham Lincoln Brigade, which raised money for the medical care and rehabilitation of the disabled volunteers. Some also contributed to the Campaign to Aid International Volunteers, organized to obtain the release of veterans of the International Brigade from internment camps in Spain and France, and arrange for their transportation to other countries.

Fascism and Communism: Are They Different?

In retrospect, the efforts on behalf of loyalist Spain proved the most successful experience of cooperation between liberals and radicals, both in general and in the ranks of social work. The two groups were otherwise in an uneasy alliance during the decade, often pulling in different directions, or divergent in their assessment of specific issues.

The root conflict was over the difference between Fascism, as represented by Nazi Germany, and Communism, as defined and practiced by the Soviet Union. Were the two really unlike, as the American Communist party and its sympathizers claimed, or were they both manifestations of totalitarianism, with greater likenesses than disparities, as many liberals believed? Was it not true, these liberals asked, that both ideologies glorified the one-party state at the expense of the individual, had no use for civil liberties, and established a police regime characterized by secret arrests, imprisonment or execution of dissidents, and the establishment of labor camps and concentration camps into which enemies of the government, real and imagined, disappeared, rarely to be heard from again?

The adoption by the Communist party in 1935–36 of the Popular Front policy all but erased these questions. Liberals were pleased by the party's seeming abandonment of its philosophy of class struggle and revolution, its avowal of a belief in the values of democracy, its support of Roosevelt and the second New Deal, its offer to work for the common good with progressives, liberals and Democrats. The foreign policy of the Popular Front, which was the new foreign policy of the Soviet Union, emphasized the common stake of the U.S.S.R. and the western democracies in halting Fascist aggression. Summed up in the term "collective security," it appealed to liberals, who saw Hitler as a greater danger to the world's peace than Stalin, and the collective security thesis as a possible answer to the

Berlin-Rome Axis. Russian aid to loyalist Spain served to demonstrate a willingness to act when the chips were down, in contrast to the ostensibly neutralist, but at bottom cowardly behavior of the United States, Britain, and France in the Spanish crisis. It reinforced the favorable picture of Russia in the middle and late thirties for many Americans, who had earlier approved of Roosevelt's recognition in 1933, and saw in the Soviet Union's joining of the League of Nations in 1934 and signing of a mutual security pact with France in the same year solid evidence that Russia was a natural ally of the democracies against the Axis powers. Another plus for Russia in their eyes was that the principal voice raised in the League against Fascist aggression was that of Maxim Litvinoff, the Soviet foreign minister.[11]

Whatever their views as individuals, officers of national social work organizations, with possibly the one exception noted below, never sought to involve them in events abroad, regarding such issues as irrelevant to their purposes. The formation as early as 1933 of the Hospites, which addressed itself to the relief and placement of refugee social workers from Germany, reflected concern in the field with the trend of events in that country. But until 1938 no national organization took it upon itself to condemn, even by implication, the government whose policies made Hospites necessary. In December of that year the governing board of the National Federation of Settlements adopted resolutions favoring amendment of the Neutrality Act to permit the sale of arms to China and Spain and urging the public not to buy German or Japanese products. The New York chapter of the AASW, about the same time, condemned racial, religious, and political persecution in Germany.[12] A special issue of the *Survey Graphic* in February 1939, put together by guest editor Raymond Gram Swing, was devoted to the persecution of minority groups in Europe by both Fascist and Communist regimes, but within the profession as a whole distress about developments abroad centered on Germany and Japan rather than on the Soviet Union. The special issue of *Social Work Today*, comparable to the *Survey Graphic* special issue, appearing later that year and devoted to the new immigration to the United States, identified the immigrants as refugees from Fascism only, a view related only in part to the unwillingness of the editors to publish anything critical of the U.S.S.R. The distinction *Social Work Today* made between the two totalitarian regimes (a term the editors found unacceptable and never used) was shared by more social workers than the readers of that journal and those otherwise associated with the Rank-and-File Movement.

A friendly attitude toward the Soviet Union was evident from the very first year of *Social Work Today*. Articles on aspects of Russian life of interest to social workers always struck an up-beat note: "Soviet Children at Play," by Eunice Fuller Barnard, March 1936; "Social Work in the

U.S.S.R.," by Nathan Berman, who had spent six months there studying the treatment of juvenile offenders, April 1936; "The New Soviet Constitution," by Kathleen Barnes and Harriet Moore, of the Institute of Pacific Relations, February 1937. Books well-disposed to the Soviet Union got favorable reviews.

References to the Nazi regime, on the other hand, and to Italy and Japan, were always critical. Articles and editorials stressed the repressions suffered by the people of Germany, the threat of war in the aggressive foreign policies of Hitler and Mussolini, and Japanese military expansion in China. "Social Work Under the Nazi Regime," November 1939, by Walter Friedlander, a refugee social worker on the faculty of Chicago's School of Social Service Administration, described the degradation of social work in the new Germany. An editorial in the October 1936 issue noted with regret the presence at the Third International Conference of Social Work, held in London that July, of delegates from Germany, and the refusal of the conference president, René Sand of France, to read a letter to the gathering written by Mary van Kleeck, who had been president of the Second International Conference in 1932. In her letter van Kleeck had criticized the destruction of parliamentary democracy in Germany, and the downgrading of women in the professions, developments she described as denials of fundamental social work principles. The *Social Work Today* editorial praised the Soviet Union for adherence to these principles, for its defense of them when under attack in other countries, and for its advocacy of collective security for the maintenance of peace.

Collective security was the centerpiece of *Social Work Today*'s foreign policy position. An editorial in November 1937 called for repeal of the Neutrality Act, which prevented the purchase of American arms by the governments of Spain and China, and endorsed the campaign for a boycott of Japanese imports. The same issue contained an article by Winifred Chappell of the Methodist Federation of Social Service, "Social Workers and War," warning of the inevitability of World War II unless the "progressive forces" of the world (the U.S.S.R. and the western democracies) learned to unite to stop Fascist aggression.

"*Social Work Today* calls on every one of its readers," said an editorial in April 1938, "to become an active and determined worker for peace and democracy through collective security. It is the most important task confronting the world today." A month later it appealed for the support of the O'Connell bill providing for cessation of economic cooperation between the United States and the treaty-breakers—Germany, Italy, and Japan; warned of plans for world conquest by the Rome-Berlin-Tokyo Axis; and renewed its call for U.S. aid to Spain and China. Post-Munich developments were examined in a symposium in the November '38 issue on Czechoslovakia. An editorial advocated severance of diplomatic relations with Germany. Roosevelt's State of the Union address to Congress in January 1939, calling, among other things, for the defense of democracy at home, and for defense against aggression through repeal of the Neutrality Act, was hailed as "one of America's great historic documents."[13]

War

August 24, 1939, the world was startled to learn that Hitler and Stalin had signed a nonaggression pact in Moscow at a conference at which Stalin toasted the German fuehrer, and von Ribbentrop, the German foreign minister, drank a toast to the health of Stalin. The pact pledged neutrality in the event of armed conflict involving either country. On September 1, his eastern front secured by the new pact, Hitler invaded Poland. Two days later a reluctant France and Britain, pledged to Polish independence, declared themselves in a state of war with Germany. On September 17, the armed forces of the U.S.S.R. crossed the Polish frontier from the east to occupy the Soviet share of the new partition of Poland provided for in the secret clauses of the Hitler-Stalin pact. World War II, so often feared during the decade, so often warned against, was finally a reality.

With the Hitler-Stalin pact, collective security as a concept, as a policy, as a slogan, died. Dead also was the Popular Front. The Moscow treaty terminated not only a period in the history of the American Communist party, but also any major collaboration between liberals and Communists. A few liberals defended the pact, including Maxwell Stewart, Corliss Lamont, and Frederick Schuman, who referred to it as a masterstroke of *Realpolitik*. But the *New Republic* called it appeasement and the *Nation* "sickening."

A few months earlier the newly organized Committee for Cultural Freedom had issued a statement, signed among others by George S. Counts, Sidney Hook, Horace Kallen, Carl Becker, Oswald Garrison Villard, and Elmer Davis, critical of Russian as well as German and Italian repressions. It described the Popular Front mass organizations, such as the American League for Peace and Democracy and the American Youth Congress, as run by Communist party stooges and made up in the main of innocents and dupes. If the left in America had a future, it seemed to say, it lay in noninvolvement with the Communist party and its fronts.

Members of the committee, along with such prominent liberals as John Dewey, John Haynes Holmes, Charles Beard, and Max Eastman, had been identified with opposition to the Communist party and the Soviet Union for a number of years. They had denounced the Moscow purge trials of 1935–38 as evidence of the final destruction of all opposition in Russia to one-man rule. They had also publicized the annihilation by the

Spanish Communist party, acting under orders from Moscow, of the anarcho-syndicalists and Trotsky adherents in the elements supporting the coalition loyalist government in Spain. The *Nation* ran the committee's statement, but the *New Republic*, which had refused to take a position on the purge trials on the ground that not all the evidence was in, and tended to view committee members as ideologues blinded by an anti-Russian bias, would not print the release because it linked the U.S.S.R. with the two principal Fascist states. The pact now lent the statement an authority among liberals it would otherwise not have had.

Social Workers in Defense of Neutrality

Social Work Today was not published during the summer months. In October 1939, in the first issue to appear after the pact and the outbreak of the war, the lead editorial, "The War and the New Deal," did not call for collective action against German aggression and for aid to Poland, France, and Britain. It attributed the war's coming to British and French appeasement, which had only fed Hitler's appetite, and recommended American abstention. A strong, prosperous, democratic America, at peace with the contending powers, had a major contribution to make to the new world which would emerge from the war. The New Deal's march toward social progress had to be accelerated. This position was reaffirmed in an editorial in the November issue captioned "Peace Agenda for Social Work."

A detailed exposition appeared in the January 1940 number, in the form of a letter addressed to the Congress convening that month, entitled "Meeting Social Need: A Peace Program." It made six points:

1. Measures for meeting basic human needs are in themselves a peace program. They include an adequate work program for the unemployed; an expanded and liberalized social security program; legislation protecting labor, consumer, and minority needs; legislation removing obstacles to the exercise of the franchise by all American citizens of voting age; and expanded public health services.
2. There must be no diversion into military channels of funds needed for social programs.
3. There must be no gearing together of civilian and military programs, which should be kept separate.
4. Sales to belligerents must be severely taxed to take the profits out of war.
5. Civil rights must be zealously guarded.

    6. Social workers are opposed to giving the United States an eco-
       nomic stake in the war.

Any impression that "Meeting Social Need" represented a manifesto of
the radical wing of social work was quickly dissipated by an examination
of the names of the seventy-five social workers who signed the letter, all
distinguished in one way or another in the field. They included Paul
Kellogg, editor of the *Survey*; such federal personnel as Ruth Blakeslee,
chief of the Division of Policies and Procedures of the Social Security
Board's Bureau of Public Assistance, and Harald Lund, associate research
director, White House Conference on Children in a Democracy; current
or former state and local public welfare officials (Joseph L. Moss, director,
Cook County, Illinois, Bureau of Public Welfare; Alice Liveright, former
state secretary of welfare, Pennsylvania); executives of national voluntary
social agencies (Linton Swift, general director, Family Welfare Association of America, and T. Arnold Hill, director, Department of Industrial
Relations, National Urban League); executives of local voluntary agencies
(Charlotte Carr, former director of New York's Home Relief Bureau and
in 1940 head worker, Hull House, Chicago, and Frederick Daniels, general
secretary of the Brooklyn Bureau of Charities); officers of the professional
associations in social work (Walter West, executive secretary, AASW, and
Fred K. Hoehler, director of the APWA); directors and other officials of
local councils of social agencies (e.g., Robert P. Lane, executive director,
Welfare Council, New York); and a raft of social work educators, among
them Walter Pettit, director of the New York School of Social Work;
Kenneth Pray, dean, and Karl de Schweinitz, director, Pennsylvania
School; Wilbur I. Newstetter, dean, School of Applied Social Sciences,
University of Pittsburgh; Isabelle K. Carter, director, School of Social
Work, University of North Carolina; Grace Coyle, of the School at
Western Reserve and president that year of the National Conference of
Social Work; Bertha Reynolds, from 1925 to 1937 associate director of the
Smith College School for Social Work.

    There were some radicals or near-radicals, among the signers, of course,
including Mary van Kleeck, Harry Lurie, and a number of officers of
social work unions, but the great bulk came from the establishment in
social work. In defining their position on the war, the editors of *Social
Work Today* had unquestionably articulated the views of many social
workers influential in the affairs of the profession.

    Following publication of the letter, additional signatures were submit-
ted to *Social Work Today* by persons of importance in the field. The
statement was endorsed by the Washington and Denver chapters of the
AASW, by the American Association of Social Work Students, by the
New York SSEU, and by the National Executive Board of the SCMWA.[14]

Further evidence of widespread agreement with the position taken by *Social Work Today* was the small number of resignations from the list of *Social Work Today* Cooperator sponsors during the period '39–'41, the two years covering the antiwar stand of the magazine, in the face of charges that the position was parallel with, if not determined by, that taken by the Communist party.

Advocacy of neutrality was general among social workers in the first year of the war. Said Edward Corsi, first deputy commissioner, New York Department of Welfare, addressing a meeting of U.S. Army chaplains in November 1939: "The European conflict should not distract the American people from their domestic problems; particularly the problem of achieving a minimum of economic security for the masses within our democratic framework .... We as Americans have no national interests in the European conflict, although as human beings none of us can ignore its tragedies. If we are to preserve our national neutrality, we must eliminate the war-interest factors in our national economy that constitute the greatest basic threat to that neutrality. After all, isn't it better that we spend millions of dollars to insure the welfare of our people through health, unemployment, old age, housing and medical programs, than to ignore these human needs and exhaust our resources on bullets and battleships?"[15]

These themes were also stresed in the meeting in New York that fall sponsored by the New York SSEU and *Social Work Today*, attended by 1,200 social workers, at which Harry Lurie presided, and the speakers were Mary van Kleeck and Len de Caux, publicity director of the CIO, an organization also opposed to any American intervention in the war.[16] *Social Work Today* printed the addresses as 10-cent pamphlets for mass distribution by social work unions.

Roosevelt's State of the Union message to Congress in January 1940, in which he promised to slash all expenditures for purposes other than defense, was not greeted in the pages of *Social Work Today* with the applause of his message a year earlier, but critically, severely. In an article, "Social Workers and the War: 1914 and 1940" (February 1940), Frank Bancroft, the managing editor, evoked the memory of the peace efforts in World War I of Jane Addams, Lillian Wald, Paul Kellogg, and the Abbotts, and contrasted that picture with the "cooptation" of Canadian social work in the new conflict. War, said van Kleeck in "Social Work in the World Crisis" (March 1940) destroys civil liberties and gains in social legislation; subordinates the needs of the people to the needs of the military. She rejected as simplistic the view of the war as democracy vs. Hitlerism, saw it as a conflict between imperial Britain and Fascist Germany, in which the best interests of the United States were served by "constructive neutrality."

The thesis of the January 1940 letter to Congress received additional exposure at a *Social Work Today* luncheon meeting held at the 1940 National Conference of Social Work in May, chaired by Harry Lurie, at which the principal speakers were the Reverend William Spofford, executive secretary, Church League for Industrial Democracy, and Carey McWilliams, chief of the Division of Immigration and Housing of the state of California. Copies of the letter, on display at the booths of *Social Work Today* and the Joint Committee of Trade Unions in Social Work, drew 1,000 additional signatures, reportedly one for every four persons in attendance at the conference. The copies were later taken to the White House for presentation to the President; accepted for him by his military aide, General Watson.[17]

Through 1940 and the first half of 1941, almost every issue of *Social Work Today* struck repeatedly at the administration for reducing the WPA and NYA rolls, for increasing expenditures for defense, and for Roosevelt's efforts, short of war, to aid Britain. Other articles called attention to the neglected social needs of the day in social security, in health services, in programs for children, in jobs for the unemployed. These and related needs, and the potential threats involvement in the war posed for gains won under the New Deal, were also the subjects of meetings and forums under *Social Work Today* auspices, and of sessions at the 1940 National Conference of Social Work under the auspices of the Joint Committee of Trade Unions in Social Work.

It was at the delegate conference held in conjunction with the 1940 national conference that the AASW finally issued its own statement on the war. It urged on the American people "their abiding obligation to our inner lines of defense, that of building permanent protection against those social and economic evils enumerated herein and which undermine the desire and capacity of men to live at peace with one another."[18] An editorial in the August 1940 issue of the *Compass* called attention to the "unprecedented expenditures for defense, [the] increasing centralization of governmental authority" and the "greater regimentation of civilian life" war involved. "Social work," it went on, "must reckon with the material and psychological environment that is created by a 'war economy'. . . . The democratic philosophy has provided a peculiarly favorable setting for social work. Dangers to the democratic thesis threaten not merely the external structure but the inmost essence of professional social work." In the same issue, an unsigned article, "Social Workers and National Defense," began with the sentence, "Social workers are particularly sensitive to the impact of events which may undermine the democratic ideals that have given social work its character and direction."[19] As late as the summer of 1940 most social workers wanted to keep the war and the issues it raised at arm's length.

Strange Bedfellows

Social workers who urged neutrality in the European conflict were not alone in their opposition to American involvement. Groups in favor of America's abstention were a varied lot, ranging politically from extreme left to extreme right and including some which fitted nowhere into the conventional political spectrum. At least five groups may be identified here; there were some social workers in most of them.[20]

The Communist party, its sympathizers, and the organizations it controlled, including some major CIO unions, described the military struggle in Europe as a clash between two imperialisms, in whose outcome the United States had no stake. Since the Axis powers were not appealing for American aid, and Axis adherents here were not calling for such aid, the party and the organizations influenced by it directed their principal fire against groups favoring help to the Allies, and against Roosevelt for his maneuvers to make such help possible. And the party, like most social workers who spoke up on the subject, advocated, on the positive side, that the administration give first priority to the preservation and strengthening of the social gains under the New Deal.

At the opposite pole, politically, was the isolationist right-wing group calling itself America First. It believed a Fascist victory in Europe inevitable, was inclined indeed to view such an outcome as a desirable barrier to the spread of Communism, and saw little point in any effort to impede it, not only because the attempt would be futile, but because it would create difficulties in doing business with a postwar Hitler-dominated Europe. America First was financed by such businessmen as Robert E. Wood, president of Sears Roebuck, and Jay Hormel of the meat-packing company bearing his name; and its views were publicized by the xenophobic isolationist press of Robert McCormick (*Chicago Tribune*), Joseph Medill Patterson (*New York Daily News*), and William Randolph Hearst.

Easily the most influential figure in America First, and Roosevelt's major foe in his battle to win public opinion to the side of aid to Britain, was Charles Lindbergh. Colonel Lindbergh had been a mass cult figure since 1927, when he made the first nonstop solo flight across the Atlantic. In the years that followed, press and radio competed in presenting to an adoring public the image of a reluctant hero, who hated publicity yet seemed to invite it by writing a best-selling book about his exploit. A poor boy, his winning the hand of the daughter of a millionaire banker was the perfect American romance; the genius he displayed in the operation and maintenance of an airplane, that central divinity in the pantheon of mechanical marvels of an age which worshiped the motor-driven machine, made Lindbergh the archetypal American. When his two-year-old son was kidnaped and found murdered in 1932, all America mourned with him.

Lindbergh visited Britain, France, and Germany in the late thirties, saw nothing but disunity, flabby will, and incompetence in the two democracies, but was impressed by, and felt great admiration for, the efficiency, the virility, the national unity, the subordination of the individual to the will of the leader he believed he observed in Germany. (He didn't bother to mute his contempt for Vice-president Wallace's common man, and for the democratic ethos.) In 1938 he accepted with gratitude the Reich's second highest decoration, the Service Cross of the German Eagle with Star, awarded him by Hitler. There were reports in the press that he was planning to transfer his residence from France to Germany, ostensibly to collaborate better with German confrères on developments in aviation which had made the *Luftwaffe* superior, in his opinion, to the British, French, and Russian air forces. In 1940 his views on the direction which events would take were reflected in his wife Anne Morrow Lindbergh's book, *The Wave of the Future*, which identified the wave with Fascism.

When the war broke out, he toured the country under America First auspices, warning the public against the perils of aid to Britain; and three months before Pearl Harbor he accused Roosevelt, Britain, and American Jews of wanting to push the United States into the war.

America First had supporters in places of power on Capitol Hill, but advocates of neutralism in Congress were by no means confined to America-Firsters. They included in the House respectable stodgy conservatives, such as Joseph W. Martin, Massachusetts Republican, and the flamboyant Martin Dies, Texas Democrat and chairman of the House Un-American Activities Committee, who saw a Communist lurking under every liberal bed; and in the Senate, such liberals as Burton K. Wheeler of Montana, and Robert La Follette, Jr., of Wisconsin, inheritors of an isolationist tradition stretching back to the days of World War I.

Mass backing for neutralism was provided by the CIO. Crusty John L. Lewis, its chief, never more his own man, had broken with Roosevelt over national priorities, and now accused the President of betraying the populist promises of the second New Deal, in particular the new deal for organized labor, in his zeal to strengthen America's defense preparations. "Within the new year, 1940," he thundered as it opened, "this nation . . . must decide whether it will listen to those who divert attention from the difficulties of our internal problems and stake the nation's future on the vagaries of wars abroad . . . . The American people . . . will require of their government that it adopt a vigorous internal program, intensifying its efforts for the welfare of the many."[21] Addressing the NAACP convention later in the year, he said, "Involvement or intervention in the European war is repugnant to every healthy-minded American."[22] Roosevelt's national defense program, a code term for rearmament in case the administration's foreign policy brought hostilities leading to participation in the war, justified in part as a contribution to the reduction of unemployment, would still leave at least 7 million persons out of work, predicted Ralph Hetzel of the CIO's research department that fall. Campaigning for reelection as the first third-term candidate in American history, Roosevelt felt obliged to promise fathers and mothers in the electorate that their boys would not be sent into any foreign wars; but the CIO leadership thought he spoke with a forked tongue. At its convention in November, the CIO adopted a peace resolution pledging itself to work "against any involvement in the present tragic and horrible war raging throughout the world."

Another group in this disparate assembly of neutralists were the non-communist radicals and liberals who identified with the disillusionment of the twenties concerning American participation in World War I, which had been attributed to one-sided assistance to the Allies and to British propaganda. They saw signs of the same propaganda in reports from Europe about the new war; and they feared what American involvement would do to civil liberties, which, they now reminded people, had taken a severe beating in 1917–19. They included president Robert Hutchins of the University of Chicago; Bruce Bliven, editor of the *New Republic*; Oswald Garrison Villard, retired editor of the *Nation*; Quincy Howe, popular author and journalist in the field of public affairs; Chester Bowles, advertising genius; and eminent churchman Harry Emerson Fosdick.

And then, of course, there were such traditional pacifists as the Friends and other principled opponents of war. Not a few of the well-known social workers who signed the letter to Congress in the January 1940 issue of *Social Work Today* were either pacifists or felt guilty about the cooptation of social work in World War I, or identified with the social work pacifist opposition in World War I represented by Jane Addams, Lillian Wald, and Roger Baldwin.

Public Opinion and the War

To what extent did these neutralist sentiments reflect the views of the public at large?

The question is worth a brief examination, not because conformity with public opinion has ever been a great desideratum in social work—social workers have often had the experience of being in a minority on social issues of moment to them—but to see in better perspective the position taken by *Social Work Today* and its supporters in the profession in relation to the great public debate over the meaning of the war and America's stake in it, which went on during the two years between the Hitler-Stalin pact and Pearl Harbor. The subject is also of interest because *Social Work Today* professed to be reflecting the views not only of social workers but of the labor movement as well, and of the silent majority of the American people. A convenient source for the views of the public on the subject may be found in the Gallup poll. Public opinion polls have been rightly criticized as ambiguous in their findings because they are influenced by the way in which the questions are put. It may be worthwhile nevertheless to look at the results of the Gallup polls taken in 1939–41 on the war, particularly since significant shifts can be observed in the answers to the same question, as well as a broad consistency among the responses to related questions.

To judge by this source, public opinion through '39, '40, and '41 was predominantly neutralist, in the sense of the desirability of American nonparticipation as a belligerent. In December 1939, for example, almost half the respondents queried thought the most important problem facing the country was to keep out of the war. American intervention in the event of a German victory was favored by only 29 percent in October 1939, only 23 percent in February 1940, 24 percent in May 1941. It took Pearl Harbor and Germany's declaration of war on the United States to induce a majority of Americans to favor participation in World War II.

On the other hand, there was no question as to where their sympathies lay. They were pro-Ally and in favor of American aid to Britain and France short of the risk of war. Between 1939 and 1941 the public's views on which side it would like to see win the war, and on the nature and extent of American aid, the use of American ships to carry aid, their protection by the American navy, the need for increasing America's defense capabilities, gradually shifted toward a more open espousal of the Allied cause.

In September 1939, 82 percent of the respondents queried said Germany was responsible for the war, and in October 84 percent said they would like to see the Allies, not Germany, win. This lopsided majority on attitudes towards the belligerents remained quite stable through the two years or so preceding our entrance into the war. It was reflected also in the choice of countries on whose behalf war-relief activities were conducted. As early as 1940, voluntary committees to raise money for civilian victims of the war in France and Britain began to proliferate, including the U.S. Committee for the Care of European Children, the American Gifts Committee, and the alliterative Bundles for Britain. The American Red Cross launched a drive to raise $20 million, to be spent in the countries fighting Hitler. Existing voluntary foreign-aid organizations such as the American Friends Service Committee and the Joint Distribution Committee doubled and redoubled campaign goals and staff in the field in Europe working with refugees fleeing the German armies. But no comparable groups emerged to solicit aid for the other side in the conflict. By January 1941, two out of three respondents in the Gallup poll sample thought America's future safety depended on Britain's winning the war.

In answer to the question, should Congress change the Neutrality Law so that the United States could sell war material to Britain and France, 50 percent of the respondents said Yes, early in September 1939, and 50 percent said No. By the end of October, the Yes ratio had risen to 62 percent. A bare majority in May 1940 favored government credits to the Allies to buy planes here, but by January 1941 almost 70 percent of the respondents approved Roosevelt's proposed Lend-Lease program for aid to Britain. Fear of involvement made 84 percent in September 1939 agree that American vessels carrying aid to Britain and France should stay out of the war zone. By April 1941 sentiment changed to the peril-inviting stand reflected in the two to one approval given the statement that the United States should help Britain even at the risk of war. And between April and June 1941, the proportion of respondents who thought it acceptable to use the U.S. navy to guard ships carrying supplies to Britain rose from 41 to 55 percent.

Views on America's participation in World War I—on which the public was asked to take a backward glance—underwent a concurrent transformation. In November 1939, two-thirds of those queried thought it had been a mistake—one in three said in December 1939 that the United States had been a victim of propaganda and selfish interests. The two-thirds dropped to 40 percent by April 1941. Under the pressure of events, history, as mirrored in popular memory, was being rewritten to conform to current emotions. The lineup of the principal European belligerents was almost the same.

Approval of an increase in American defense capacity drew heavy support from the very beginning. Eighty-six percent said Yes in November 1939 to a question about increasing the size of the army, and as early as June 1940 two-thirds favored universal military training for one year for youths of twenty.[23]

These changing views were basically a response to the progress of the war in Europe. The partition of Poland in October 1939 between Germany and the U.S.S.R. was followed by the Russo-Finnish War of 1939–40, ending in Finnish cession of 12 percent of her territory to the U.S.S.R.; then the Nazi conquest of Yugoslavia and Greece in April 1940, and the simultaneous occupation of Denmark and Norway. In May and June, the Netherlands, Belgium, and France were overrun. The Baltic states of Lithuania, Latvia, and Estonia were absorbed into the U.S.S.R. between June and August. The summer of 1940 saw the whole of Europe in the effective control of Germany and Russia. With the continent secure (Italy, Spain, Hungary, Rumania, and Bulgaria were in the grip of allied or friendly Fascist regimes), Hitler ordered the aerial bombardment of Britain in August in preparation for invasion. The Battle of Britain began. U-boat attacks on ships carrying war supplies to Britain intensified.[24]

What had initially been mild identification with the democratic countries of the West and dislike of the rapacious, brutal, barbaric Nazis, grew in strength with the fall of France and the occupation by Hitler and his allies of almost all of Europe west of the U.S.S.R., the public's revulsion at the devastation wrought by the Nazi air onslaught on Coventry, its admiration of British aplomb under the London blitz and of the RAF's success in defeating the *Luftwaffe*. The image of a beleaguered , isolated Britain defying the world's mightiest war machine, symbolized in the bulldog jaws of Churchill, clamped on a cigar, captured the American imagination. By '41 most Americans supported Roosevelt's ardent search for ways of helping Britain short of war itself.

Roosevelt's Strategy

Changes in foreign policy and in defense capabilities consistent with the gradual shift in public opinion, and the reciprocal influence of one on the other, had been carefully—his critics said guilefully—orchestrated in the meantime by Roosevelt. In his famous quarantine speech of October 5, 1937, he had said that the foundations of civilizations were threatened by the lawlessness of aggressor nations, that America could not assume it would not be attacked in turn, and suggested that, to preserve the health of the international community, countries pursuing their aims through war or the threat of war should be quarantined by the peace-loving nations of the world. But it was not until several years later that Congress was willing to endorse this sentiment and put teeth in it. In the meanwhile he asked for and got increases in defense authorizations; and in his budget message of January 1939, requesting funds for fiscal year 1940, projected defense outlays topped the relief budget for the first time in his presidency.

"I hope the United States will keep out," he said when war came with the German invasion of Poland. "Every effort of your government will be directed toward that end."[25] That was one side of the picture, as he saw it and as reflected in public opinion. The other side was help to the countries fighting Hitler. (He had no intention of repeating Woodrow Wilson's call in 1914 to be "impartial in thought as well as in action.") The Neutrality Act of 1939 repealed the arms embargo of the 1935 Neutrality Act (against which the supporters of loyalist Spain had repeatedly stubbed their toes), making possible the shipment of war materiel, particularly planes, to Britain and France. And in September 1940, Congress went along with the President's executive order trading fifty "overage" destroyers to Britain for bases in Newfoundland and the Caribbean.

But even if acceptable to public opinion, other meaningful help was not an immediate possibility since there was no large armaments industry in America. Conversion of existing industrial capacity would take time. Moreover our own armed forces lacked military readiness, particularly in weaponry, a realization brought home by the stunning success of the Nazi army in overrunning Poland in thirty days and knocking France out of the war in a little over a month. We had nothing to compare with that military machine.

Roosevelt's answer was the national defense program of July 1940, providing for a two-ocean navy and a corresponding increase in the army and its air wing. In September came the Selective Service Act, the first peacetime draft in American history. That the President had broad public support for these moves was indicated in the results of the 1940 election. The platforms of both major parties pledged U.S. neutrality, but aid to the countries fighting the Axis powers. Roosevelt won handily over Wendell Willkie, who struck most voters as a Johnny-come-lately, me-too figure. Minor party candidates drew the smallest vote in decades. Under the pressure of events abroad popular opinion tended to rally to the administration and as at no time in the thirties, both the radical left and the radical right were largely isolated.

By this time—1940—America had recaptured its earlier role as the leading nation in the democratic West. In the person of Roosevelt, a world figure, America had produced a leader to whom the embattled democracies of Europe now looked for counsel and material assistance in its struggle against the seemingly invincible forces of Fascism.

Their faith seemed vindicated by the Lend-Lease Act of March 1941, granting Roosevelt almost unrestricted freedom to furnish the Allies with war materiel and the authority to waive repayment. The following month the United States occupied Danish-owned Greenland to forestall German occupation, and in July the defense of Iceland was taken over from Britain. In the same month the Navy began convoying ships carrying war supplies across the Atlantic. In August Roosevelt and Churchill, at a meeting in Newfoundland, issued the Atlantic Charter, pledging solidarity and cooperation in the peace to be established "after the final destruction of Nazi tyranny." German-American hostilities short of formal declaration of war seemed assured by the orders given American naval escorts in September, to shoot first in any conflict with German U-boats, which had been active in the Atlantic since the first days of the war and were sinking British vessels at an alarming rate.[26]

The AASW Adapts

These changes, particularly the immense expansion of both the armed forces and defense-related industries, had their impact on the position of the American Association of Social Workers. Initially, as noted earlier, the association was concerned with the threat defense preparations posed to the federal government's social welfare and social insurance programs, to civil liberties and to democracy in general. The threat proved illusory. Increasingly association attention focused on the second of its concerns, due recognition by the government of the contribution social work could make to the solution of the social problems created by the defense program. Unlike the editors of *Social Work Today*, the leadership of the AASW did not, at least explicitly, argue the merits of neutrality vs. aid to the Allies. It was interested in matters closer to home.

Over the years, it said in effect, social work had developed certain skills. The defense program brought in its train problems crying for the utilization of these skills. Through the pages of the *Compass* and in statements issued by the Division of Government and Social Work, the association seemed to be saying, in almost imploring terms—don't overlook us, please use us, we have much to give. For example, help to meet the problems— inadequate housing, health, educational, and recreational facilities— caused by the rapid growth of communities around the expanding military installations and the new defense plants; help to develop and administer dependency allowances for families of men in the armed forces; help to plan for the rehabilitation of men rejected for selective service.[27]

This attitude was encouraged by the government itself. AASW officers and committee chairmen, by reason of their positions in the association and as federal and state agency officials, found themselves increasingly drawn, from 1939 on, into federal programs auxiliary to the defense program. They were invited to join committees to develop "cooperative relationships" between the Social Security Board, the Children's Bureau, and other federal agencies employing social workers, and the departments and special agencies whose principal purpose was the expansion of the nation's defense forces and its defense plants. Their response was strongly affirmative.[28] Concurrently the national AASW office urged members to join state and local defense councils "to direct attention to state and local problems inadequately understood and to interpret the relationship of these problems to the growing concept of total defense."[29]

It was taken for granted that chapters and individual members would cooperate in the defense effort. To keep apprised of developments, the national office in May 1941 addressed an inquiry to sixteen selected chapters located near major military camps and defense plant concentrations. The replies provided a revealing checklist of the variety of social problems in such communities, and of the utilization of social workers in their amelioration, particularly those employed in the Red Cross, the YM and YWCA, and other private agencies, which had doubled and tripled staff.[30] In March 1941 the USO (United Service Organizations for National Defense, Inc.) was formed to facilitate cooperation between the YM and YWCA, the National Catholic Community Service, the Salvation Army, the Jewish Welfare Board, and the National Travelers Aid Association, in their activities on behalf of servicemen and their families, and to campaign jointly for the millions of dollars their programs required.[31] In August 1941 the AASW's Division of Government and Social Work sought to go beyond the elementary services offered by the USO group by identifying as appropriate objectives "in relation to National Defense" the utilization of social work skills in services to draft boards and in the armed forces. "We are also trying to get social work personnel in the National Selective Service Administration." [32] The AASW effort may have been prompted by the use of psychiatrists in the selective service program under arrangements developed by the American Psychiatric Association, the surgeon-generals of the army and navy, and the Selective Service Commission, a use criticized editorially by *Social Work Today* in Marcy 1940, but hailed by the *Survey* in its December 1940 issue as a "heartening . . . recognition" that mental health was a "definite element in national defense."

Social Workers in Conflict

All this was not very different from what social agencies had done in World War I, which had been the subject of a savage attack by *Social Work Today* in 1934, had been implicitly disapproved of in its January 1940 statement, "Meeting Social Need," and, in an article in February 1940, had been denounced by managing editor Frank Bancroft as cooptation of social work in the war effort, with reference to America in World War I and Canada in World War II. *Social Work Today* refrained, however, from any criticism of the AASW, concentrating its fire instead on the government's program. The silence on the subject may have been prompted by editorial unwillingness to recognize the presence within the ranks of social work of views on the war other than its own, or it may have been a reluctance to take issue with the AASW, with which it had made its peace some years earlier. It was a position not difficult to maintain as long as no organized group openly called for aid to the Allies. This was no longer possible by the spring of 1941. The shift in attitude toward the war among the public at large had also affected social workers. Early that year Social Work Unionists for Britain and Democracy was formed, dedicated to approval of aid to Britain by the United States, repudiation of totalitarianism in all its forms (Communism as well as Fascism), opposition to Hitlerism, and affirmation of faith in the principles of freedom and self-government. John Fitch of the New York School of Social Work was chairman of the sponsoring committee; Philip Klein, also of the New York School, was vice-chairman; and Elinor Pettengill, secretary. A flier advertising a meeting of the group at the 1941 National Conference of Social Work, held in the first week of June, arraigned the SCMWA and the UOPWA for their opposition to the administration's Lend-Lease bill prior to its passage, and charged that the two unions were being used as channels for propaganda against defense measures and against aid to the enemies of totalitarianism. The new group wished "to dissipate the idea . . . that social work unionists "were opposed to aid to Britain, or minimized the significance of Hitlerism in its war to destroy democracy." Among the eighty names signing the flier were a number which had appeared a year and a half earlier appended to *Social Work Today*'s statement "Meeting Social Need," which affirmed strict neutrality in the war, including John Fitch and Lester Granger of the National Urban League, two of the four speakers at the June 3 meeting advertised. The flier was answered by another issued in the name of the Joint Committee of Trade Unions in Social Work, calling on social workers to bring pressure on the government to reverse the trend to involvement in the war, to extend and improve the social services supported by public funds, and to safeguard the Bill of Rights.[33]

These clashing views were aired at separate meetings of the two groups at the 1941 national conference, a conference dominated by the "defense" theme in all its multifold aspects, including an address, via radio, by Britain's minister of labor, Ernest Bevin. The Joint Committee of Trade Unions in Social Work held four sessions at which speakers reaffirmed the unions' position on the war, on the urgency of domestic problems, on their neglect by the government. The meeting of Social Work Unionists for Britain and Democracy heard Clinton Golden of the CIO's Steelworkers Organizing Committee assert that the administration's defense and aid-to-Britain effort was supported by a majority of CIO unions, as well as by the AFofL as a whole. "A victory by Hitler is a defeat of the democratic ideal," said Lester Granger of the National Urban League, another speaker; and the Reverend J. M. Hayes, of the National Catholic Welfare Conference, declared a Nazi victory would be a spiritual disaster for the world.[34]

That the position of Social Work Unionists for Britain and Democracy had broad support among social workers in general may be presumed from the treatment given the war and the American defense effort in the pages of the *Survey*, the social-work journal with a circulation four or five times that of *Social Work Today*. While there were no open appeals for military aid to Britain and its allies, there was no questioning either of the increasing magnitude of administration involvement in such aid, and the commitment, in Lend-Lease and other efforts, to the defeat of Germany. Numerous articles and news notes on the plight of the refugees in war-torn Europe, the fortitude of the British people in the defense of their homeland, the "heroic R.A.F." in the Battle of Britain, the contribution of British social work agencies in meeting the emergencies created by war shortages and Nazi bombing, the cooperative British-American program to evacuate children to the United States, and other aid-to-Britain volun-tary efforts—subjects avoided by *Social Work Today*—all assumed an identification with the British side of the war. Articles and news notes reflected an unquestioning acceptance—paralleling the position of the AASW—of the desirability of the coordination of social work and defense agencies to develop programs that would make use of social work facilities and social work skills to meet the problems created in communities affected by the defense effort. Identification of activities related to the American defense effort with the "defense of democracy," as it was put in a study guide issued by the American Association for the Study of Group Work, "Meeting New Responsibilities for Defense,"[35] was taken for granted, as was the belief that the defense of democracy did not stop at the water's edge.

A controversy somewhat similar to that between the Joint Committee of Trade Unions in Social Work and Social Work Unionists for Britain and Democracy had also taken place in the Spanish Refugee Relief Campaign, affecting the affiliated social workers committee. With the outbreak of hostilities, differences developed within the board of the campaign and among members of the staff, traceable to basic disagree-ment on the nature of the war. A majority favored using the American Friends Service Committee for distributing the campaign funds, charging that the International Coordinating Committee of the Campaign, whose offices were in Paris, was under Communist party control and therefore not to be dealt with under the terms of an earlier agreement to take a nonpartisan position on relief distribution. The minority preferred work-ing directly with the International Coordinating Committee and advo-cated criticism of the French government for its alleged ill-treatment of refugees and for an alleged decision to order the refugees back to Franco Spain, i.e., to imprisonment or execution. The charges were denied by French government officials, who termed them Communist propaganda. Some members of the minority group on the board and among the staff picketed French consulates in the name of the Campaign, carrying signs based on the charges. Three minority group members on the staff mailed an unauthorized letter to Campaign contributors inviting signatures in the name of the Campaign to a letter of protest to the French government. The executive director of the Campaign, the Reverend Herman Reissig, felt obliged to fire the three.[36]

The controversy darkened the last days of the Spanish Refugee Relief Campaign, which disintegrated with the Nazi occupation of France, and heightened tensions within the affiliated social workers committee between alleged Communist sympathizers, who identified with the minority, and the other members of the committee. It was an unhappy period for both groups.

Resolution

Then, like the plot resolution following the appearance of the *deus ex machina* in a Roman play, the issues dividing social workers on the war were suddenly resolved. The miracle in this case was the invasion of the Soviet Union by the Germans on June 22, 1941. Overnight many of the neutralists in the United States disappeared. Unions and organizations under Communist party control or influence became all-out supporters of aid to Britain—and Russia. In their Manichean world there were still two sides, but now they had different names. Before June 22, the two were warmongers and peace-lovers. After June 22, the two were pro-Nazis and anti-Nazis. The only pro-Nazis in the United States were a handful of members of the German-American Bund, some Italian Fascist sympathizers, and possibly some diehard America-Firsters. There were none among social workers. Other than a small group of dedicated pacifists, all social workers, it seemed, were now for American aid to the countries fighting Germany and Italy, the two principal Fascist belligerents.

In *Social Work Today*'s first issue to appear after the invasion of Russia, November 1941, the lead article, "Let's Face Facts This Time," written by Albert Deutsch, welfare editor of the New York daily *PM*, identified the war in Europe as one between "two mutually incompatible worlds—democracy and fascism. The future course of humankind for centuries to come will be decided by who survives—we or they. Social workers . . . have as large a stake in victory as any other single group in the population, for fascism is the annihilation of social work."

It was the Popular Front foreign policy again. All that had happened and been said between August 1939 and June 1941 was folded and put away, as though it had never happened or been said, nonhistory, and therefore not a subject for examination or discussion. Meeting in convention that fall, both the SCMWA and the UOPWA passed resolutions of endorsement of the administration's policy of aiding all nations allied against Hitler.

The executive committee of the AASW was in session December 7, 1941 when the news of Pearl Harbor broke on the radio. In a boxed statement on the front page of the next issue of the *Compass*, Kenneth Pray, executive committee chairman, urged the membership to give their unquestioning support in the "national emergency" to the association, which "must represent the profession of social work" as a whole.[37] Implicit in the plea, and so taken for granted that it was not even hinted at indirectly, was unquestioning support of the administration in the national emergency. World War II was not World War I. There would be no opposition to the war effort, either in social work, or elsewhere on the national scene.

It was the close of another chapter in social work history.

V At Decade's End:
Summary and Assessment

Chapter 18

The Economy: Winners and Losers

As the decade ended the Depression was by no means over. Gross National Product, it was true, was back to the 1929 level and better on both an absolute and per capita basis, when adjusted for price changes. But the scars left by the thirties were visible on all sides. Persons on public aid in December 1940 numbered 7 million. Another 2 million were employed on federal work programs based on need, and payments from National Youth Administration funds were going to three quarters of a million young people at the end of the year.[1]

Some of the other consequences were revealed by the 1940 census. The thirties registered the smallest ten-year population growth rate since the first census was taken in 1790—7 percent, or less than half the 16 percent gain from 1920 to 1930. The underlying reason was not the fall in the birth rate, a long-term phenomenon which had been going on since at least the middle of the last century, but the precipitate drop in immigration. (The marriage rate declined several points from '29 to '32, but quickly recovered and was above the '29 level by the end of the decade.) For the first time in its history, America no longer beckoned as the land of opportunity. "Give me your tired, your poor, . . . the wretched refuse of your teeming shore," the Statue of Liberty still proclaimed at its base, but the poor and the wretched were here and in number, and few Americans wanted more from the Europe to which Emma Lazarus had addressed her generous welcome in 1883. And as bad as things were there, few Europeans saw any advantage in migrating to America. Between 1929 and 1934 annual immigration from all countries decreased from 280,000 to 29,000, almost 90 percent. Immigration rose only moderately after recovery set in, reaching 83,000 by 1939, much of it induced not so much by better job prospects as by Nazi repressions in Germany and its newly-acquired territories, and the flight of emigrés which followed.[2]

The '40 census also documented the large shifts in the nation's population resulting from the search for jobs, the collapse of farm prices, and the great drought in the Middle West. With fewer employment opportunities, the movement from farm to city was temporarily halted during the decade and farm population actually grew slightly, but six states, largely farm states in the Middle West, lost population. The principal gainers were the states that presumably offered employment in the emerging agribusiness economic sector, notably California and Florida, and the District of Columbia, the seat of government and the new address for several score thousand additional federal workers.[3]

Mass unemployment, that most characteristic feature of the Great Depression, and its most vivid memory for those who lived through it, remained high throughout the decade. It dropped from a monthly average of 13 million in '33 to 8 million in '37, but it rose again to 10 million in '38 and receded only a million in each of the relatively good years of '39 and '40. In the latter year the average monthly number of jobless was 8 million, as it had been in '31 and '37, despite the gains in employment attributable to the defense effort. (The impact of the latter and of the increase in the armed forces didn't show up dramatically until 1941, when monthly average unemployment fell to 5.6 million.) By '39, however, the total number of persons at work was back to the '29 level, and in '40 it was higher than it had been in any previous year.[4]

And in composition the nation's working force was somewhat different from what it had been at the beginning of the decade. There were a million fewer farmers and farm laborers, but more workers in manufacturing, construction, and the service industries. The largest growth took place in government employment, reflecting the increasing role of the public sector in the economy. The number of federal workers rose 89 percent. Partly as a result of the several new federal-state programs, state and local government employment also went up, but not as much; the gain here was 22 percent.[5]

The paradox of a return to '29 levels in GNP and in employment, accompanied by continued high unemployment, was the result of two factors: the growth in the labor force, which added over 7 million persons to the job market in the decade '30–'40,[6] and the 25 percent gain in productivity per worker (as measured by output per manhour), data on which were emerging from the National Research Project referred to in chapter 14.[7] The sick economy was regaining its health, not fast enough, however, to pick up the additional demands put on it by a larger population and a more efficient utilization of its work force.

The Depression was by no means over as the decade closed, but the focus of administration effort was no longer recovery; it was the war in Europe and the strengthening of America's defenses. Public sentiment was pro-Ally but opposed through 1939 and 1940 to any governmental action that would give the United States a stake in the conflict. Its neutrality was prompted by a concern with the possible threat American involvement in the war posed to the social gains of the New Deal. It rejected, however, the antidemocratic ethos at the heart of Fascism and its sympathies in the main were with the victims of the Fascist triumphs in the initial years of the war.

It was World War II that abolished unemployment and wiped out the last remnants of the Depression. By 1944, with over 11 million persons in the armed forces and production for war at its peak, the number of jobless fell below a million for the first time since 1926.[8] Business failures, from a high of 32,000 in '32, sank below 10,000 in '36 and '37, and below a thousand by the last year of the war.[9] And agriculture had not only revived, never had its output been so high or in so much demand.[10]

As in other depressions in America's past, there were winners and losers in the thirties. The great majority were losers: the jobless, the families with earners on part-time or intermittent work or reduced wage levels, indebted and dispossessed farmers and sharecroppers, the many who went hungry, young people who took to the road to seek jobs and subsisted often on handouts, oldsters cut off from family support by the reduced income or lack of income of a son or daughter.

The winners, few in number, were a mixed lot: Wall Street scavengers who bought up bankrupt companies for a song at the bottom of the market, discarded the decayed parts and sold what was left at a high profit when the worst was over; bankers who foreclosed failing companies or farms and acquired assets far in excess of the debt owed; exporters of scrap metal to an iron-hungry, rearming Japan; advertising geniuses who started new companies and were smart enough to sign up popular radio personalities to huckster their clients' products over the air; popular songwriters; movie stars with million-dollar contracts, and the executives and the owners of the companies in whose productions they starred. Even in the lowest year of the Depression, 1932, there were twenty persons who reported a net income of one million dollars or more to the Bureau of Internal Revenue.[11]

When recovery set in, not all shared equally in the gain in income. Corporation net profits more than tripled from '34 to '39, but total wage and salary income rose by less than half in the same period. Some of the growth in wage and salary income represented more persons at work, some a longer workweek, and some a rise in the wage level.[12]

The strong not only survived but acquired additional strength. Fifty-nine corporations reported a net income of $5 million or more in 1932; by 1937 the number had gone up to 248.[13] Concentration in industry, documented by Berle and Means in 1932 in *The Modern Corporation and Private Property*, was accelerated by the Depression. The larger corporations swallowed or destroyed their frailer competitors, emerging at decade's end to dominate the economy from greater heights.

The wage gains in the main went similarly to workers in industries where the unions were strongest. A revived labor movement, encouraged by a sympathetic administration and protected by new legislation, was largely responsible for the growth in hourly rates in the latter half of the decade. As compared with the twenties, there were more unions, they had more members, they were more aggressive, and the bigger ones were organized on an industry-wide rather than a craft basis.

Paradoxically, the split in the labor movement with the establishment of the CIO in 1935 augmented rather than reduced the size and influence of the AFofL, thanks in part to recovery, in part to a more aggressive leadership, in part to a new legislation requiring collective bargaining by management. By 1939, after vigorous organizing drives marked by sit-down strikes and police and National Guard violence, the CIO could claim almost 4 million members, as many as were in the revived AFofL. The CIO was solidly entrenched in the auto, steel, rubber, and coal industries. For the first time in their history some of the largest corporations in the country, including General Motors, Ford, Chrysler, U.S. Steel, Goodyear, were under union contract.

It was this development which accounted largely for the post-1933 gains in wages made by workers in manufacturing, mining, construction, railroad transportation, communications and public utilities. After falling a little over one third from '29 to '33, for example, the average annual earnings per full-time employee in mining rose 38 percent from '33 to '39. Similarly, average annual earnings in construction, which had dropped 48 percent between '29 and '33, made a gain of 46 percent in the succeeding six years; workers in manufacturing, whose average annual earnings had fallen 30 percent from '29 to '33, experienced a gain of 26 percent from '33 to '39; while railroad workers and workers in communications and public utilities were earning more in '39 than in '29.

On the other hand, such an unorganized field as domestic service regained less than a third of the loss in average annual earnings sustained between '29 and '33. A like comment may be made about changes in earnings in laundries, hotels, hospitals, offices, and retail establishments, industries characterized by either weak or nonexistent union activity in the thirties.[14]

(The differences between the workers in industries that prospered in recovery and those in industries that did not were not all attributable, of course, to the extent of unionization. The second group of industries was, and to a very large extent still is today, marked by low skill requirements, few technological advances, and a relatively high proportion of women and minority group workers, traditionally discriminated against in wages and salaries paid, all factors making for a disadvantaged position in the economy in both recession and recovery.)

In the aggregate, these mixed trends yielded a slight gain in income equality in the population as a whole. In 1929, it has been estimated, 31 percent of all families and unattached individuals had personal incomes below $2,000; this percentage had dropped to 28 by 1941. Similarly, the percentage of households with incomes of $10,000 or more fell from 19 to 13 percent over these eleven years. The share of total income received by the top 5 percent of the population dropped from 26 to 22 percent; of the top 1 percent from 15 to 11 percent.[15]

There were other winners in the thirties, not in money but in other rewards. These were the lawyers, the engineers, the economists, natural and social scientists of all kinds, persons with administrative or managerial experience, who flocked to Washington and to federal regional offices all over the country to man the agencies created by the New Deal. Some had civil service appointments in new and old agencies; some were on the WPA payroll. For nearly all, FDR was a hero because he was the first President in modern times to give government employment in any substantial numbers to artists, scholars, and intellectuals—painters, actors, musicians, dancers, writers, historians, economists, statisticians, psychologists, anthropologists, political scientists of all kinds, and people in the humanities.

They were more fortunate than most of their fellow-Americans in having jobs and job security and in earning a little more than their compeers in private employment. But the compensation many cherished most was their sense of participation in one of the greatest adventures that could befall a person beginning a career, the attempt to redress the social and economic wrongs of the old order, to help fashion a new order, to rescue a nation. They were for the most part young, enthusiastic, idealistic. They considered themselves lucky to have been born when they were, to be fitted by education and some experience to meet the requirements of the jobs that needed filling, and to be chosen. And indeed they were lucky. The country was in bad shape, but paradoxically it was also a time of hope, of great expectations. The great bulk of their fellow-Americans may have felt despair about the future; they felt the optimism and excitement of a brave new world coming.

The brave new world was not the future Lincoln Steffens saw in the U.S.S.R. in 1919, the future that worked; or even the planned economy, made-in-the-U.S. model, that Soule, Bingham, Dewey and other liberals saw in the early thirties as the only way out of the bind into which old-fashioned laissez-faire capitalism had put America. The basic order survived. The economic and political systems that prevailed in 1929, were still very much with us in 1940. America was still a citadel of capitalism, its economy dominated by privately owned corporations, its politics by two parties, neither of which challenged the system.

The brave new world envisaged by both Communists and noncommunist, more-or-less radicalized liberals assumed a scenario which never developed. There was, to begin with, a conviction that the Depression was so severe that capitalism could not survive and would be, had to be, replaced by an economic system based on central planning and designed for production for use, not profit. So sweeping a change required for implementation a radicalized and politically potent working class, for which Europe provided the only model. In the pure form of the model in socialist theory, the working class was driven to revolt by exploitation and by hunger resulting from repeated breakdowns in the system. Unfortunately the only nation in which a successful socialist revolution had taken place in the twentieth century was that industrially backward country, Russia. Short-lived socialist revolutions of a sort had been suppressed in postwar Germany and Hungary. In Germany and the other advanced industrial countries, the ascendant Socialist party was a social-democratic parliamentary party committed to majority rule, not the kind of party that took to the streets, as in Russia, gun in hand, to change the system.

Whether the transformation to a centrally planned production-for-use economy followed the revolutionary or the parliamentary social-democratic path, a class-conscious, politically united working class was essential, since it furnished the mass base for the party providing the leadership for the changeover from capitalism to socialism.

What went wrong with the scenario?

The class consciousness characteristic of the European industrial worker was not felt by the great majority of wage and salary earners in the United States, critics of the scenario were to say later. It was not felt because of factors present here but absent or only minimally present in the old world.

Diversity of national origin was one factor, promoting distinctions expressed in ethnic pecking orders and exacerbated by periodic outbreaks of nativism. This was exploited by employers through such devices as preferment in employment and promotion opportunities for persons of selected ancestry, intended to encourage divisiveness among employees and to reinforce, at both extremes of the pecking order, ties based on ancestry rather than economic class.

Geographic mobility was another, loosening attachments formed by plant or city of employment, and foreign to the experience of Europe's place-bound settled wage earners. Social mobility was a third factor, long-range in its nature, to be sure, but observed by the parents' generation, particularly among immigrants, in the more favorable circumstances of their children's generation. This was interpreted by the parents as evidence of the nonexistence of fixed socio-economic classes in America, a social attitude rarely observed in the class-ridden society of the typical European country.

And there was popular sovereignty, which, where present in Europe, had been won only as a result of political struggle by the working-class party. It was taken for granted in the United States, where every citizen who wanted to could vote (the blacks in the South were an exception), fostering the illusion that, because the people elected the President and Congress, they controlled the government and the further illusion that, because in voting they chose between two parties, they were exercising a genuine choice, overlooking or perhaps indifferent to the fact that both were committed to the preservation of the system.[16]

These factors, advanced by some historians to explain the failure of America's wage and salary earners to develop a political party of their own, had been operative, to be sure, since at least the industrial explosion of the post–Civil War period, for almost three quarters of a century. But they had a particular relevancy in the Great Depression of the thirties, when, if ever, a serious threat to the prevailing order might have developed.

Other influences were at work to dampen such a threat.

"Farewell to reform," a disillusioned John Chamberlain had said in 1932, but the America of 1940 was a capitalist America reformed, purged of some of its grosser abuses, yet basically the same America it had been in '32 and '29. The reforms had put the protection of the law behind labor's right to collective bargaining via the National Labor Relations Act, vigorously enforced in the thirties by a pro-union National Labor Relations Board and staff, and taken advantage of by a militant, resurgent labor movement to organize big industry and to win higher wages and fringe benefits for its members. Social welfare and social insurance programs had been established, underpinning family income among the poor, the near poor, and the potentially poor.

These measures gave both groups, whose membership overlapped, a form of property right in prevailing political and economic arrangements, hardly as valuable as the property rights given big industry via tax loopholes, guaranteed markets, government contracts, tariffs, and a foreign policy which favored and protected American investment abroad; or the land and water development giveaways to the mining, lumbering, agribusiness, and grazing interests; but a property right nevertheless. Wage earners who could afford to buy their own homes benefited also from the new federal housing-mortgage guarantees intended to help the middle class, still another form of property right in the system. Giveaways, made possible by America's enormous wealth, had been part of its history from the beginning, starting with the land grants of the crown, preceding the first English settlements here. The biggest and most powerful, to be sure, got the most—the railroads in the nineteenth century, for example, were given more free land for spanning the continent than the family farmers who picked up a measly 160 acres under the 1862 Homestead Act—but nearly every group got something, some property right; and property rights have been at the heart of the American system since at least 1787 and account for the loyalties which bind individuals to it, despite periodic clashes among the different interests when in conflict.[17]

The reforms of the thirties created new forms of property rights for wage earners, the poor and near poor, and for farmers receiving benefit payments, reforms which by the end of the decade yielded a somewhat greater income equality in the population as a whole. It was a gain which appealed to the only groups from which an effective demand for a fundamental change in the system could come, and sustained an attachment to it too firm for either the Socialist or Communist parties to disturb. It was this loyalty which made possible the success of an improvising, often baffled, but never discouraged Roosevelt in bringing the country through the decade with its economic, social, and political order essentially intact.

Chapter 19

Social Work:
The Thirties as a Watershed

Meeting Need

The thirties were a watershed in social work. The decade saw a profound revolution in the country's concept of responsibility for the treatment of economic need, actual and potential. Programs established to give it expression had a significant impact on the understanding the public and the profession itself had of social work's basic role, on the nature and scale of the activities in which social workers were engaged, on the size of expenditures and funding sources for social welfare (broadly defined to include social work, social insurance, and related programs) on the number of social workers, and on social work education.

It took perhaps a depression as severe as that of the thirties to bring the United States into the twentieth century and into the company of other developed industrial countries, in accepting public responsibility for meeting needs arising out of disparities in the volume, regularity, and distribution of the income the economic order created. Until the thirties, wage loss due to unemployment, illness, disability, death, or retirement by reason of age of the family earner, had been met by such sources as savings, borrowing, gifts, or loans from relatives, friends, fraternal and friendly societies, the church, and, as a last resort, charity in the form of assistance by social agencies under voluntary auspices.

This last-resort function fixed social work in the public mind as a net into which society's failures fell, from the penniless oldster to the homeless alcoholic, a net with holes, but a net nevertheless which caught in every generation the people who had exhausted the traditional resources available in an earlier society to the poor. By 1929, true, a beginning had been made in public provision for meeting economic need for selected groups in the population, in the form of mothers' aid and old age pensions in a number of states, but the grants were small, eligibility was restricted, and geographical coverage limited by the county-option feature of the law. Social workers, employed for the most part in voluntary agencies, tended to look askance at such programs, because of the generally untrained character of the staff employed and the fixed size of the grant, violative of one of the fundamental axioms of social work, which was to vary assistance according to family circumstances. With some exceptions, they preferred to have the poor remain a responsibility of voluntary social work, in the same last-resort sense as seen by the public at large, a concept living in uneasy partnership with the social casework philosophy dominant in the twenties, which tended to minimize the economic-need component present in the problems deemed appropriate for and amenable to the services offered by social agencies.

The inability of voluntary sources, despite heroic fund-raising drives, to meet destitution on the scale created by the Great Depression forced state and local governments to assume an increasing share of the cost of assistance to needy families. It was a shift welcomed by social work's leadership, which recognized as early as 1930 that the burden was not only beyond the capacity of the traditional community-supported social work structure, but in principle a public rather than a private obligation. By 1932 at least 80 percent of the assistance to families in need was administered by public agencies funded from tax sources. The establishment of the Federal Emergency Relief Administration (FERA) in 1933 marked the beginning of federal sharing in the cost of public assistance and of the development of minimum standards of eligibility and grants related to need. Although terminated in 1935 for the total needy population, federal responsibility for financing all or part of the assistance needs of selected groups in the population has been continuous since.

From considerably fewer than a million in 1929, the number of persons on assistance or work-relief programs rose to 9 million by 1940. During the same period, annual expenditures increased from somewhat under $100 million to $3.6 billion. The growth was entirely in public aid. Assistance derived from voluntary sources fell from something like a fourth of the total in 1929 to one percent or less in 1940, a shift of the most far-reaching consequences for the relative role of the public and private sectors in social work.[1]

Some of the increase in the volume and relative importance of public aid reflected the growth from 1936 on in the three categorical assistance programs (Aid to Dependent Children, Old Age Assistance, and Aid to the Blind) under the Social Security Act. The requirement of state (and in most states also local) participation in funding these programs, as well as the withdrawal of the federal government from general assistance after 1935, was responsible for the dominant place of the states in sources of funds for public assistance in 1940: 47 percent, as compared with 29 percent from the federal government and 24 percent from local governments.[2]

We may attribute to the establishment of public assistance programs in almost every city and county in the country in the first half of the decade, and to the public assistance titles of the Social Security Act after 1935, the substantial growth which took place in the thirties in the number of social workers. "Social and welfare workers" numbered 31,000 in the 1930 census; 70,000 in the 1940 census. The increase, 117 percent, was greater than that of any other professional group.[3] The figures from both census years exclude social agency employees classified as nonprofessional, not only clerical and maintenance workers, but case aides, receptionists, and others who conducted initial interviews with relief applicants or assisted in the completion of forms required for the determination of eligibility and the amount of the assistance grant. Marion Hathway estimated in 1939 that 150,000 persons were employed in social work in that year in a professional or semiprofessional capacity.[4]

Among her 150,000 were, of course, fully qualified social workers, as defined by the membership requirements of the American Association of Social Workers (AASW), who had earlier been drafted to run the FERA and its state and local counterparts, to fill strategic slots in WPA and local work-relief programs, to flesh out the Bureau of Public Assistance when the Social Security Board was created in 1935, and to make possible an enlarged and strengthened federal Children's Bureau. The great majority worked, however, in the newly established or newly expanded local public welfare departments, were newly recruited and untrained, except for such training as they acquired on the job.

Although it doubled in size between 1930 and 1940, the AASW had only 11,000 members in the latter year,[5] perhaps one in ten or fifteen of the personnel in the field with professional or paraprofessional responsibilities. The contrast is eloquent, not of AASW's high admission standards, but of the rapid expansion of employment opportunities in the field and the lack of qualified personnel to fill all the positions created.

To help overcome the gap, seventeen new schools of social work were established between 1930 and 1940, raising to forty the number in operation in the latter year.[6]

Perhaps the most significant change in the decade for social work was the establishment of a public welfare department in almost every county, stimulated initially by FERA but made almost mandatory under the public assistance and child health and welfare titles of the Social Security Act. Where only a few hundred were in existence in 1930, there were several thousand in 1940, permanent in character, and beginning to meet the requirements of the 1939 amendments to the act relating to the establishment of a merit system. The federal-state character of the public assistance and child health and welfare titles, expressed in making the state the recipient of the federal share, and in the requirement of an approved state plan to qualify for federal aid, strengthened and enlarged state public welfare units. Where nothing had existed in 1930, there was in being in 1940 a complex skein of federal-state-local relationships, defining mutual responsibilities, setting standards, and authorizing the monitoring of operations and performance. It had, and would continue to have, a transforming influence on social work.

Many social workers, of course, remained outside these programs, working in voluntary agencies and in the traditional public institutions and hospitals left relatively untouched by the changes of the thirties. But the profession as a whole was deeply affected by the new place in American life of national social welfare programs, towards the creation and operation of which it contributed not only personnel, but goals, philosophy, structure, and standards of operation.

Important as were the public assistance and the child health and welfare titles of the Social Security Act, its principal significance lay in the social insurance titles. They made the act one of the major achievements of the New Deal. It established the principle, new for the United States, that unemployed and retired workers, and (as amended in 1939) the dependents of retired workers and the dependent survivors of deceased workers, were entitled to benefit as of right, and need not, as in the past, turn to private or public assistance when resources were exhausted. In this respect the act, if only in principle, since experience in the forties and fifties demonstrated the need for public assistance supplementation of benefits for some individuals, met a cherished goal in social work by relieving it of the obligation to meet the basic requirements of persons who were the responsibility of society as a whole, rather than private philanthropy or government in its role as a last resort (public assistance) for the needy.

The act, to be sure, fell short of the social insurance programs in the advanced industrial countries in Europe in terms of risks to income covered (disability and temporary illness were absent, for example, in the American system) and benefit amounts as a percent of wages, and in the absence of a government contribution to the cost of the program. Neither did it include, as in some other countries, any provision for meeting the costs of medical care. Friends in both the administration and the public at large viewed it as a first step only and were not long in proposing expansion and improvement. Some of the limitations noted were overcome in amendments enacted in later decades, but not entirely, and the issues and the political controversies they arouse have remained as a claim on America's social conscience, and a part of the unfinished business of Congress in the years since. Among them is health insurance, a want met only in small part by the Medicare program for the aged adopted in the 1965 amendments; and the battle social work fought and lost in the thirties for a general assistance title, which is periodically revived, most recently in the form of guaranteed minimum income or negative income tax plans.

Social workers took the lead in the development of the public assistance and child welfare titles of the act; their role in the evolution and adoption of the other titles is more difficult to assess. There were social workers on the staff of the Committee on Economic Security whose recommendations were the basis for the administration-supported Wagner-Lewis bill which, as amended, became the act. Social workers were among the most persuasive witnesses heard in the hearings on the bill in House and Senate, just as they were earlier in the decade in hearings on bills putting the federal government into the relief business. The American Association of Social Workers was divided on whether to endorse the administration bill, but its strong support for the principle of social insurance was clear as early as 1930. To attribute to social work a major role in the passage of the bill, or even its introduction and serious consideration by Congress, is to exaggerate its influence. Administration endorsement and congressional support may be more convincingly linked to the educational and lobbying efforts of such organizations as John Andrew's American Association for Labor Legislation, Abraham Epstein's American Association for Social Security, the support of church, consumer, and women's groups, and above all to the work on its behalf by organized labor. Not to be overlooked is the pressure from the left contributed by the endorsement given the more ambitious Lundeen bill by the Unemployed Councils of America, and some of the more militant unions; in a turbulent decade receptive to radical ideas, this lent the administration's Wagner-Lewis bill, if not a conservative image, the politically attractive aspect of a minimum, sensible, realistic program.

The Dissenting Left and its Legacy

One of the more striking aspects of the response of social work to the Depression was the rise of a dissenting left which questioned the moral validity of the economic and social order and pressed for changes going beyond the reforms just listed. The views expressed by such eloquent spokesmen for the left as Mary van Kleeck, Harry Lurie, and Bertha Reynolds, linked social work in the thirties with the larger vision of a just social order given high priority in the program espoused by social work in the Progressive Era, and served as a reminder as well of the profession's kinship with the liberal-radical tradition in American political life.

Such mass base in social work as the dissenting left had was provided by the Rank-and-File Movement.

To assess the Rank-and-File Movement in social work, particularly in relation to the extent to which it achieved its goals by the end of the decade, presents a number of problems. Some arise out of the changing nature of the goals, some from the restraints imposed by limiting to ten years the examination of developments whose impact requires a longer period to measure.

The broad aim of the group founding the Rank-and-File Movement was to raise the political consciousness of social workers. The emphasis on the breakdown of the economic system and its responsibility for widespread distress was meant to wean social workers away from an absorption in the individual and his problems, a basic aspect of the social casework philosophy dominant in the twenties, taught in social work schools, explicated in standard social work texts, and from which derived the accepted wisdom that the primary task of the social worker was to adjust the individual to his environment. Raising the political consciousness of social workers would, it was hoped, radicalize them; that is, persuade them of the need for a fundamental reorganization of an oppressive unplanned economic and political order, in which the rewards went to the rich and the well-placed, and which was responsible not only for deprivation among the poor and near poor, but for emotional problems regarded by social workers as amenable only to the special insights provided by social casework. In a socially just, rational order, not only would the basic economic needs of people be met, but the incidence of emotional maladjustment would diminish sharply, if not disappear altogether, since it was social and economic, not individual or family, in origin.

Measures of the level of political consciousness, and of the number of adherents each level attracted, whether the old-fashioned ideological kind conveyed by that term in the thirties, or the more recent kinds embodied in the black-is-beautiful and women's liberation movements, still await development. There is some reason to believe that several hundred social workers were politically radicalized in the early thirties. It is difficult to determine the relative contribution to the process of the founding group of the Rank-and-File Movement, on the one hand, and, on the other, the broad influence of the swing to the left among liberal writers and journalists, which shaped the ideas teachers, lawyers, and other professionals, as well as social workers, had of the nature of our society.

One is on firmer ground in moving to the activities through which the Rank-and-File Movement expressed itself programmatically: advocacy of a closer alliance with the labor movement via the organization of social work unions; support of the demands by organizations of the unemployed, and later of WPA workers, for a more adequate federally aided public relief program for people in need, a full-time federal job program paying union wages for all the unemployed, and a social insurance system covering all risks to wage income, financed out of general revenues; nondiscrimination in the treatment of blacks and other minorities as recipients of public assistance or work relief jobs, and as employees in

public welfare departments; opportunities for a fair hearing of the grievances of persons on assistance or job programs; support of a federally
financed program of jobs, vocational training and educational opportunities for youth; and lastly, of a more general character and related to the
broad objective of raising political consciousness, promotion among
social workers of an awareness of, and an appropriate response to, the
growing danger of a Fascist triumph in Europe.

The social welfare and social insurance elements in the Rank-and-File
Movement's program staked out more advanced positions in these two
areas than were taken by the establishment in social work as represented
by the AASW. The latter's stand was to some extent influenced by the
Rank-and-File Movement adherents among its members, few in number
but articulate, and by the persuasive voices of van Kleeck, Lurie, and
Reynolds in its leadership. On these and related issues, however, the
tendency of the profession was to identify with the policy of the administration in Washington, taking issue with it only on its abandonment of
federal aid for general assistance, both in prematurely closing down the
Federal Emergency Relief Administration program and in omitting general assistance from the public assistance titles of the Social Security Act,
and on the size and timing of changes in the federal work program for the
unemployed.

Support for the social welfare and social insurance positions of the
Rank-and-File Movement, even during the years of the second New Deal,
when the Movement switched its image from rebels to part of the flag-
waving majority, never extended beyond a minority of the social workers
in the country. At its peak, the circulation of its magazine, *Social Work
Today,* was 6,000, as compared with the 25,000 or so of the *Survey,* the
leading general periodical in the field, always more representative of the
central direction of the profession in issues examined and positions taken.

The principal triumph of the Rank-and-File Movement in the thirties
was the introduction of unions in the field of social work. It was frustrated
by the jurisdictional claims of other unions in its initial aim of one big
union for employees of social agencies, but by the end of the decade unions
affiliated with the CIO and the AFofL claimed 10,000 or so members in
the public welfare field and approximately 3,000 in voluntary agencies.
Unions were appropriate in a social work characterized by government as
the principal employer; by large agencies; by a bureaucratic structure
regulating staff relationships, authority layers, and personnel practices; by
recognition by employees of shared economic interests with fellow-em-
ployees engaged in other programs and providing other services, and of
the advantages of joint action in defending these interests at budget
hearings and in hearings before appropriation committees. The destruction of these unions during the anti-Communist hysteria of the early fifties

takes us beyond the period covered by the present narrative, but does not diminish the significance of the achievement effected in the thirties in acceptance by the profession of the place of unions in social work, in union recognition by public welfare departments and boards of voluntary agencies, and in the economic gains unions won for their members.

Mixed results attended the attainment of the more difficult goal of sensitizing social workers to the menace of Fascism in Europe in the years 1935–39, and its successor as a menace in 1939–41, American involvement in the war in Europe. As a concept for the solution of international tensions, as a slogan, collective security attracted little attention in social work outside the movement. The Movement's most successful effort in terms of general approval in the profession, as expressed in the prominence of the persons represented on its executive committee and money raised, was the Social Workers Committee to Aid Spanish Democracy, perhaps because social workers by and large saw themselves as liberals, and support for the loyalist side in the civil war in Spain engaged the sympathies of American liberals as no issue had since the Sacco-Vanzetti case of the twenties.

The Rank-and-File Movement also succeeded in giving expression to the general yearning for neutrality among social workers in the first year of the war in Europe, in its January 1940 statement in *Social Work Today,* "Meeting Social Need: A Peace Program," a statement signed by most of the top social workers of the country. The adherence of the movement to this fixed position until Russia was invaded, its disregard of the moral differences between the belligerents, particularly its sudden blindness to Fascism as a menace after the Hitler-Stalin pact of 1939, contributed in no small measure to the loss of Movement adherents after 1940 and to the demise of *Social Work Today* in 1942.[7]

Initially hostile to what it regarded as the Establishment in social work represented by the AASW, and the American Public Welfare Association (APWA), the Rank-and-File Movement adopted a more conciliatory attitude towards the profession in the middle and later years of the decade, advocating joint action on issues of common concern, such as personnel practices, in-service training, and the administration's social welfare program. Among some of the liberal leaders of the AASW there was a sympathetic attitude toward the aspirations of the Movement; conservatives viewed it with reserve and at times with hostility. Perhaps the biggest victory achieved by the movement in its relationship with the profession was to obtain acceptance by the APWA, and by leading committees and the larger chapters of the AASW, of the legitimacy of unions in social work.

Viewed in its broadest aspect, the Rank-and-File Movement and the ripples it raised in social work may be regarded as one manifestation of the ferment in political and economic ideas and the drift to the left in the liberal professions which marked the decade. It left no lasting legacy, but at least it contributed to a heightened awareness among social workers of the need for a broad, adequately financed, integrated social welfare and social insurance system appropriate to the problems created by an advanced industrial society, comprehending a guaranteed minimum income, government work and retraining programs for the unemployed not absorbed by the private sector of the economy, and of the need for health insurance, goals only partially realized in the four decades since. In its emphasis on nondiscrimination, and recognition of the right of public assistance recipients to a hearing for and the adjustment of their grievances, the movement in some measure anticipated the civil rights legislation, government affirmative action employment programs for minorities, and the antipoverty measures of the sixties, measures that stressed recipient participation in policy-making and democracy in the relations between administration and program beneficiaries.

Perhaps to see these thumbprints of the future in the not fully articulated causes supported by the Rank-and-File Movement is to exaggerate its contemporary significance. At least it helps diminish the distance which separates the seventies and the eighties from the thirties in social work.

Notes and References

Abbreviations, Symbols, and Short Titles Used in Notes and References Cited

Archives   Social Welfare History Archives Center, University of Minnesota.
Compass   Monthly organ of the American Association of Social Workers,
              the *Compass* was published from 1921 to 1947, when the name
              was changed to the *Social Work Journal*.
HSUS   *Historical Statistics of the United States: Colonial Times to 1970.*
              U.S. Department of Commerce, Bureau of the Census, 1975.
NCSW   Proceedings of the National Conference of Social Work.
NYT   The *New York Times* on microfilm.
Survey   The *Survey Midmonthly.*
SWT   *Social Work Today.*

Introduction

1. Books found helpful in locating changes in social work thinking within the
   broader stream of the political and intellectual currents of the period
   include (year of first publication given in brackets): Daniel Aaron, Writers
   on the Left, New York: Harcourt, Brace and World, 1961); James B.
   Gilbert, *Writers and Partisans: A History of Literary Radicalism in Amer-
   ica* (New York: Wiley, 1968); Richard Hofstadter, *The American Political
   Tradition* (New York: Vintage, 1974 [1948]); Irving Howe and Lewis
   Coser, *The American Communist Party: A Critical History* (1919–57)
   (Boston: Beacon Press, 1957); Richard Pells, *Radical Visions and American
   Dreams* (New York: Harper and Row, 1973); Arthur Schlesinger, *The Age
   of Roosevelt*, vols. 1–3 (Boston: Houghton Mifflin, 1957–60); Rita James
   Simon, ed. *As We Saw the Thirties* (Urbana: University of Illinois Press,
   1967); Harvey Swados, ed. *The American Writer and the Great Depression*
   (Indianapolis: Bobbs-Merrill, 1966); Studs Terkel, *Hard Times* (New
   York: Avon, 1971 [1970]); Frank A. Warren, *Liberals and Communism:
   The "Red Decade" Revisited* (Bloomington, Ind.: Indiana University
   Press, 1966); Edmund Wilson, *The American Earthquake* (New York:
   Octagon, 1971 [1958]). A good part of Wilson's book originally appeared
   in *The American Jitters: A Year of the Slump* (New York: Scribner's,

1932). The books cited here also served as sources for some of the general background referred to in the text of the book. Page references are to the editions given above.

Chapter One. A World Turned Upside Down

1. Archives. Excerpt from address by Joanna Colcord at Conference of American Association of Social Workers on National Economic Objectives for Social Work, April 22, 1933.
2. *HSUS*. p. 511.
3. *World Almanac and Book of Facts, 1933*. Entry for January 2 under chronology for 1932.
4. Edmund Wilson, *The American Earthquake*, 1971, p. 171.
5. *NYT*, May 31, 1931.
6. Richard Hofstadter, *The American Political Tradition*, 1974; pp. 386, 387.
7. Arthur Schlesinger, *The Age of Roosevelt*, vol. 1, p. 238.
8. Hofstadter, *American Political Tradition*, p. 391.
9. Wilson, *American Earthquake*, p. 487.
10. *NYT*, September 28, 1932.
11. *HSUS*, p. 126.
12. Schlesinger, *Age of Roosevelt*, vol. 1, p. 249.
13. Schlesinger, *Age of Roosevelt*, vol. 1, p. 241.
14. Schlesinger, *Age of Roosevelt*, vol. 1, p. 175.
15. The events cited in this section may be found in the *NYT* for the dates given in the text.
16. *NYT*, January 23, 1931.
17. *Compass*, November 1936, p. 15.
18. Wilson, *American Earthquake*, p. 307.
19. Hofstadter, *American Political Tradition*, p. 399.
20. Hofstadter, *American Political Tradition*, p. 400.
21. *Public Welfare News* (American Public Welfare Association), November 1932.

Chapter Two. An Unprepared Social Work

1. HSUS, pp. 126, 199, 211, 224.
2. *Social Case Work, Generic and Specific*, p. 17.
3. Russell Sage Foundation, *Social Work Year Book 1929*, 1930. Article on education for social work.
4. Russell Sage Foundation, *Social Work Year Book 1929*, 1930; *Social Work Year Book 1933*, 1933. Articles on social work as a profession. The count of 36,000 in Walter West's 1933 article included 31,241 "social and welfare workers," 4,270 "probation workers," and 500 "keepers of charitable institutions." The reference in the text to the admission requirements of the AASW comes from an article in the *Compass* for September 1932. The same article notes that minimum education and training admission re-

quirements would be raised on July 1, 1933, under a standard adopted at
the 1929 annual meeting, to two years of college, plus a year of training at
a school of social work, plus two years of experience in social work.
5. A brief general treatment of the Progressive Era will be found in Richard
Hofstadter's *The Age of Reform* (New York: Knopf, 1955). Representative
documents from the period appear in *The Progressive Movement 1900–15*,
ed. with introduction by Richard Hofstadter (Englewood Cliffs, N.J.:
Prentice-Hall, 1963); and *Years of Conscience: The Muckrakers,* ed. with
introduction by Harvey Swados (Cleveland: World, 1962). The role of
social workers and the mutual influence on one another of social workers
and Progressive Era leaders is treated in Robert H. Bremner's *From the
Depths: The Discovery of Poverty in the United States* (New York: New
York University Press, 1956).
6. *Proceedings of the Thirty-Ninth National Conference of Charities and Corrections*, 1912, pp. 376–395.
7. Donald Johnson and Kirk Porter, eds. *National Party Platforms, 1846–1972*,
1973, pp. 175–182.
8. *HSUS*, p. 1073.
9. Hofstadter, *Age of Reform*, p. 241.
10. Sources cited in note 5, supra.
11. Jacob Fisher, "The Early Social Insurance Movement in the United States,"
1951, p. 10. (Unpublished manuscript in the Archives Collection, Library
of the Department of Health, Education and Welfare, Washington, D.C.)
12. Bremner, *From the Depths*, p. 254.
13. Treated in detail in Fisher, "Early Social Insurance Movement."
14. Bremner, *From the Depths*, p. 138.
15. Russell Sage Foundation, *Social Work Year Book 1935*, 1935. Articles on state
mother's aid and old age pension laws.

Chapter Three: Social Work in Dissent

1. Compass, December 1930.
2. *Compass*, November 1930.
3. Wilson's articles, as noted in the text, appeared in book form in *The American
Jitters*, 1932, now out of print. They were incorporated, however, in *The
American Earthquake*, 1958.
4. Ralph G. Hurlin, "Need for a Permanent Program for National Relief
Statistics," in *This Business of Relief: Proceedings of the Delegate Conference of the American Association of Social Workers*, Washington, D.C.,
February 14–16, 1936, pp. 120–127.
5. *Social Security Bulletin*, May 1942, "Public and Private Aid in 116 Urban
Areas, Calendar Year 1941." The article includes annual data for the years
1929–41 on expenditures for assistance in 116 urban areas, by source and
program. Expenditures from "private funds" increased from $11,430,000
in 1929 to $58,903,000 in 1932. The data were derived from the statistical
series referred to in n. 4.

6. Schlesinger, *Age of Roosevelt*, vol. 1, p. 172; *Compass*, October 1931.
7. *HSUS*, p. 340; *Social Welfare Expenditures under Public Programs in the United States, 1929–66*, U.S. Department of Health, Education, and Welfare, Social Security Administration, Office of Research and Statistics, Research Report no. 25, 1968, pp. 87, 207, 208. The reference in the text to "at least 80 percent" is based upon the relationship between the public aid data for 1932, cited here, and the "private funds" data for 1932, cited in the source given in n. 5, after account is taken of the differences between calendar year and fiscal year and in coverage (116 urban areas vs. the country as a whole).
8. Schlesinger, *Age of Roosevelt*, vol 1., p. 250.
9. *Compass*, October 1931.
10. *Compass*, June 1931.
11. *Compass*, December 1931.
12. *Compass*, October 1932.
13. *Compass*, December 1931, January 1932, February 1932.
14. *Compass*, October 1931.
15. *Compass*, December 1931.
16. *Compass*, May 1932.
17. *Social Service Review*, September 1932, p. 498.
18. *Social Service Review*, September 1932, p. 504.
19. *Compass*, May 1932.
20. *Compass*, October 1932.
21. *Compass*, December 1932.
22. *Compass*, January 1933.
23. *Compass*, February 1933.

Chapter Four. In the Promised Land

1. NCSW, 1933; *Compass*, March, May, July 1933; *Public Welfare News*, May 1933; Schlesinger, *Age of Roosevelt*, vol. 2, pp. 20, 264–267, 337–340.
2. *Compass*, November 1933.
3. Schlesinger, *Age of Roosevelt*, vol. 2, pp. 269–271.
4. *NCSW*, 1933.
5. *HSUS*, p. 1073.
6. Donald Johnson and Kirk Porter, eds. *National Party Platforms, 1846–1972*, 1973, pp. 331–333, 339–351.
7. Schlesinger, *Age of Roosevelt*, vol. 2, pp. 20, 21.
8. Summarized from Schlesinger, *Age of Roosevelt*, vol. 2 as a whole.
9. Schlesinger, *Age of Roosevelt*, vol. 2, chapter 6.
10. Schlesinger, *Age of Roosevelt*, vol. 2, chapters 2,3,4.
11. *HSUS*, pp. 483, 489, 491.
12. *HSUS*, pp. 224, 126.
13. *Compass*, May 1934.
14. *Public Welfare News*, October 1934.
15. *NCSW*, 1934.

16. *Public Welfare News*, June 1934.

Chapter Five. *The Critical Eye*

1. Compass, March 1934.
2. *Compass*, March 1934.
3. *NCSW*, 1934.
4. *Compass*, May 1934.
5. *Public Welfare News*, November 1934.
6. *Public Welfare News*, December 1934.
7. *Compass*, January 1935.
8. *Public Welfare News*, June 1935.
9. *Compass*, January 1935.
10. *Compass*, March 1935.
11. *Compass*, December 1935.
12. *Compass*, January 1936.
13. *Compass*, October, November, December 1935.
14. *Public Welfare News*, June 1934.
15. *Compass*, March 1934.
16. U.S. Committee on Economic Security. *Report to the President*, January 15, 1935.
17. *Compass*, January 1935; *SWT*, February 1935.
18. The hearings before the House Ways and Means Committee and the Senate Finance Committee revealed broad support for the bill. Serious opposition was voiced from expected quarters only—the National Association of Manufacturers and other business and industry groups. It had been discounted in advance and received scant sympathy in either committee, except from some of the Republican party members.
19. Social Security Act, approved August 14, 1935, Public Law 271, 74th Congress.
20. *Public Welfare News*, September 1935.

Chapter Six. *The Emergence of a Left Wing in Social Work*

1. Compass, March 1935.
2. The *Family*, February 1933.
3. *Compass*, May 1933.
4. *NCSW*, 1933, pp. 639–651.
5. *NCSW*, 1933, pp. 3–19.
6. *NCSW*, 1933, pp. 20–28.
7. *NCSW*, 1933, pp. 43–56.
8. *Compass*, November 1933.
9. *Compass*, April 1934.
10. *Compass*, November 1934.
11. *Survey*, June 1934.

12. *SWT*, June 1934.
13. *Archives*. Letter, Gertrude Springer to Paul Kellogg, n.d. (May 1934?)
14. Ibid.
15. *Compass*, November 1934. *Archives*. Draft memorandum, H.L. Lurie, chairman to members of the AASW Committee to Outline a National Social Welfare Program, January 30, 1935.
16. More graphically revealed than in the official report in the *Compass* for March 1935, in a memorandum on the conference by Marion Hathway, a delegate from the Seattle-Tacoma chapter, n.d., available in *Archives*.
17. *NCSW*, 1935. The Grace Marcus paper was reprinted in full in the June 1935 issue of the *Compass*, from which the present excerpts are taken.

Chapter Seven. The Liberal Connection

1. Some but not all of the books mentioned served as sources for the summary presented in the present chapter, which was derived for the most part from the sources listed in n. 1 of the Introduction.

Chapter Eight. The Rank-and-File Movement in Social Work: Social Workers Discussion Clubs

1. Jacob Fisher, The Rank and File Movement in Social Work 1931–36, New York School of Social Work, 1936. This 49-page bulletin constitutes the primary source for chapters 8 to 11, supplemented by relevant articles in *Social Work Today*, the *Proceedings of the First National Convention of Rank and File Groups in Social Work*, Pittsburgh, February 22–24, 1935; also by bulletins, fliers, memoranda, correspondence, and other documents issued by the organizations referred to in the four chapters, material now in the Social Welfare History Archives Center at the University of Minnesota. The author's personal recollections are also drawn on.
2. One trail to follow is the possibility that, as the children and grandchildren of immigrants, they had to fashion in their own lives a value system relevant to their American experience, often in conflict with that cherished by the older generation, and were therefore more receptive to new concepts and less embedded in the matrix of traditional values than their counterparts in the nonsectarian and Catholic agencies.
   Before the subject is left, it may not be amiss to reject also any possible link with the traditional Jewish concept of social justice, referred to in Hebrew as *Yoysher*, which goes back to the Prophets, particularly Amos and Hosea, and to which some members of the Jewish rabbinate in Western Europe and the United States appealed to justify their identification with ideas of social reform—the analog in a way of the Social Gospel among Protestant ministers in the late nineteenth century. With very few exceptions, most social workers in Jewish agencies in New York were

alienated from and ignorant of Jewish traditions, including *Yoysher;* they were nonbelievers, agnostics, atheists.

3. In a "Dear Bill" letter, Lurie disassociated himself from the polemical rhetoric of the Open Letter. To avoid misunderstanding, he presented his own recollection of the meeting. Hodson had agreed with the delegation on the inadequacies of the relief program; had said that he had made efforts to convince city, state, and federal officials of the need for more money, but because of his position was not free to voice criticism of their decisions. In general, Hodson had said he was doing all he could to better the situation and expressed the hope that social workers would recognize this. Lurie commented in his letter that he didn't find Hodson's attitude very encouraging and felt with the discussion club that more public pressure was necessary. He saw a real problem, he said, in reconciling professional social work standards with the limitations imposed by a restrictive government program, and thought that local administrators yielded too easily on this issue. He praised Hodson's fairness and courtesy and regretted that he—Lurie—was not given an opportunity to see the Open Letter before publication (*Archives*, Letter, Lurie to Hodson, June 22, 1934.)

Chapter Nine. The Rank-and-File Movement: Social Work Unions

1. The principal sources for chapter 9 are given in n. 1, chapter 8.
2. Data from bulletins issued by Association of Community Chests and Councils and Family Welfare Association of America and cited in undated bulletin issued by New York Association of Federation Workers in 1933. (Archives)
3. Marion Hathway paper dated December 13, 1935. (*Archives*).

Chapter Ten. The Rank-and-File Movement: Social Work Today

1. Chapter 10 is based on a review of Social Work Today for the period 1934–36.

Chapter Eleven. The Rank-and-File Movement: The Wider Involvement

1. The principal sources for chapter 11 are cited in n. 1, chapter 8.

Chapter Twelve. The New Deal in its Populist Phase

1. The principal sources for chapter 12 are Arthur Schlesinger, The Age of Roosevelt, vol. 3, 1960, and the chapter on Roosevelt in Hofstadter, *The American Political Tradition*, 1948.

2. *HSUS*, pp. 1073, 1075, 1083; *World Almanac*, 1937.
3. Hofstadter, *American Political Tradition*, pp. 430, 431.
4. Hofstadter, *American Political Tradition*, pp. 444, 445.
5. *HSUS*, pp. 126, 224, 235, 236.

Chapter Thirteen. The Lost Battle for a Federal General Relief Program

1. Compass, April 1936.
2. *Public Welfare News*, April 1936.
3. Ibid.
4. *Public Welfare News*, January 1936.
5. *Compass*, July 1936.
6. *Compass*, June 1936.
7. *Compass*, February 1936.
8. *Compass*, July 1936.
9. *NCSW*, 1936; *Compass*, July 1936.
10. *Compass*, March 1937.
11. *Compass*, June, October 1937.
12. *NCSW*, 1937.
13. *NCSW*, 1936; *Compass*, July 1936; *Archives*. Bulletins issued at National
    Conference of Social Work, 1936, by National Coordinating Committee of
    Social Service Employee Groups.
14. Donald Johnson and Kirk Porter, eds., *National Party Platforms, 1846–1972*,
    1973, pp. 360–363, 365–370.
15. *HSUS*, p. 357.
16. *Compass*, October 1937.
17. *Social Welfare Expenditures under Public Programs in the United States, 1929–*
    66, U.S. Department of Health, Education and Welfare, Social Security
    Administration, Office of Research and Statistics, Research Report no. 25,
    1968, p. 208.
18. *HSUS,* p. 356.

Chapter Fourteen. Social Work's Left Wing Sets a New Course

1. SWT, April 1936.
2. *Archives*. Documents from the *Proceedings of the Second Conference of the*
    National Coordinating Committee of Rank and File Groups in Social Work,
    Cleveland, February 22, 23, 1936, including "A National Social Welfare
    Program," and "Resolutions Adopted."
3. Some of the more striking photographs appear in Dorothea Lange and Paul
    Taylor, *An American Exodus* (New Haven: Yale University Press, 1969);
    Walker Evans, (New York: The Museum of Modern Art, 1971); Roy
    Stryker and Nancy Wood, *In This Proud Land* (New York: Galahad
    Books, 1973); Arthur Rothstein, *The Depression Years* (New York: Dover

Publications, 1978). Similar in coverage to the Farm Security Administration effort were the photographs taken by Margaret Bourke-White and published by Modern Age Books in 1937 under the title *You Have Seen Their Faces*, with a text by Erskine Caldwell. In 1941 James Agee's *Let Us Now Praise Famous Men* (Boston: Houghton Mifflin) appeared, the result of an assignment in 1936 by *Fortune* magazine to do a series of articles, which it never published, on the lives of sharecroppers in the South. This idiosyncratic book, which has become a legend and has been reprinted several times, contains sixty-two photographs (in the 1960 edition) Walker Evans took for the FSA while working with Agee on what was a joint effort; they show the people, the homes, and the land Agee writes about in his moving text. When Eudora Welty came home to Mississippi from college during the Depression, she got a job with the WPA as a "publicity agent." The photographs she took while traveling all over the state may be seen in *One Time, One Place* (New York: Random House, 1973).

4. *Archives*. Documents issued by and relating to NCC developments, 1935; *SWT*, July 1935, December 1935.
5. *Archives*. Documents issued by and relating to NCC developments, 1936; Jacob Fisher, *The Rank-and-File Movement in Social Work 1931–36*, 1936, pp. 40–43; *SWT*, April 1936; Russell Sage Foundation, *Social Work Year Book 1937*, 1937, article, "Trade Unionism in Social Work."
6. *Archives*. Bulletins issued by NCC at National Conference of Social Work, 1937.
7. References cited in notes 5 and 6, supra.
8. *Archives*. "Statement on the Negro Issue at the National Conference of Social Work," NCC, January, 1937.
9. *Archives*. Bulletins issued by NCC at National Conference of Social Work, 1937.

Chapter Fifteen. Social Work: Acquiescence in the Administration Program

1. HSUS, pp. 126, 224, 357.
2. *SWT*, March 1938.
3. *Compass*, April 1938.
4. Ibid.
5. *Compass*, October 1938.
6. *HSUS*, pp. 356, 357.
7. *Compass*, April 1940.
8. *Public Welfare News*, December 1938.
9. The Social Security Amendments of 1972 amended Title XVI to provide Supplemental Security Income (SSI) for the Aged, Blind, and Disabled, a change which federalized the public assistance program for these three groups, but did not enlarge the types of need for which the federal government assumed responsibility.
10. Social Security Act Amendments of 1939, approved August 10, 1939, Public Law 379, 76th Congress.

Chapter Sixteen. Social Work: The Unconverted Dissidents

1. Archives. Lurie papers.
2. *SWT*, June 1938.
3. *SWT*, June 1938, October 1938, June 1939, June 1940; Marion Hathway, *Trade Union Organization for Professional Workers*, United Office and Professional Workers of America, CIO, 1939; Russell Sage Foundation, *Social Work Year Book 1939*, 1939, article, "Trade Unionism in Social Work."
4. John Haynes, "The 'Rank and File Movement' in Private Social Work," *Labor History*, Winter 1975; *SWT*, April 1941.
5. *SWT*, April 1937; Hathway, *Trade Union Organization for Professional Workers*.
6. *SWT*, October 1938.
7. *SWT*, February 1939.
8. *SWT*, December 1938.
9. *SWT*, October 1937, January 1938, April 1938, May 1938, June 1941.
10. *SWT*, June 1937, May 1939.
11. *SWT*, April, May, June 1938.
12. *SWT*, January 1938.

Chapter Seventeen. Social Work and Politics Abroad: Becoming Involved

1. HSUS, p. 884.
2. The developments cited are conveniently summarized in the *Harper Encyclopedia of the Modern World*, ed. Richard B. Morris and Graham W. Irwin, (New York: Harper and Row, 1970). The details may be traced in the annual issues of the *New York Times Index*, among other sources.
3. House of Representatives, Special Committee on Un-American Activities, *Investigation of Un-American Activities in the United States, Appendix, Part IX: Communist Front Organizations with Special Reference to the National Citizens Political Action Committee*, 1944, pp. 382–383.
4. House Special Committee on Un-American Activities, *Investigation etc.*, p. 380.
5. *SWT*, October 1936.
6. *Compass*, March 1937; *SWT*, May 1937.
7. *Archives*. Correspondence, financial reports, and related documents concerning Social Workers Committee to Aid Spanish Democracy. *SWT*, June 1938.
8. *SWT*, October, November 1937.
9. *SWT*, January 1938.
10. *SWT*, April, October, December 1938. *Archives*, Correspondence concerning Social Workers Committee to Aid Spanish Democracy.
11. Sources cited in n. 2.
12. *SWT*, January 1939.
13. *SWT*, February 1939.
14. *SWT*, March, April, June 1940.

15. *SWT*, February 1940.
16. *SWT*, January 1940.
17. *SWT*, June 1940.
18. *SWT*, June 1940.
19. *Compass*, August 1940.
20. Annual issues of *The New York Times Index* for the years 1939–41. Scattered references to the principal neutralist groups in 1939–41 will be found in Robert Sherwood, *Roosevelt and Hopkins* (New York: Harpers, 1948), chapters 5, 6 and 7; and in the books by Howe and Coser, Pells, and Warren cited in n. 1, *Introduction*.
21. *SWT*, February 1940.
22. *SWT*, June 1940.
23. *The Gallup Poll: Public Opinion 1935–71* (New York: Random House, 1972), Vol. I, pp. 178–288.
24. *Harper Encyclopedia of the Modern World* and annual *New York Times Index*.
25. Hofstadter, *American Political Tradition*, p. 449.
26. *Harper Encyclopedia of the Modern World* and annual *New York Times Index*.
27. *Compass*, "Social Workers and National Defense," August 1940; "Social Problems and National Defense," December 1940; "Local Impact of Defense Activities," May 1941.
28. *Survey*, August 1940, p. 240.
29. *Compass*, December 1940.
30. *Compass*, August 1941.
31. *Survey*, March 1941, pp. 75–77.
32. *Compass*, August 1941.
33. *Archives*. Copies of fliers issued by Social Work Trade Unionists for Britain and Democracy and Joint Committee of Trade Unionists in Social Work, June 1941.
34. *Survey*, July 1941, p. 217.
35. *Survey*, June 1941, p. 185.
36. *Archives*. Memorandum by Paul Kellogg, attached to letter of April 15, 1940, from Helen Harris, chairman, Social Workers Committee of the Spanish Refugee Relief Campaign, to members of the executive and national committees.
37. *Compass*, November 1941

Chapter Eighteen. The Economy: Winners and Losers

1. HSUS, pp. 224, 356, 357.
2. *HSUS*, pp. 8, 49, 105.
3. *HSUS*, pp. 24–37.
4. *HSUS*, p. 126.
5. *HSUS*, pp. 138, 139, 1102, 1104.
6. *HSUS*, p. 126.
7. *HSUS*, p. 948.
8. *HSUS*, p.126.

9. *HSUS*, p. 912.
10. *HSUS*, p. 481.
11. U.S. Treasury Department, Bureau of Internal Revenue, *Statistics of Income*, 1932.
12. *HSUS*, pp. 235, 236.
13. U.S. Treasury Department, Bureau of Internal Revenue, *Statistics of Income*, 1932 and 1937.
14. *HSUS*, pp. 166, 167.
15. *HSUS*, pp. 300, 302.
16. The theses summarized briefly here are taken from and discussed in fuller detail in an article, "The Reasons Why," *The New York Review of Books*, February 8, 1979, by Jerome Karabel, Senior Research Associate, Huron Institute, and Associate, Center for European Studies, Harvard University. The article is ostensibly a review of a new translation of Werner Sombart's *Why Is There No Socialism in the United States?* (1905), but this is only an occasion for an elaboration and amplification of the Sombart thesis, and includes references to later books and articles written on the same general subject, which the interested reader may wish to examine.
17. The dominant role of property rights, of all kinds, in America's major political traditions is persuasively discussed in the Introduction to Richard Hofstadter's *The American Political Tradition* (1948), from which the following key sentences are quoted: "However much at odds on specific issues, the major political traditions have shared a belief in the rights of property, the philosophy of economic individualism, the value of competition; they have accepted the economic virtues of capitalist culture as necessary qualities of man . . . . American traditions also show a strong bias in favor of equalitarian democracy, but it has been a democracy in cupidity rather than a democracy of fraternity." (p. xxxvii in 1974 Vintage edition.)

Chapter Nineteen. Social Work: The Thirties as a Watershed

1. HSUS, pp. 340, 357; *Social Security Bulletin*, May 1942, "Public and Private Aid in 116 Urban Areas, Calendar Year 1941."
2. *HSUS*, p. 356.
3. 1930 data from Russell Sage Foundation, *Social Work Year Book 1933*, 1933, article on social work as a profession. 1940 data from *Social Work Year Book 1943*, 1943, article on social work as a profession. The reference to the greater percentage increase in the number of social and welfare workers than in that of any other professional group is based upon an examination of data on 1930–40 changes in the number of professional, technical, and kindred workers, by detailed occupation, in *HSUS*, p. 140. The latter source unfortunately lumps "social and welfare workers" with "recreation and group workers" in 1940, and both groups with "religious workers" in

1930, which is why the *Social Work Year Book* is used here as the source for the data on "Social and Welfare Workers."

4. Marion Hathway, *Trade Union Organization for Professional Workers*, United Office and Professional Workers of America (CIO), 1939.

5. Russell Sage Foundation, *Social Work Year Book 1943*, 1943, article on social work as a profession.

6. Russell Sage Foundation, *Social Work Year Book 1943*, article on education for social work.

7. The death of *Social Work Today* in 1942, which Bertha Reynolds felt "as if it were the loss of a member of my family," (*An Uncharted Journey* [New York: Citadel Press, 1963], p. 240) falls a little outside the time span of the present book. It invites a comment nevertheless. With the whole-hearted support given U.S. entry into the war by the political left, including the left in social work, a support which covered every aspect of the administration program, extending to its hold-the-line position on social welfare and social insurance, the distinctive feature which had marked the Rank-and-File Movement from its beginning, dissidence—as an attitude, as an ideology, as the intellectual spine of a different structural view of the world about us, as a phenomenon—disappeared. It seems plausible to believe that with little to distinguish *Social Work Today* from the *Survey*, the *Family*, and other social work magazines, there was, many readers must have felt, little reason for its continued existence. The Rank-and-File Movement lived on only in the form of unions in the social work field. With respect to social welfare policy and programs, it had nothing to say that the AASW, the APWA, and other pillars of the social work establishment were not saying. It was not stirred by the concerns which led in wartime Britain to the Beveridge Report of 1942, accepted in principle by the government in 1943, enacted in stages between 1944 and 1946, and giving postwar Britain a comprehensive universal social insurance and social assistance system providing minimum income maintenance for all families and a national health service. In this country, the tendency to defer until after the war any consideration of a more comprehensive approach to an integrated social welfare and social insurance program was, of course, true of the social work field as a whole. But in a magazine (and the movement for which it spoke) committed to a dissenting radicalism, the silence on the subject represented a critical failure.

Index

Abraham Lincoln Brigade, 199;
Friends of the, 201; Veterans of the,
201
Administration-social work disagreement on social welfare policy,
40, 42, 53, 57, 66–71; reconciliation
of, 180; in second New Deal period,
143–52, 153–55, 182–83, 239; social
work unions dissent, 186; "Third
Viewpoint," 66–71
Advisory Committee on Social Secu-
rity, 180
Agricultural Adjustment Act, 50, 51–
52; criticism of, 75, 89; and racial discrimination, 133; ruled unconstitutional, 89, 139
Agricultural Adjustment Administration, 52
America First, 209–10, 220
American Academy of Political and
Social Science, 40
American Association for Labor Legislation, 33, 237
American Association for Old Age Security, 33
American Association for Social Security, 33, 237
American Association for the Study of
Group Work, 219
American Association of Social Workers (AASW): Chicago chapter protest, 43, 117; criticism of, 111, 184;
and Dawson case, 118; delegate con-
ference, 1935, 59, 60–61, 66, 69, 78,

81, 146–47; delegate conference,
1937, 148; established, 20; executive
committee statement (1930), 34, 36–
40; growth of, xiv, 235; lack of discrimination in, 135; Milford Conference Reports, 16, 71; national delegate assembly, 1932, 42; New York
chapter, 116, 117, 202; position on
W.W. II, 208, 216–21 *passim*; practitioner groups, 92, 99–100; and Rank-
and-File Movement, 99, 240; report
on public assistance, 177; and second
New Deal, 143, 144, 146–147, 153;
and social insurance, 63, 65, 66–71,
77-83, 237; and social work unions,
116–18, 169–70; mentioned, xiv, 21,
40, 43–44, 49, 115, 179, 235
American Association of Social Workers (AASW), organizational: Committee on the Coordination of Governmental Services (1934), 74;
Committee on Current Relief Programs (1935), 56–57; Committee on
Federal Action on Social Welfare
(1933), 73, 74; Committee on Federal
Action on Unemployment (1932), 43,
71–72, 73; Committee on Unemployment (1931), 40, 41, 42; Committee to
Outline a National Social Welfare
Program (1934), 74, 77–83; Conference on Governmental Objectives for
Social Work (1934), 55, 59, 63, 73–
74; Conference on National Economic Objectives for Social Work